The PHILOSOPHY OF SĀDHANĀ

SUNY SERIES IN TANTRIC STUDIES
Paul Muller-Ortega, Editor

The PHILOSOPHY OF SĀDHANĀ

With Special Reference to the Trika Philosophy of Kashmir

Deba Brata SenSharma

Foreword by Paul Muller-Ortega

STATE UNIVERSITY OF NEW YORK PRESS

Reproduction of Indian miniature used on front cover courtesy of Kumar Gallery Ltd., New Delhi.

Published by
State University of New York Press, Albany

Printed in the United States of America

For information, address State University of New York
Press, State University Plaza, Albany, N.Y., 12246

Library of Congress Cataloging-in-Publication Data

SenSharma, Deba Brata.
The philosophy of sādhanā : with special reference to the Trika
philosophy of Kashmir / Deba Brata SenSharma.
p. cm. — (SUNY series in tantric studies)
Reprint. Originally published: 1983.
Includes bibliographical references.
ISBN 0–7914–0347–5. — ISBN 0–7914–0348–3 (pbk.)
1. Kashmir Śaivism—Doctrines. 2. Spiritual life (Hinduism)
3. Self-realization—Religious aspects—Hinduism. I. Title
II. Title: Trika philosophy of Kashmir. III. Series.
BL1281.1547.S26 1990
181′.4—dc20 89–27739
CIP

10 9 8 7 6 5 4 3 2

To
the sacred memory of the swami Vidyaranya
and
the Mahamahopadhyaya Dr. Gopi Nath Kaviraj
as a humble offering

Contents

Foreword

It is a great joy to introduce this third volume in the State University of New York Press series on Tantric Studies. Deba Brata SenSharma's *The Philosophy of Sādhanā* introduces the essentials of Tantric sādhanā in the light of the process of śaktipāta—the divine descent of the power of Śiva. It contains a systematic and careful exposition of aspects of the tantric worldview as seen through the texts of the Trika-Kaula traditions of non-dual Kashmir Shaivism. It is an exceedingly useful and readable study of the technical components of Hindu tantric thought as these relate to sādhanā.

After reading this book, I had wondered what kind of a person comes to write in such an erudite and deeply insightful way. I was therefore happy that I had the pleasure of meeting Professor SenSharma on a recent trip to India. We coincided for a few days in the beautiful environs of the Gurudev Siddha Peeth in Ganeshpuri near Bombay. I came to know the author of this book as a very refined person, of deep humility and possessed of a great love for the ancient wisdoms of India. In our conversations, Professor SenSharma recounted to me his many years at Banaras Hindu University studying under the direction of the late Gopinath Kaviraj, probably the leading Indian expert on the Śaiva and Śākta traditions of the Tantra. SenSharma spoke of his explorations of a variety of tantric texts under the guidance of Kavirajji (as he affectionately referred to his teacher). He told me of his increasing appreciation for the works of the tenth century Śaivācārya, Abhinavagupta, such as the Tantrasāra, the Tantrāloka, the Parātriṃśikā, and many others. In fact, these works form the textual horizon of the present volume. SenSharma explained that his teacher, Gopinath Kaviraj, was not just a scholar but an initiate and practitioner of these traditions. He spoke with deep feeling about the times he had been privileged to accompany Kaviraj on expeditions to meet some of the extraordinary beings that embody sādhanā such as the great saint Ananda Mayi Ma. SenSharma then went on to tell me something about his distinguished career as a university professor and administrator at Kurukshetra University.

In the following pages, readers will accompany SenSharma as he guides them through an exploration of the conceptual bases at the heart of the tantric sādhanā. As the fruit of many years of textual study as well as the attempt to gain accurate insight into the meaning of these texts, SenSharma presents a detailed survey of tantric Shaivite sādhanā. He treats in a careful and systematic fashion the notion of the supreme reality of Śiva, as well as the various Śakti-s that expand his power. If there is one theme that seems to be at the heart of SenSharma's book, it is the notion of śaktipāta, the divine descent of grace. In order to properly elaborate his analysis of śaktipāta, SenSharma carefully explains the structure of the tattva-s or principles of Shaivism, as well as the way these result in the contraction of the supreme consciousness of Śiva by the agency of three successive impurities (mala-s). He then goes on to elaborate the variety of conscious experiencers (pramātṛ-s) that arise as a result of the contraction of the infinite consciousness. This leads him to a detailed consideration of the nature of grace and its transmission through the guru by the process of initiation (dīkṣā). There then follows a detailed exposition of the nature of the various upāya-s or methods of the tradition, all of which lead to the final goal of perfection or self realization, and, in some cases, jīvanmukti liberation while still alive.

In India, the encouragement to persist in sādhanā is often phrased as "Making, making, someday made." We would probably say: Practice makes perfect. If we were to translate this into the vocabulary of the Hindu Tantra, it would be: sādhanā leads to siddhi, that is, spiritual practices lead to attainment and perfection. Sādhanā represents the life-blood of tantric Hinduism. Indeed, it is in the doing of sādhanā that its structures—ritual, doctrinal, experiential—take on a living vitality and relevance for the practitioner. For the sādhakā, the practice of sādhanā unlocks the secret, experiential realms of the Tantra. It gives access to the transformative experiences which are thought to lead to liberation. It is thought to allow entry into the domain of the "center" from which the baroque complexity of the Hindu Tantra resolves into an elegant simplicity.

Sādhanā represents the tantric crucible of transformation. It is conceived as the involving arc of return, the mechanism by means of which Śiva recuperates himself from his self-shadowing play of cosmic existence. The universal actor releases himself from bondage and contraction. S/he extricates herself from her part in the drama and steps off the stage. Or, s/he does *not* step off the stage, but heroically continues to explore the part s/he was once compelled to play.

This book on the philosophy of sādhanā represents a sustained attempt to explore, in the light of the traditions of the nondual Shaivism of Kashmir, the elaborate theoretical matrix that informs sādhanā and undergirds its ritual and meditative prescriptions. One often reads that the Tantra is unoriginal and that it has borrowed most of its doctrines from elsewhere; that its originality is precisely limited to the concoction of a series of practical, and somewhat experimental techniques. Moreover, and somewhat inconsistently, the Tantra is simultaneously charged with holding doctrines that are irrational, impenetrable, "magical", and so on. Those who would launch such accusations inadvertently reveal their own incapacity or unwillingness to understand. SenSharma's book goes a long way toward introducing the lineaments of the Hindu tantric worldview. Once that worldview is penetrated, the structures of sādhanā take on deep resonance as a means toward that which is of ultimate value.

Because it deals with the holomovement, the philosophy of sādhanā is open, and provides a bridge between closed intellectual systems and open experiential flow. SenSharma's book provides insight into the tantric view of Śiva—the uncontainable and finally unnegatable implicate order which is beyond intellectual apprehension. From the realm of infinite potentiality implicately enfolded on itself, one particular reality unfolds. A universe of actuality arises from the vast ocean of possibility. As this presently perceived actuality unfolds or explicates itself, vast infinities of the potential remain obscured. Thus, to explicate is simultaneously to affirm and to negate. The absolute implicate becomes the relative explicates. In this process, something vital is lost, even as something essential—explication—is gained. Therefore, the Tantra recommends that the practitioner experientially replicate the implicate. It holds that in order to know Śiva the sādhaka must become Śiva. From one point of view, this is very easy. After all, Śiva is everything. All finite beings already *are* Śiva. There is a poignant futility here. Nothing need be done to become what one already is. At the same time, it is very hard to recuperate the consciousness of Śiva *as* Śiva.

The link that joins the sādhaka to this process of recovery, of self-recognition, is Śakti, the intrinsic and fundamentally non-dual power of Śiva. It is thus no accident that SenSharma treats in great detail the process of śaktipāta. There is a sense in which this mysterious process of opening is neither explicable nor rationalizable. Nevertheless, SenSharma allows readers to see what the tradition itself has had to say about it. Śaktipāta overturns the apparently closed causal systems of the individual's physical and psychological being. Another reality begins to flow into the practitioner—a reality, new and perhaps alien, but which nevertheless comes eventually to be recognized as the intrinsic truth, the innate being, the very Self of Śiva. Yet the experience of śaktipāta may violently challenge the relative autonomy of ordinary life and its small systems of safe contraction and closedness. This challenge comes in the name of a higher order, an order of wholeness which may appear initially chaotic, random, violent, irrational, and even destructive. This higher order of wholeness has traditionally received the name Śiva. ITI ŚIVA. Thus Śiva, tell us the traditional āgama-s, the revealed texts of Shaivism. To yield gradually into the holonomy, into this higher pattern of wholeness, may at times be painful, disconcerting, and bewildering. Or, it may appear at other times as ecstatic, truth-revealing, and comforting. At all times, the process of yielding the relative autonomy of the explicate orders into the absolute holomony of the implicate order is intrinsically liberating.

It is in this context that there develops the notion of kuṇḍalinī which is said to unwind and unravel in the yogic body of cakra-s and nāḍī-s. In its own way and time, it unlocks the secret keys of consciousness, the entryways into liberation. The kuṇḍalinī burns the temporary and small universes of safety and relative order which have until that moment provided a haven of security at the price of keeping the transmigrating self entrapped in its own constructions of ignorance. ITI ŚIVA. Thus Śiva invades and restores himself to his own primordial dignity, trampling under foot the demon of forgetfulness, who is none other than the embodiment of Śiva's will to dance the dance of life and death and transmigration. Śiva, the undefinable and omnipresent flux of reality, recuperates his wholeness continuously, and continuously sunders that wholeness into the shards and fragments that constitute the relative worlds of form in which he dances. This function of dispersal into form and subsiding back into the formless is carried out by the visargaśakti, the Emissional Power of Śiva, a power which is said to reside in the Heart of all beings.

To practice tantric sādhanā, then, is conceived as a process of attuning ever more closely to the operation of this power. Sādhanā, seen in this way, represents the cosmic process by means of which Śiva recuperates the wholeness he has apparently relinquished in order to make the dance possible. In actuality, the holomovement is never sundered. The apparent fractionation and limitation of the unbounded Śiva by the appearance of myriad planes of transmigration and of finite, bound experiencers never occurs. This is the delightful realization of the sādhaka: that s/he is at once a limited human being and also the unbounded Śiva. This simultaneity of form and formless, of the finite and the infinite, of the bound and the unbounded, of ignorance and enlightenment is the precise nature of Śiva's reality. It is always both. Śiva is always embracing the Śakti that gives rise to his eternal dance. The reality of Śiva and Śakti is always nondual yet dyadic.

The great masters and gurus of the Hindu Tantra marvelled at this cosmic process and attempted to explicate it to themselves even as they lived it. The texts of the Hindu Tantra represent the unfolding into words and language of the intrinsic nature of the enlightened consciousness of those who wrote them. To read the words of a great master like Abhinavagupta is to be caught up, a thousand years after their composition, into the ever-fresh and shimmering reality of the wave-form of Śiva-Śakti undulating through Abhinavagupta's awareness.

Thus, SenSharma's book is an immensely valuable account of this living wisdom, of this experientially-charged knowledge, which unfolds in its very structures the dynamic pattern of human life as continuously enclosing and disclosing the holonomy. As we have said above, the Tantra has often been accused of being irrational, unsystematic, magical. These charges are unfounded, but they also betray preconceptions of what a system of "thought" should be—uncontradictory, complete, apodictic, etc. However, the Hindu Tantra, in the hands of its most gifted exponents, responds to a higher and more subtle pattern of order. It is a system of "life" as much as a system of "thought." To insist on subjecting it to certain modern preconceptions of what "philosophy" should be causes its structures to elude comprehension.

The philosophy of sādhanā, as SenSharma demonstrates so capably, lies embedded in the fundamental inner and outer gestures or mudrā-s of the Hindu Tantra. The outer gestures are embodied in the displays of Hindu tantric ritual; the inner gestures are expressive of a variety of higher states of consciousness. Both inner and outer gestures dynamically and ecstatically unfold the inherent pattern of the implicate order. We are barely beginning to understand and existentially encompass either the outer or inner gestures of the Hindu Tantra. All the more reason why SenSharma's book is such a valuable contribution. It is a careful, technical and highly-detailed rendition of the backdrop of these gestures. It is not, however, a work of dry scholarship, but one of enormous existential relevance. It allows the reader to enter into the wonder of the process of sādhanā. To understand the implicate order that flows through life is to begin to yield to sādhanā, to the flow of this order as it leads from small, closed patterns of intellectual and emotional contraction to ever-expanding and more inclusive patterns of wisdom and enlightenment. This study is itself clearly a product of this process. It is the result of an intellect clarified, widened, and emboldened by the removal of the contractive mala-s. We are therefore grateful to Professor Sensharma for his profound and systematic investigation of the pattern of sādhanā.

Paul E. Muller-Ortega
Department of Religious Studies
Michigan State University

Preface

This book aims at an exposition of the philosophy of spiritual discipline (*sādhanā*), especially of the Trika philosophy of Kashmir. Several decades ago N. K. Brahma published his pioneering work *Philosophy of Sādhanā* based on his study of spiritual discipline as formulated in the texts of some orthodox schools of Indian philosophy, and since then there has been no supplement to his studies on the subject. Therefore I have attempted to shed some light on this important but thus far neglected branch of philosophical studies.

I have made a critical examination of the philosophy of *sādhanā* as presented mainly in the Sanskrit texts of the Trika school, especially those of Abhinavagupta in which the *sādhanā* aspect occupies a prominent place. I am conscious of the fact that the aspect of *sādhanā* in general and in the Trika texts in particular is, by its very nature, abstruse and is also garbed in secrecy, and that only those spiritual seekers who have been bestowed with divine grace by the teacher and are actually on the way to spiritual realization are capable of knowing the profound mysteries that the subject involves. Nevertheless I have attempted, despite my limitations, to understand the problem intellectually and to decipher whatever I could from the published texts. How far I have been successful in my attempt, I leave it to my readers to judge.

My study is divided into seven chapters. The first chapter gives an outline of the metaphysics of the system relevant to the understanding of the nature of man and of his present condition in the worldly existence. Advocating a purely monistic system of the thought, the Trika school postulates the existence of one Ultimate Reality, called *Parama Śiva,* who pervades and permeates the entire cosmos as the cosmic Reality and yet, at the same time, transcends it as the Absolute Being. Exercising his divine Śakti, he assumes self-contraction (*saṅkoca*) out of his free will (*Icchā*) and reveals himself as the world consisting of thirty-six levels of creation in which he assumes different roles as the limited experience (*pramātā*), the objects of experience (*prameya*), and so forth.

The second chapter is devoted to the examination of the origin and nature of man, and what the Trika system refers to as the *malas*, or different kinds of defilements that cover his real nature. The human component in the various levels of creation as envisaged in the Trika texts is discussed in the third chapter.

The fourth chapter, entitled "The Way to Ultimate Self-Realization," is divided into three sections. The first deals with such topics as the role of different types of defilements (*malas*) which prevent man from getting a glimpse of his real Self and the various means to overcome them. The second section deals with divine grace (*śaktipāta*), a crucial factor in spiritual discipline. The third section examines the concepts of *guru* (teacher) and *dīkṣa* (spiritual initiation), important ingredients of spiritual discipline as envisaged by the system.

The fifth chapter, entitled "The Ways of Spiritual Discipline," is divided into five sections discussing different kinds of spiritual aspirants (*sādhakas*) and the four recognized ways of spiritual discipline (*upāyas*) called *anupāya, śāṁbhava upāya, śākta upāya,* and *āṇava upāya,* which are prescribed for as many kinds of aspirants. The *āṇava upāya* prescribed for aspirants receiving grace in very mild form is of great importance to ordinary human beings who are incapable of adopting other *upāyas.* This section has been revised and enlarged. Although other schools of Indian philosophical tradition also recognize the necessity for prescribing different ways of *sādhanā* in conformity with the varying temperaments of spiritual aspirants, the Trika texts make these distinctions according to the difference in the intensity of the divine grace received by the aspirants.

The sixth chapter is devoted to the examination of the nature of perfect integral Self-realization, technically called *Śivatva.* When a spiritual aspirant attains *Śivatva,* he does not experience any difference between himself and the Supreme Lord. He experiences complete identity with him, and simultaneously develops within himself all of the divine powers, such as omnipotence, omniscience, omnipresence, fullness, and so forth, which were until then lying dormant within him. This, however, does not lead to his obliteration or absorption in the Universal Self, a position unlike that of the Advaita Vedānta of Śaṅkara. The reason for such a view is that the Śaivācāryas recognize the existence of both aspects of reality—the individual and the universal—in the Supreme Self, *Parama Śiva*.

The concluding chapter examines the concept of *jīvanmukti* (liberation while existing in bodily state). Although all men are said to be eligible for the achievement of this state, the Trika system lays down three conditions for it: first, possession by the *sādhaka* of the appropriate inclination, technically called *bhogavāsanā* (desire for enjoyment); second, receiving the appropriate kind of initiation from the *guru* (spiritual teacher); and third, the continuance of the residual impressions of *karma* in the form of *prārabdha karma saṁskāra* (residual impressions of *karma* starting their fruition).

An apology is due here for my using Sanskrit technical terms freely and frequently, which may create difficulty for those who are not familiar with the technical terminology of the system. I have used these reluctantly for want of suitable synonyms in English. I was reluctant to follow the lead given by some scholars using English technical terms in the place of Sanskrit, for two reasons. First, English words have an associative meaning besides the dictionary meaning which may, at times, brew confusion and lead to misunderstanding. And second, the Sanskrit technical terms, especially of this system, which tends toward the mystical, have a depth of import that cannot be conveyed by a single synonym in English. For the readers' convenience, however, I have given English equivalents in parentheses wherever possible, and have provided a glossary at the end.

In conclusion, I wish to acknowledge my debt of gratitude to the scholars and friends who have rendered help in various ways in the preparation of this work.

I express my heartfelt gratitude to the late revered Swami Vidyāraṇya of Pushkar (Dr. B. B. Dutta of Calcutta University in his *pūrvāśrama*) who was the first to suggest to me a careful study of Kashmir Śaivism; to my teacher, the late Professor P. L. Vaidya, then Mayurbhanj Professor of Sanskrit and Pali, Banaras Hindu University, for encouraging me in my studies and providing me the facilities for research; to my teacher Professor Baladeva Upadhyaya, for inspiring me to undertake the study of abstruse systems; and to Professor Arabinda Basu, former Spalding Lecturer in Indian Philosophy and Religion, Durham University, for discussing many intricate problems and removing many doubts on the subject.

I am also grateful to my colleagues in the Department of Sanskrit, Pali, and Prakrit at Kurukshetra University, especially Professor Gopika Mohan Bhattacharya, and to Professor Ajit Kumar Sinha of the Philosophy Department for constantly encouraging me in the publication of this work.

It is my duty to express my deep sense of gratitude to the late Mahāmahopādhyaya Dr. Gopinath Kaviraj at whose feet I had the privilege of sitting and studying the abstruse texts of the Trika system. His illuminating discourses on Indian philosophy in general and on the Trika philosophy in particular, helped me to grasp the spirit of Indian thought and to understand the philosophy of *sādhanā*. As an expression of my gratitude to him and to Swami Vidyāraṇyaji I dedicate this humble volume in the memory of these two departed souls.

I am also grateful to Dr. Gauri Nath Sastri, Vice-Chancellor, Sampurnanand Sanskrit University, Varanasi, for very kindly writing the foreword to the first edition.

Last but not the least, I am thankful also to my wife, Mrs. Dipika Sen Sharma, for helping me in many ways in preparing the original manuscript for the press.

I acknowledge my thanks to Dr. (Mrs.) Mango Rani for readily undertaking the publication of the first edition of this work, gladly and expeditiously seeing it through the press.

I express my deep sense of gratitude to Mr. William D. Eastman, Director of SUNY Press, for very kindly consenting to publish the second revised edition in the SUNY Series of Tantric Studies and to his team of editorial staff for preparing the revised manuscript and seeing it through the press.

I am also grateful to Dr. Paul Muller-Ortega for contributing a learned introduction and supervising publication of the second edition.

Despite all help, errors and shortcomings might have crept in, for which I crave the indulgence of my learned readers.

Abbreviations

APP	Anuttara Prakāśa Pañcāśikā (Kashmir Series of Texts & Studies)
Āh	Āhnika.
AMBH	*Aspects of Mahāyāna Buddhism and Its Relation to Hīnayana*, by N. Dutta (Calcutta, 1973)
Br. Up.	*Bṛhadāraṇyaka Upaniṣad*
Chand Up	*Chāndogya Upaniṣad.*
I.P.V.	*Īśvarapratyabhijñā Vimarśinī* (Bhāskarī Ed.)
I.P.V.V.	*Īśvarapratyabhijñā Vivṛti Vimarśinī* (KSTS)
JNM (JMV)	*Janma-Maraṇa-Vicāra* (KSTS)
Ka Śaiv	*Kashmir Shaivism*, by J. C. Chatterji (KSTS)
KSTS	Kashmir Series of Texts & Studies
Ma Up.	*Maitri Upaniṣad*
Mbh.	*Mahābhārata*
MM	*Mahārthamañjarī* (KSTS)
MVV	*Mālinīvijayavārttika*
PC	*Paramārtha Carcā*, Published in the appendix of *Abhinavagupta, An Historical and Philosophical Study:* K. C. Pandey, Varanasi, 1936
Par. Sār.	*Paramārtha Sāra* (KSTS)
Para Trim.	*Paratriṁśikā* (KSTS)
Pr. Hd.	*Pratyabhijñā Hṛdayam* (Adya)
ŚD	*Śiva Dṛṣṭi* (KSTS)
Śiv Sū	*Śiva Sūtra Vimarśinī* (KSTS)
Śiv. Sū Va	*Śiva Sūtra Vārttika* (KSTS)
Sp. Kā.	*Spanda Kārikā* (KSTS)
Sp. Nir.	*Spanda Nirṇaya* (KSTS)
STTS	*Saṭtriṁśattat Vasaṅdoha* (Kuruksetra)
Sva. Tan.	*Svacchanda Tantra* (KSTS)
Svet. Up	*Svetāsvatara Upaniṣad*
T.A.	*Tantrāloka* (KSTS)

T.S.	*Tantrasāra* (KSTS)
TV (TVD)	*Tantravaṭadhānikā* (KSTS)
V	Volume
Ved. Sar	*Vedānta Sāra* of Sadānanda (Poona)
Vāj Sam	*Vājasaneyī Saṁhitā*

Introduction

Philosophy, in its wide Indian connotation, has sprung from religion and has developed side by side with religion. It has therefore been inseparably fused with religion to such an extent that philosophy minus religion is almost unthinkable in India. Indian philosophy has never been speculative in character, indulging in scholastic acrobatics for the satisfaction of the intellectual elite. It has always been practical in its outlook and methods, aiming at the realization of the spiritual ideals of life. Indian philosophy is not content with propounding abstract theories about Reality, or with the mere description of it as experienced intuitively by seekers of Truth. It has always prescribed ways for the realization of the Supreme Goal of life.

It is indeed for this reason that the Indian philosophers, right from the Upaniṣadic times, have paid so much attention to the aspect of *sādhanā* which forms an integral part of Indian philosophy as such. All schools of Indian philosophy, theistic or atheistic, monistic or dualistic or pluralistic, whether constituting the Vedic stream of thought such as Nyāya, Vaiśeṣika, Sāṁkhya, Yoga, Mīmāmsā, Vedānta, etc., or the Āgamic stream of thought, such as Vaiṣṇava, Śaiva, Śākta, etc., formulate their own disciplines and prescribe their own methods for the achievement of the Supreme Ideal which they promulgate. Hence, to grasp the true spirit of Indian philosophy and to comprehend fully the essence of the metaphysical thinking of different schools of thought, it is essential to make a special and methodical study of the philosophy of *sādhanā* of each school without which our knowledge of the metaphysics of a particular school of thought would remain incomplete. This is especially true of all those schools of Indian philosophy which belong to the Āgamic stream where *sādhanā* forms the core and kernel. The Trika school of Kashmir, popularly known as Kashmir Śaivism, is one such school which is based on the Śaivāgamas, wherein the various modes of spiritual discipline were given more importance than epistemology or metaphysics.

Before we discuss the philosophy of *sādhanā* as enunciated by the different Śaivācāryas of Kashmir, it would not perhaps be out of place to give, by way of introduction, a bird's-eye view of the philosophy of *sādhanā* as can be gleaned from the philosophical literature right from the time of the Upaniṣads.

If we study the religio-philosophical literature from the earliest times to look for elements of the philosophy of *sādhanā,* we discover two distinct trends in the development of this thought. The first trend is discernible in the literature prior to the rise of different schools of philosophical thinking in India. Here we come across sages and *ācāryas* vividly describing their personal visions of the Truth[1] and also indicating to their disciples ways to reach the Supreme Goal. The ancient literature is characterized by the dominance of intuitive knowledge over dialectical thinking,[2] hence the philosophy of *sādhanā* is only implicit in the form of discourse on *yoga* given by sages (*ṛṣis*) who spoke from their personal intuitive experience of the Truth.

The reason for this is that the *ṛṣis* did not feel the necessity of discussing the rationale of all that they preached or talked about; they merely concerned themselves with the description of their vision of the Truth. The Upaniṣads, which constitute historically as well as traditionally the source book of Indian philosophy and religion, are replete with passages vividly describing the sages' intuitive vision of the Supreme Reality, but they also sometimes allude to the various modes of *sādhanā* or give practical tips to aspirants on *yoga* (way to Self-realization).

For example, the sage Yājñavalkya in the *Bṛhadāraṇyaka Upaniṣad* does not only describe the nature of *Ātman* and *Brahman,* but he also declares that "this *Ātman,* O Maitreyi, ought to be seen, ought to be meditated upon, for it is only when the *Ātman* is seen, heard, thought about, and meditated upon, does all this become vividly known."[3] The *Chāndogya Upaniṣad* also ex-

1. *Vedāhametam puruṣam mahāntam ādityavarṇam tamasaḥ parastāt /Tameva viditvā atimṛtyumeti nānyaḥ panthā vidyate ayanāya/Śvetāsvatara Up., III.,* 8.
2. Cf. . . . *naiṣā matiḥ tarkeṇa āpaneyā. Kaṭhopaniṣad I,* 29.
3. Op. cit., II, 4, 2–5.

presses the view that man does not remain satisfied with little happiness, which is, indeed, perishable. He aspires for 'the great happiness' which is full and eternal by its very nature. 'Little' happiness consists in seeing, hearing, and meditating upon other things besides the *Ātman*, while 'the great happiness' (*bhūma*) is experienced when the Infinite is seen everywhere in front and in the back. When the *Ātman* is seen everywhere and is realized as identical with everything that exists, 'great happiness' is experienced. He who realizes the unity of the Infinite, the individual, and the *Ātman* and thus experiences himself as *'So'ham Ātmā'* (I am the *Ātmān*), he enjoys the highest happiness.[4]

The *Muṇḍaka Upaniṣad* tells us that 'we should verily leave away all words, i.e. give up discussions about the Reality, we should devote ourselves to the knowledge of the *Ātman;* for this alone is capable of bestowing immortality. Meditate upon the *Ātman* with the help of the symbol *oṃ*, for this alone makes it possible for one to go beyond the ocean of darkness.'[5] The *Kaṭhopaniṣad* declares that 'the Self cannot be realized through words, through discursive thought, through the study of scriptures. It can directly be visualized by the *yogins* through meditation by purified mind.'[6]

The second trend in the development of the philosophy of *sādhanā* is to be seen in the later philosophical literature which was produced through systematization and rationalization of different philosophical ideas by different *ācāryas* who are known as the propounders of different schools of thought, such as Kapila, Gotama, Akṣapāda, Kaṇāda, and Patañjali. These *ācāryas* provided the religious experiences of their predecessors with a rational basis and organized them under different schools of philosophy. In this phase of development, Indian philosophy grew into rationalistic philosophy and as a consequence, the philosophy of *sādhanā* was also provided with a somewhat sound rationale, each system first indicating the goal of life to be achieved by an individual and then laying down the way to achieve the Supreme Goal. It is probably in this period that the theory of

4. *Chānd. Up.*, VII, 22–25.
5. Op. cit., II, 2, 3–4.
6. Op. cit., II, 3, 4.

puruṣārthas, or the goals of life, corresponding to the four stages of man's life (*āśrama*), was first enunciated and developed. In the course of time it was recognized that there could not be one particular mode of *sādhanā* prescribed for all individuals; it had to be different in accordance with different supreme ideals postulated by different schools of thought. For example, some schools of thought, such as Sāṁkhya[7] and Advaita Vedānta, considered ignorance to be the root cause of all miseries. Hence they laid emphasis on the acquisition of spiritual knowledge or *jñāna*, which alone, according to them, was capable of eradicating ignorance and leading the individual to the achievement of the Supreme Goal.[8] Some philosophical schools, such as those of the Mīmāmsakas, thought that performance of *karma* (actions), especially those prescribed by the scriptures, was essential for the achievement of the *summum bonum* since one cannot fully give up action, or escape from it while he is in embodied state. *Karma* has therefore to be utilized in such manner as to be instrumental in achieving the Supreme End. The *Bhagavadgītā* has prescribed the performance of *niṣkāma karma* (desireless action) or *karma* with fruits dedicated to the Supreme Being, technically called *Karma Yoga*, as the easiest way for an embodied individual to achieve the Ultimate Goal. Some schools of philosophy belonging to Vaiṣṇava stream considered *bhakti* as the best mode of *sādhanā*. Later during this phase of development, attempts were made at synthesizing the different modes of *sādhanā* by postulating some kind of hierarchy in the different ways.

A careful examination of the philosophy of *sādhanā* enunciated by different schools of thought would reveal certain common traits which may be noted here. First, all schools of Indian philosophy and religion consider the human individual to be the central figure for whom the different modes of *sādhanā* are prescribed. All systems postulate an extensive range of creation, consisting of many levels of existence[9] (according to popular belief, 84 lakh[10] *yonis* or types) in which man is said to occupy the

7. Cf. *Sāṁkhya Kārikā*, kā 1, and *Ved. Sār.*, p. 2 (Poona ed.).

8. Ibid.

9. Cf. *Sāṁkhya Kārikā*. kā 53, *Ved. Sār p.* 5 (*Poona*).

10. One lakh = 100,000.

central position on account of his being endowed with *karmadeha*, and therefore possessing the unique capacity for evolution up ward or having a fall downward in creation through his personal endeavor or through wrong actions. All other creatures possess *bhogadeha*, that is, a body-apparatus which can serve as an instrument for enjoyment only; hence they are incapable of performing purposeful actions and achieving the highest Goal. Man alone has the singular privilege of achieving the Supreme End out of his free will and through personal efforts.

Second, all schools agree (with the exception of the Buddhists and the materialist Cārvāka) that man in essence is pure and free, and therefore is not subject to misery and suffering. But in his present form, he is not aware of his real nature. Hence, he is in bondage, and undergoes pain and suffering in this world. Looking from the highest state of perfection, his present state represents him as one having fallen from his original status, a descent into the world of misery. What he seeks to achieve through his *sādhanā* therefore is his restoration to his real nature, the Essence.

Third, almost all schools of Indian philosophy (with the exception of the materialist Cārvāka) agree in holding the human personality to be complex by its very nature. It is said to consist of several layers of gross and subtle matter that exist one over the other, covering the noumenal self or spiritual self. In a normal state of his existence in the world, man is not aware of his real nature, owing to these sheaths of gross and subtle matter. He has, therefore, his ego-experience (*ahaṁbodha*) arising out of the false superimposition of the not-Self (*anātmani*) on the Self (*Ātman*), thus hiding his real Self. Thus the individual identifies himself with not-Self in the form of the gross physical body as he is ignorant of his real spiritual nature. Ego-experience also has the gross physical body as its basis. The aim of *sādhanā* is therefore to put an end to this false identification of not-Self with imagined self (*kalpita ahaṃbodha*) by directing man's "gaze" inwards,[11] as it were. It is sometimes metaphorically represented by journey from without to the innermost core of man's being.

11. This is precisely the reason for the Upaniṣadic seer to declare that the *Ātman* (Self) 'should be seen' (*drastavya*) first, and then it can be

While it is true that the Advaita Vedāntins, following the statement in some Upaniṣads that the real spiritual Self cannot be known through finite mind (*yan manasā na manute*), speak of the unknowable nature of Self, but it must be admitted that the veil of ignorance which covers the Self and thereby prevents its knowledge by the individual can be removed only by knowledge of the real Self on the intellectual plane. *Buddhi* (intellect) thus is the substratum of both knowledge and ignorance, which cancel each other. All schools, therefore, have to admit the important role that intellect plays in removing ignorance and causing the rise of knowledge of Self. The intellect in a fettered embodied individual is highly contaminated by the layers of residual impressions (*saṁskāras*) of past actions and *vāsanās* (desires) since the beginning of creation. So long as the intellect remains contaminated, man cannot hope to get a glimpse of his real Self. Hence, as a first step towards Self-realization, it must be cleansed and purged of all kinds of impurities so as to become the perfect medium for the vision of the Self. An intense and persistent endeavor is necessary for accomplishing this task, and it is here that ethical practices play a crucial role. The practice of such ethical means as *śama* (control of internal sense organs) *dama* (control of external sense organs), *titikṣā* (tolerance), etc., and such yogic devices as *yama* (control from without), *niyama* (control from within), *āsana* (posture), etc., are considered to be the first preparatory step in *sādhanā* which may be broadly called "purgation."

Before discussing in the following chapters the philosophy of *sādhanā* as enunciated by the different Śaivācāryas of Kashmir, it would perhaps be useful to give a survey of the rise and development of the Śaiva school of thought, especially the Trika school of Kashmir.

The origin of Śaivism as a powerful religious-philosophical current lies in the hoary past. On the basis of archaelogical evidence unearthed at several places in India, historians believe that

---

known through scriptures and meditation. (*Śrotamya mantavya.*) The direct experience of Self should precede its apprehension on the intellectual level (see: *Br. Up.* II, 4, 5).

it existed as a cult among the aboriginal tribes of India long before the advent of the Āryans on the Indian scene.[12] Tradition has ascribed the beginning of this cult to an Āgamic current which is believed to flow side by side with the Vedic current.[13] There is, however, no concrete evidence to support the traditional view, as no Āgamic literature belonging to the Vedic time has come down to us.

But there is enough evidence to show that the Śaiva cult was in existence even in the Vedic times. For instance, *Sūkta* 136 of the *Maṇḍala* X of the *Ṛgveda* refers to the *ṛṣi* Keśin, who was probably the leader of a sect of *ṛṣis*. From the interesting description of the members of this sect who wore dress of *piṅgala* (ochre) color and moved from one place to another in semi-naked condition, it appears that they were Śaiva *sannyāsins* (ascetics) of a Śaiva order. It has been said that members of this sect sometimes used to drink *viṣa* (poison) with the Vedic god Rudra. This description of the members of this sect is suggestive of the worshipers of Rudra Śiva.

It is true that the name of Śiva as god does not figure in the Vedic Saṁhitās, but the word *Śiva* occurs at a number of places, especially in the *Vājasaneyi Saṁhitā*,[14] as an adjective of Rudra. This has led scholars to identify Śiva with the Vedic god Rudra. The *Śatarudrīya* portion of *Yajurveda*[15] describes the Vedic Rudra through enumeration of one hundred names of Rudra in which the word *Śiva* occurs. Some scholars have linked Śiva with Mahādeva of the Vrātya hymns of the *Atharvaveda*, who is represented there as the protector of the Vrātyas.[16] Though the identification of Mahādevā of the Vrātyas with Śiva has been questioned, it is significant to note that the Vrātya hymns record a particular religious practice in which *yoga* is important—a fact that again brings the Vrātyas nearer to Śaivites.

Some scholars see a link between the phallus-worshipers of the *Ṛgvedic* time and the Śaiva cult, and are of the opinion that

---

12. Cf. Marshall, J., *Mohenjodaro and the Indus Civilization*, p. 25.
13. Cf. Abhinavagupta in *Parātrimśikā*, p. 4.
14. Op. cit., 3, 63.
15. *Taittirīya Sam.* 4, 5, 1; *Vaj Sam.*, 16.
16. *Atharvaveda* XV, 2.

the disapproval of the phallus-worshipers in the *Ṛgveda* indicates the tribal nature of the Śaiva cult.[17] R. G. Bhandarkar, however, considers that *liṅga* worship was not in vogue even at the time of Patañjali or Wema Kadphasis.[18] F. Kittel[19] and Barth trace the origin of *liṅga* worship to the Greeks.[20]

Though the reference to *ṛṣi* Aitas in the *Aitareya Brāhmaṇa* is highly suggestive of ascetics of a Śaiva order, positive evidence about the existence of Śaiva cult is, however, found only in the *Śvetāsvatara Upaniṣad.* It is in this Upaniṣad (composed probably in the third century B.C.) that Śiva appears as the prominent deity who has been given the epithet of Maheśvara. In fact, so much attention is paid to the delineation of Śiva as the main deity[21] that some scholars thought that this Upaniṣad marked the beginning of the rise of Śaivism as a distinct school of thought. The *Aṣṭādhyāyī* of Pāṇinī (500 B.C.) gives definite evidence about the existence of Śiva-worshipers in a *sūtra* laying down the rule for the formation of a word denoting Śiva-worshiper.[22] In the *Mahābhāsya* of Patañjali there is a reference to Śiva and his devotees, called *Śiva Bhāgavatas.*[23] Different names of Rudra Śiva, Girīśa, Mahādeva, Tryambaka, Bhava, Sarva, etc., are mentioned there.[24] The *Mahābhārata* gives clear indication of the existence of the Śaiva school of thought in the *Śāntiparva,* where five schools of thought including the Pāñcarātra and the Pāśupatas, have been mentioned.[25] Kauṭilya in the *Arthaśāstra*[26] refers to the construction of the shrine of Śiva with the shrines of other deities in the center of the city.

Certain numismatic articles and archaeological evidences discovered at various places also support the view that Śaivism

17. Cf. *Ṛigveda* X, 99, 3, VII, 21, 5. Also see Bagchi, P.C., p. 404, quoted in the *History of Śaivism* by P. Jash, p. 2.
18. *Vaiṣṇavism and Śaivism and other Minor Religions,* p. 164.
19. Kittel F, *Uber der Urspring des Linga Kultno in India,* p. 46.
20. Barth, *Religions of India,* p. 261.
21. Cf. *Śvet. Up.* Chapters. III & IV.
22. Op. cit. IV, 1, 112; V, 3, 99.
23. Op. cit., II, pp. 387–88 (Kielhorn).
24. Loc. cit.
25. *Mbh.,* Adhyāya 349 v. 64–68 (Poona).
26. Op. cit., Bk. II, Ch. IV. p. 64 (Shamshastri Ed.).

as a cult existed in the period between the second century B.C. and the first century A.D. A bronze seal discovered by John Marshall on a site near Taxila dated in the first century B.C. contains a figure of Śiva and the legend *"Śiva-rakṣita"* in Brāhmī and Kharoṣṭi characters.[27] Some early Yaudheya coins contain the figure of Śiva as symbol,[28] while the *triśūla* (trident) is depicted on the coins of Rudragupta, the Pāñcāla king.[29] Coins of foreign rulers in India, such as Wema Kadphasis,[30] Manes, Gondophares, Kaniṣka,[31] etc., not only reveal the leanings toward the Śiva cult but also vouchsafe the popularity of Śaivism in that period.

Śaivism as a distinct school of religious philosophy developed probably at a later date. Abhinavagupta, in his *magnum opus Tantrāloka,*[32] refers to three distinct streams of Śaivism, viz., dualistic, dualistic-nondualistic, and monistic, propounded, respectively, by Śiva, Rudra, and Bhairava. This division of Śaivism into three distinct currents is, however, based on the difference in outlook of the three schools of thought as well as the number of Śaivāgamas on which these are said to be based. For instance, the dualistic Śaiva stream is said to be based on ten Saivāgamas, the dualistic-nondualistic on eighteen Śaivāgamas, and the monistic Śaiva stream on sixty-four Śaivāgamas.

Historically speaking, the Śaiva stream consists of as many as eight schools of thought that developed at different times in different parts of India. These are the Pāśupata, Lakulīśa Pāśupata, Śaiva Siddhānta, Vīraśaiva, Nandikeśvara Śaiva, Raseśvara Śaiva, Trika Śaiva, and Viśiṣṭādvaita Śaiva of Śrīkaṇṭha. From the philophical point of view these schools can be classified under the three broad heads mentioned above. The dualistic stream is represented by the two southern schools of Pāśupata and Śaiva-Siddhānta, the dualistic-nondualistic by the Lakulīśa-Pāśupata and Viraśaiva schools, while the monistic stream con-

27. *Comprehensive History of India,* vol. II, p. 401.
28. Allan, J. *Catalogue of Ancient Indian Coins in British Museum* (London, 1936), p. 307.
29. Banerji, J. N. *Development of Hindu Iconography* (Calcutta, 1956), p. 11.
30. Ibid., p. 117.
31. Ibid., p. 118.
32. Loc. cit., I, 37–48.

sists of Nandikeśvara Śaiva, Raseśvara Śaiva, Trika Śaiva, and the Viśiṣṭādvaita Śaiva of Śrīkaṇṭha.

Of the eight schools of Śaivism mentioned above, historically speaking, the earliest school was probably that of the Pāśupatas, which is said to be founded by Śrikaṇṭha.[33] He is mentioned as the author of *Piṅgalamata*,[34] and is believed to have flourished prior to Patañjali. It is probable that Patañjali refers only to his followers as *Śiva-Bhāgavatas*. Lakulīśa Pāsupatas flourished at least a century later[35] and formed a different sect of the Pāśupatas. In light of the Mathura Pillar inscription, D. R. Bhandarkar has shown that he flourished in the second century A.D.[36]

The richest school of Śaivism, however, is the Trika school, which possesses exceptional philosophical literature. This school of Śaivism, which propounds monistic philosophy, developed in the beautiful valley of Kashmir around the eighth century A.D. It is popularly called "Kashmir Śaivism," though this is actually a misnomer. Kashmir saw the rise of as many as four Śaiva schools which, according to orthodox tradition,[37] were started by Durvāsā through his three "mind-born" sons, viz., Tryambaka, Āmardaka, and Śrīkaṇṭha, who were founders of the monistic, monistic-cum-dualistic, and dualistic schools respectively; the fourth was founded by a descendant of Tryambaka on the daughter's side. This fourth school was called the Ardha Tryambaka, which probably is the same as the Kaula school, or Kulaprakriyā, referred to by Abhinavagupta and Jayaratha.[38] This school, however, merged with the Trika school in the course of time, though some of its doctrines are mentioned here and there in the works of Abhinavagupta and other writers.

A word of explanation is necessary for our using the name Trika in preference to Pratyabhijñā, which has been used by Mādhavacārya in his compendium *Sarva-darśana-samgraha* to denote this school of Śaivism. Various reasons have been adduced

33. Cf. *Mahābhārata*, Adhyāya 349, v. 150–51.
34. See Pathak, V. S. *Śaiva Cults in North India* (Varanasi 1960), p. 7.
35. Ibid.
36. *Journal of Bombay Branch of Royal Asiatic Society*, vol. XL, pp. 21ff.
37. *T.A.Āh* I, 35.
38. Ibid., *Āh*. I, v.7 and 30. comm.

and various explanations have been given in the Śaiva texts, which can be summed up as follows:

1. It is said that of the sixty-four Āgamas recognized as authoritative by this school, the triad (*trika*) of the *Mālinī, Siddha,* and *Nāmaka Āgamas* is of greatest importance. In fact this monistic school of Śaivism is based on these three famous Āgamas;[39] hence it is called the Trika system.
2. This school venerates three important triads,[40] viz., *Śiva, Śakti,* and their union; or *Śiva, Śakti,* and *Nara;* or *Parā, Aparā,* and *Parāpara śaktis;* hence it is named as the Trika system.
3. It explains three modes of the knowledge of Reality, viz., nondual (*abheda*), nondual-cum-dual (*bhedābheda*), and dual (*bheda*); hence the name Trika.
4. The literature which has come down to us can be divided under three heads, viz., *Āgama Śastra, Spanda Śāśtra,* and *Pratyabhijñā Sāśtra,* constituting three streams[41] which represent three phases of development of this school that later merged to the Trika school.

The Trika system in the form of *Āgama Śastra* is believed to have eternal existence. Of the large number of Āgamas that have come down to us, the chief ones are the *Mālinīvijaya Tantra, Svacchanda Tantra, Vijñānabhairava Tantra, Mṛgendra Tantra,* and *Netra Tantra,* which are available in print. The founder of the Trika school of Śaivism as a systematic system of philosophy, however, was Vasugupta (*c.* 825 A.D.), to whom the *Śiva Sūtras* are said to have been revealed. The *Śiva Sūtras,* also known as the *Śiva-rahasya-āgama-śāstra-saṁgraha,* constitute the most important text under the head, *Āgama Śāstra.* On the *Śiva Sūtras,* three commentaries are available, viz., *Vṛtti,* by an unknown author; *Vārtika,* by Rājanaka Bhāskara; and *Vimarśini,* by Kṣemarāja. Commentaries were also written on the principal Āgamas at a later date by Śaiva writers of this school. For example, Ksemarāja wrote *Udyota* (commentary) on the *Netra Tantra, Svacchanda Tan tra,*

39. Ibid., *Āh.* I, 25.
40. Ibid., *Āh.* I, v. 7.
41. Chatterji, J. C. *Kashmir Shaivism,* p. 2.

and the *Vijñānabhairava Tantra,* available only in part. Abhinavagupta wrote a gloss on the *Mālinī-Vijaya Tantra,* which came to be known as the *Mālinīvijayavārtika.* He also wrote a commentary on the *Parātrimśika,* which is said to contain verses from *Rudrayāmala Tantra,* available only in fragments.

The *Spanda Śāstra* elaborates the purely monistic principles enunciated in the *Śiva Sūtras* but does not adduce logical support to the principles. The first and foremost work belonging to this branch is the *Spanda Sūtra,* better known as the *Spanda Kārikā.* Though the authorship of the text is traditionally attributed to Vasugupta himself, most probably these were composed by his disciple, Kallaṭa. Kallaṭa also wrote a commentary called *Vṛtti* on the *Kārikās,* which together are known as the *Spanda Sarvasva.* Three more commentaries on the *Kārikās* are available, viz., *Vivṛti* by Rāmakaṇṭha, *Pradīpa* by Utpalabhaṭṭa, and *Nirṇaya* by Kṣemarāja. The *Spanda Sandoha* is yet another work by Ksemarāja belonging to this stream. It is in fact only an abridgement of his larger work, *Spanda Nirṇaya.*

The Pratyabhijñá Śástra may be regarded as the philosophical branch of the Trika system wherein an attempt was made, for the first time, to rationalize the tenets of the system. Siddha Somānanda, probably a pupil of Vasugupta, is credited with introducing dialectics into this system, and is therefore spoken of as the founder of logic (*tarkasya kartā*). His only available work, the *Śiva Dṛṣṭi,* laid the foundation of this branch. On this work, Utpaladeva, a pupil of Somānanda, is said to have written a commentary called *Vṛtti,* which is available in part only. Another important and scholarly work belonging to this branch is the *Īśvara-pratyabhijña-kārikā* by Utpaladeva. In this work, he has tried to present a summary of the philosophical work of his teacher in lucid language. Though this work is shorter in volume than that of his teacher, it gained so much popularity that the entire philosophical system of Trika Śaivism came to be known after it, even in ancient times outside of Kashmir. A number of commentaries were written on it, the most famous and popular among them being *Vimarśinī* by Abhinavagupta. Besides this commentary, he wrote a more comprehensive commentary on this work, called *Vivrti Vimarśinī.* Bhāskarakaṇṭha wrote a commentary on the

Vimarśinī to elucidate the explanation given by Abhinavagupta, which came to be known as the *Bhāskarī Ṭīkā*.

Abhinavagupta, who is perhaps the greatest genius of his time and its most prolific writer, wrote as many as sixteen original books expounding the philosophy of this system. Among his scholarly works, mention must be made of the *Paramārtha Sāra*, the *Tantrāloka*, and the *Tantrasāra*. His voluminous work the *Tantrāloka* is a veritable encyclopedia of the system and as such it forms a class by itself. He successfully synthesized different currents of Advaita Śaiva thought, which is his greatest contribution to this school. Jayaratha wrote a lucid and elaborate commentary on it, which runs into twelve volumes. Another important writer belonging to this school of thought is Kṣemarāja, who is equally a versatile and prolific writer. He wrote commentaries on a number of important works and thus enriched the system by his scholarly works. His original work, *Pratyabhijñā Hṛdaya*, has been very popular in Kashmir and describes Śaivayoga in a nutshell.

CHAPTER 1

The Metaphysics of the Trika School

THE HIGHEST REALITY in the Trika system is the Supreme Experiencing Principle (*Parāsaṁvit*), that is of the nature of Pure Consciousness (*śuddha-cit-svabhāva*). It is by its very nature eternal immutable, and infinite. Though it is eternal and immutable, it underlies, as the innermost and true Self,[1] every manifestation in the universe, both individually and collectively, and hence in that all-pervasive or cosmic aspect, it is called the *Ātman* and the *Caitanya*.[2]

At the same time, the *Parāsaṁvit* is one, indivisible, and infinite. It is not exhausted by its innumerable and diverse manifestations in the universe, nor is limited or conditioned by space (*deśa*), time (*kāla*), or form (*rūpa*). It transcends all, and is beyond all; and hence in that all-transcending aspect, it is called the Supreme Consciousness (*Parācit* or *Parāsaṁvit*), the *Tattvātīta*, the Absolute, the *Anuttara*.[3]

The *Parāsaṁvit* or *Caitanya* thus has a two-fold nature[4]—as the underlying reality of everything and all. It is the all-pervasive and all-inclusive cosmic Reality, the Universal Consciousness. At

1. *Śiva Sū.;* I p. 3 Comm.
2. Ibid.
3. *Par. Sār.*, Kā. I, p. 2; Ibid. p. 5. Comm.
4. *Pr. Hd.* Comm., p. 44.

the same time it is also the all-transcending Supreme Reality, the Absolute Being.

The *Caitanya*, according to the Trika system, is essentially of the nature of Pure Illumination (*Śuddha Prakāśa*) that is always self-luminous (*sphurat*) and self-revealed (*svayamprakāśita*). The *Caitanya* as Pure Illumination (*Śuddha Prakāśa*) is the substratum of all things that exist or have a being (*sattā*),[5] because the existence or being must necessarily be (by its very nature) either revealed to experience or capable of being revealed (*prakāśya*). That is to say, the concept of existence (*sattā*) is co-extensive with being manifest.[6] We cannot conceive of anything which has existence or being but is unmanifest or unrevealed or incapable of being revealed, and thus lies outside the realm of *Prakāsá*.[7] It is indeed for this reason that the Trika system holds that everything that exists or has a being must necessarily be of the nature of *Prakāśa* or Pure Illumination.[8]

The *Caitanya*, as we have stated, is held to be self-luminous by nature. This means that the *Caitanya* is not merely Pure Illumination (*Śuddha Prakāśa*) which always shines and illumines, it is also at the same time the Illuminator (*Prakaśāka*), which illumines and reveals (*prakāśati*). The aspect of *Caitanya* as the Illuminator must be one and identical with that of the Illumination, since it cannot exist outside the *caitanya* which is held to be the sole Reality. In the same way, the Illumined (*Prakāśita*) also revealed by the Illumination cannot be different from the Illumination (*Prakāśa*).[9] This, in other words, means that the *Caitanya* is not merely of the nature of Pure Illumination, it is also at the same time the Illuminator of itself as the Illumined (*Prakāśita*), the three aspects being one and identical in essence.

It is indeed for this reason that the *Caitanya* is described in the Trika system as of the nature of Pure Illumination (*Śuddha* Prakāśa)[10] which always shines and reveals itself in the absence of a second.

---

5. *I.P.V.V.*, p. 4.
6. *TV.* v. 17
7. Ibid., v–17; *I.P.V.*, I, 5,3.
8. *I.P.V.V.*, p. 5.
9. *I.P,V.V*, ,I, p. 73.
10. *Pr. Hd.*, Su 1 Comm. p, 21.

The identify of Illumination, Illuminator, and the Illumined may no doubt seem strange as it is contrary to our ordinary experience in which we always find them as separate and independent entities. But in the case of *Caitanya,* which is the sole Reality, it is true, both logically and factually.

When the *Caitanya* is described as being intrinsically self luminous (*svayaṁprākāśa*) and self-revealed (*svayaṁprakāśita*), it automatically follows that the *Caitanya,* i.e., the *Prakāśa,* possesses the innate capacity of self-revelation, whereby it always shines and reveals itself. This capacity of self-revelation, which is unique in *Caitanya* or *Prakāśa,* is technically called the *Āmarśana Śakti* of *Caitanya,* or simply the *Vimarśa Śakti,* and the act of self-revelation as the *Parāmarśa* of *Caitanya.* The *Vimarśa Śakti* is the eternal "attribute" of *Caitanya*[11] as it is inalienable from its essence.

From the above description of *Caitanya,* namely that *Caitanya* possesses the power of self-revelation or *Vimarsa Śakti,* one might conclude that the *Caitānya* or *Prakāśa,* as the possessor of the *Vimarśa Śakti,* must be distinct and separate from the possessed, i.e., the *Vimarśa Śakti,* and that the *Vimarśa Śakti* as an attribute of *Caitanya* must be something external to and independent of *Caitanya.* This conclusion, according to the Trika system, is erroneous and logically unwarranted. It is undoubtedly true, says the Trika system, that we sometimes, from the practical point of view, distinguish Śakti from the *śaktiman,* viz., the difference observed in their application and the result noticed therefrom;[12] but that kind of distinction is merely a conceptual distinction or logical distinction made by us, for our convenience in understanding their nature. It is not a real difference that actually exists. For instance, the fire (*agni*) and its power of burning (*dāhikā śakti*) are not independent entities, though we might sometimes distinguish the power of burning (*dāhikā śakti*) from the fire (*agni*) in order to understand the difference between the power of burning and the power of heating (*uttāpa śakti*), which is another power of the fire having practical application in life. On the basis of this logical distinction, which is made to understand more comprehensively the nature of things, we cannot conclude that the Śakti exists independently of *śaktimān* or the *guṇa* (attribute) of *dravya* (substance).

11. *Parāpravesika,* p. 1; I, 5, 11.
12. *T.A.,* 1, 69, p. 110 Comm.

That being so, the Trika system, being strictly a monistic system, does not believe, unlike the dualist Naiyāyikas, in the duality of Śakti and the *śaktimān*,[13] *guṇa* and the *dravya*. It does not believe, for instance, that the burning power (*dāhikā śakti*) can exist independently of its substratum, fire (*agni*[14]) or the coldness (*śaitva*) of the ice (*hima*). The Śakti and the *Śaktimān*, the *guṇa* and the *dravya* are, in the opinion of Trika system, not only inseparable as entities, but they are also one and identical in essence.

Hence it can be said that the *Caitanya*, as the self-revealing power, the *Vimarśa Śakti*, and the *Caitanya* as the Pure Illumination (*Śuddha Prakāśa*) are not the two different aspects that exist independently of each other. They are, really speaking, one and identical in essence. The *Caitanya* as the Pure Illumination (*Śuddha Prakāśa*) always implies and involves the *Caitanya* as the self-revealing power (*Vimarśa Śakti*), so that it is impossible to think of one without the other even for the sake of logical abstraction. As a matter of fact, we cannot, strictly speaking, call the *Prakāśa* and the *Vimarśa Śakti* the two aspects of the Reality, for they are biune in nature.

Since the *Caitanya* is held to be always self-revealed, *Prakāśa* is said to be always with *Vimarśa*.[15] The *Vimarśa Śakti* always functions, otherwise the *Prakāśa* will not be manifest, a state which is logically unthinkable. The *Vimarśa* is the essence of *Caitanya*,[16] its integral nature (*svabhāva*). It is, in fact, the unique character which distinguishes it from non-*Caitanya*, i.e., matter (*jaḍa*).

The Supreme Reality, which is of the nature of *Caitanya* in the Trika system, is therefore always described as *Prakāśa-Vimarśa-Maya*. In the Supreme Reality, the aspect of Pure Illumination (*Śuddha Prakāśa*) represents the *Caitanya* in the quiescent or static form, in which it is the ever-changeless self-same Principle, and therefore is also called Śiva, in the masculine form, while the aspect of *Caitanya* as the self-revealing power (*Śuddha Vimarśa*) represents *Caitanya* in the pure dynamic form in which it is the ever-

---

13. *Vijñānabhairava Āgama*, v. 18, p. 13.
14. Ibid., v. 19, p. 13; *T.A.*, I, 69, p. 110.
15. *I P.V.V.*, p. 5
16. Ibid., Vol. 1. p. 73.

vibrating (*spandita*), the ever-active Principle of dynamism, and is therefore called the Śakti in the feminine form.[17]

The Supreme Reality is absolutely silent, the Pure Statis. At the same time, it is the ever-active, the Pure Dynamis. Neither the aspect of Pure Statis, Śiva, nor the aspect of Pure Dynamis, *Śakti*, is dominant, so that it is the equilibrium of the both. That is to say, Śiva and Śakti are held in perfect equilibrium in the Supreme Reality, which is, therefore, technically designated as the *Parama Śiva.*[18]

The *Parama Śiva*, being endowed with Śakti, which is held to be identical with his Essence, is also described by virtue of it as the Supreme Lord (Parmeśvara or Maheśvara). The *Parama Śiva,* as the Supreme Lord, has the absolute freedom (*svātantrya*) inasmuch as his Śakti is absolutely free from any kind of restriction or limitation.[19] It is indeed for this reason that his Śakti is sometimes technically called the *Svātantrya Śakti* (divine freedom).

His possession of *Svātantrya Śakti* as his integral nature is indicative of his fullness[20] and absolute character. His *svātantrya* consists of his forming divine resolve (*saṅkalpa*), and of translating those resolutions into actuality through his power of action (*kriyā śakti*).[21] Thus, he possesses not only an unlimited freedom of will (*apratihata ichhā*)[22] of forming resolve, but also an absolute freedom of carrying them out in actuality,[23] i.e., the freedom of action (*kriyā*) both of which constitute the essence of his divine nature (*Pārameśvarya*).

Exercising his divine freedom, the Supreme Lord, sometimes, i.e., during the period of creative activity, reveals himself to himself as the universe (*viśva*). Of this self-revelation as universe, which he does out of his free and independent will

---

17. *T.A.*, Ah. I, 69, p. 109.
18. Ibid. II, I, Comm.
19. *I.P.V.*, I. V. 13.
20. *T.A.*, I, 92 p. 137.
21. *I.P.V.V.*, Vol. I, p. 82.
22. It must be noted that the divine *Ichhā,* when crystallized, forms the divine *Sankalpa. I.P.V.*, I. v. 15.
23. *I.P.V.* I, v. 14, Comm.

(*svecchayā*) with himself as the background (*svabhitta*),[24] he is the Supreme Agent (*kartā*), the Ultimate Experiencer (*pramātā*), and the Supreme Enjoyer (*bhoktā*).

The manifestation of the universe is thus only a mode of his self-revelation in which he utilizes no other material than his own Śakti. Or to put it perhaps in a more precise language, the Supreme Lord's self-manifestation as the universe is only a self-expansion in the aspect of Śakti, (*sva-śakti-sphārau*).[25] As such, the manifestation of the universe symbolizes his divine glory (*aiśvarya*), in the revelation of which the Śakti plays the most important role.

As the Śakti is held to be responsible for bringing out his divine glory expressed as the universe, which was until now absorbed and identified with his Essence, as well as his essential *svarupa* as the self-manifestation only, it is described in the Trika system as the essence of his divinity, the heart of the Supreme Lord.[26] Always identified with him, the Śakti is said to be ever-active and ever-functioning, always revealing his divine nature (*aiśvarya*).[27]

It would not be out of place here to examine critically the Trika conception of Supreme Reality in the light of the conception of the *Brahman* of the Advaita Vedānta of Śaṅkara for the sake of better and critical appreciation of the Trika viewpoint.

Although both the systems of the Advaita Vedānta of Śaṅkara and the Trika agree in describing the Supreme Reality as essentially of the nature of pure *Caitanya*, they differ vastly in their conception of its nature. While the Trika system considers the pure *Caitanya* to be endowed with Śakti that is held to be identical with itself, and whereby the *Caitanya* is always self-aware and self-revealed, the Advaita Vedānṭa maintains that the pure *Caitanya* is inactive, pure Existence only. Vedānta thus does not admit the existence of Śakti in the *Caitanya*.

Being endowed with Śakti, the Supreme Reality of the Trika system, technically called *Parama Śiva*, differs fundamentally from

24. *Pr. Hd.*, Sū. 2.
25. *T.A.*, 1, Comm. p. 121.
26. *I.P.V.*, I, V, p. 124.
27. *Pr. Hd.*, Sū. 12, Comm. p. 63.

the *Brahman* of the Advaita Vedānta of Śaṅkara inasmuch as the former has also been described as the Supreme Lord (Maheśvara) and the Free Agent (Svatantrah Kartā). As such, he possesses absolute freedom (*svātantrya*), exercising which he causes himself to appear as the universe, with himself as the background.

The universe, with its infinite variety of objects (*prameya*), means of experience (*karaṇa*), and experiencers (*pramātā*), thus is not something different from himself; it is, in fact, a manifestation of the immanent aspect of the Supreme Lord. It is a mode of his self-manifestation (*ābhāsa*),[28] resulting directly from his divine resolve (*saṅkalpa*) of appearing as the many.[29] For the initiation of this process of self-manifestation as well as its dissolution, nothing is needed beyond the play of his free will (*svecchā*).[30]

The Advaita Vedānta of Śaṅkara, on the other hand, regards the Supreme Reality, *Brahman,* to be the Transcedent Pure Being (*Śuddha Sat*), ever immersed in its essential nature. As such, the *Brahman* is absolutely inactive in itself. Though it is said to be the underlying Reality of every and all appearance, it is in itself one and indivisible Pure Existence. It has no relation whatsoever with the appearance of the universe, of multiplicity.

The transient world with its infinite variety, in the Advaita Vedānta's view, is an appearance, a perverted experience of *Brahman* due to *Ajñāna* (ignorance). Though the *Brahman* is the ultimate locus or the substratum of all appearances and experience, it is in no way connected with the appearance or perverted experience as it is essentially inactive.

It is held, therefore, that the appearance of the world is due to the functioning of a *śakti* which, though distinct from the *Brahman,* is held to be mysteriously subservient to it. The *śakti,* technically called the *māyāśākti,* is described as of the nature of neither *is* (*asti*), nor *is not* (*nāsti*), therefore, indescribable in logical terms. It functions ceaselessly in the *Brahman,* causing the multiplicity to appear.

---

28. For a comparative account of the doctrines of *abhāsa* and *vivarta,* see *I.P.V.V.* Vol: 1, p. 8–9; for a lucid account of the doctrine of *abhāsa* see Chatterji, *Ka. Śai,* p. 53–61; Pandey, *Abhinavagupta, A Study,* p. 195–96.
29. Cf. *Eko ham bahu syām.*
30. *Sp. Ka.,* v–1, Comm. p. 4–5; Ibid. p. 11; *Pr Hd.,* Sū. 2.

The *Brahman* is thus reduced to an actionless locus (*āśraya*) in which the *śakti* operates without any beginning. Thus, though the Advaita Vedānta of Śaṅkara does not admit the existence of *śakti* in the *Brahman,* it does not deny the existence of *śakti* altogether. To account for the appearance of multiplicity in the immutable unity of *Brahman,* the operation of *śakti* has been admitted; but it has been regarded as material (*jaḍa*), as against the Trika view, which holds the Śakti to be essentially divine and spiritual.

The divergence of opinion in the conception of the Supreme Reality between these two systems, we find, rests mainly on the differences in their conception of the nature of Śakti. While the Advaita Vedānta considers *śakti* to be material by nature and as such, different from the *Brahman* which is regarded as spiritual, the Trika system holds Śakti to be spiritual in essence, and as such an integral aspect of the Supreme Lord.[31]

By recognizing Śakti as the inalienable nature of *Parama Śiva,* the Trika system enlarges, as it were, its conception of the Supreme Reality which is both Transcendent (*viśvottīrṇa*) Reality as the Absolute, and Immanent existence (*viśvātmakasattā*) as the universe. As compared to this, the Vedānta's conception of Supreme Reality as *Brahman* appears as exclusive and based on a renunciatory outlook (*sannyāsa-mūlaka-pravṛtti*).

We have observed that the Śakti is the essence of the Supreme Lord's divinity. Always functioning as identified with him and thus revealing his divine glory (*aiśvarya*), it has innumerable forms or aspects,[32] which can, however, be subsumed under five principal heads,[33] viz., *cit, ānanda, icchā, jñāna,* and *kriyā śaktis,* arranged in the order of their intrinsicalness.

The *cit śakti* is the most intrinsic aspect of Śakti, symbolizing the Supreme Lord's power of self-revelation (*prakāśa-rūpata*).[34] As it is held in identity with the Supreme Lord, he always shines

31. *Pr. Hd..* Sū. I, Comm p. 21.
32. *T.S.,* Āh. iv. p. 28.
33. Ibid. Āh I, p. 6. Five *śaktis* are like "five faces" of the Supreme Lord from which "the five-streamed" *śāstra* has emerged. See *T.S.,* p.4; they are even reduced to three—*iccha, jñāna,* and *kriyā*—which are the three main aspects of Śakti. See *T.S.,* I, p.6.
34. *T.S.,* Āh. I, p.6.

and reveals himself to himself in the absence of a second. This self-revelation, it is said, is of the nature of "being experience" (*Aham*) of the Supreme Lord, and as such, it is eternal (*nitya*) and "full-in-itself" (*pūrna*).

Next in the order of intrinsicalness is the *ānanda śakti*, by which the Supreme Lord, who is "full-in-himself" (*pūrna-svabhāva*), feels ever-satisfied (*ātmatṛpta*) and ever at rest.[35] He does not experience any deficiency or want, for which he might feel the necessity of moving out of himself for satisfaction or joy. He remains, as it were, resting always in himself (*svātmaviśrānta*), immersed in his *Essence*,[36] and experiencing the ever-undisturbed peace.

The *icchā śakti* is that aspect of Śakti by which the Supreme Lord feels himself supremely able, possessed of absolute will and of forming divine resolve (*saṅkalpa*) as to what to do, or what to create.[37] The divine resolve is at the root of all his movements and acts (*kriyā*),[38] including the manifestation of duality (*dvaitābhāsa*) with himself as the background.

The *jñāna śakti* is that aspect of Śakti which brings in and holds all his self-manifestations as objects (*prameyakalpa*) in conscious relation to himself.[39] It is true that the very act of bringing in relationship presupposes the existence of duality, but in the case of *Parama Śiva*, the Sole Reality, the question of existence of something apart from him cannot arise. The *Parama Śiva*, therefore, never experiences complete duality between himself and his self-manifestation as object (*idam*), which is symbolized by the universe. The reason for this is said to be that he always feels and experiences his objective self-manifestation to be held in him and bound by a thread of unity. Thus, the duality of self-manifestation as the universe is always revealed in his experience, as it were, in the background of all-embracing unity.

The *kriyā śakti* is that aspect of Śakti exercising which the Supreme Lord becomes the universe assuming any and every

---

35. *S.D.*, Āh. I, 20, Comm. p. 17.
36. *T.S.*, Āh. I, p. 6.
37. *Bubhuṣālaksaṇā*.
38. *Sp. Ka.*, Niṣ I, i, Comm. p. 7; *S.D.*, I, L 16–17, p. 16; *STTS*. V–2, p. 2.
39. *S.D.*, Āh. I, 21, Comm., p. 18.

role,[40] and thus actively participates in the display of his glory as the universe.

With these five principal aspects of his Śakti functioning eternally and thus revealing his divine nature, the *Parama Śiva* always appears as the Supreme Lord. The ever-functioning Śakti exists in a two-fold condition in the Supreme Lord. First, it functions while involved in and identified with him, when it brings out his integral nature (*svarūpa*) as self-manifestation only (*svaprakāśa*); and second, it functions sometimes somewhat distinctly as his inalienable nature, when it is expressed as the manifestation of the universe.

As the Śakti functions identified with *Parama Śiva,* he reveals himself to himself as one undifferentiated Principle. This self-revelation of *Parama Śiva* to himself must necessarily be of the nature of self-experience (*svānubhava*). And since in his self-experience there is no other principle which can limit it, or from which it can be distinguished, the self-experience must be of the nature of Self or *Aham.*[41] This, in other words, means that when the Śakti functions as completely absorbed in and identified with him, it reveals his absolute nature (*svarūpa*) as *pūrṇa Aham.*[42] This self-experience as *Aham* is said to be *pūrṇa* (full) in the absence of anything external to it.

Being free of all kinds of restrictions or limitations, it is regarded as pure in nature. It is described as the self-centered (*svātma-viśrānta*) self-experience of *Parama Śiva* as it implies no outward movement or self-expression. Flowing directly from his self-shining and self-revelatory nature, as it does, his self-experience as *Aham* is eternal in the sense that it is beyond the limits of time-process (*kāla*).[43] It is unique and infinitely potential. It forms the foundation of all his self-experiences.[44]

As such, it must be distinguished from the ego-experience of the common man, which, according to the Trika system, arises

---

40. *T.S.*, Āh. I, p. 6.
41. *Aj. Pr. Siddhi,* v–15; *T.A.*, Āh. I, 67, Comm., p. 107.
42. *Sp. Nir.*, III, 13, Comm., p. 65.
43. *T.A.*, I., 127; p. 165.
44. For the nature of Self-experience, *pūrṇa ahaṁtā,* see *Sp. Nir.*, III, 13, Comm., p. 66.

from the superimposition of the Self on the not-Self, i.e. body and its constituent *tattvas,* and is, therefore, limited and impure by nature.

Sometimes when the Śakti functions distinctly, as it were, as his inalienable nature, *Parama Śiva* appears as the Supreme Lord, and his Śakti is expressed as the manifestation of the universe. The process of manifestation of the universe can be described in the following manner from *Parama Śiva's* point of view. The Supreme Lord, exercising his free will, reveals himself to himself—which is the same as his Śakti—as the universe. Obviously, the self-revelation of *Parama Śiva* as universe is only a manifestation of his immanent aspect, i.e, Śakti, as universe, which lies prior to manifestation, as absorbed in and identified with his Essence.[45] To *Parama Śiva,* the manifestation of universe appears, as it were, as a mode of his self-experience, since he is the ultimate Experiencer (*para-pramātā*) and the Spectator (*sākṣī*) of this self-manifestation.

In this way, the Trika system holds that the self-manifestation as the universe is also a mode of his self-experience in the same way as *Aham* is the mode of his integral Self-experience (*akhaṇḍa-anubhava*). These two modes of self-experiences are held to be simultaneous. That is to say, when the *Parama Śiva* has the self-experience as the universe, he does not cease to have his integral self-experience as *Aham;* the former does not obliterate the latter.

Outwardly this may appear somewhat incongruous, but if we try to understand the real nature of these self-experiences, we would find that they are not mutually exclusive. They are, rather, intimately connected, for the self-experience as universe implies and presupposes the self-experience as being or *Aham.* Unless the *Parama Śiva* has the self-experience as *viśva,*[46] *Aham* or Being-Experience is thus the foundation of *Parama Śiva's* self-experience as *viśva,* or the universe.

All that happens when he has the self-experience as the universe is that his absolute self-experience as *pūrṇa-Aham* becomes somewhat "covered up" as it were, and grows less prom-

45. *Pr. Hd..* Sū. 4, Comm., p. 30.
46. This is true of even all our ordinary experiences.

inent, due to the imposition of self-limitation (*ātma-saṅkoca*). That is to say, he then does not have the absolute self-experience as *pūrṇa-Aham;* he has the self-experience as *Aham* only in the stages of involution (*sṛṣṭi*).

The Supreme Lord is said to have five principal kinds of functions,[47] or *kṛtyas* forming a cycle as it were through which he is said to manifest his *svātantrya* eternally. They are technically designated as the *nigraha*, the *sṛṣti*, the *sthiti*, the *saṁhāra*, and the *anugraha*.[48] We have enumerated these functions in a particular order (*krama*), but that should not be taken to mean that there is a rigid succession or order in which these functions are bound to take place, or that the Supreme Lord is bound by that order. The Supreme Lord, being absolutely free (*svatantraḥ*) in all respects, is not bound in principle by a logical succession of *kṛtyas*. It is only for our convenience to explain the cycle of five functions that we have arranged them in a logical order, taking the *nigraha* to be the starting point of the cycle of *kṛtyas*.

The *nigraha*, also called the *tirodhāna*, literally means self-limitation. In order that the Supreme Lord can make the multiplicity as universe to appear, he first, exercising his divine *svātantrya*, imposes limitation on his limitless nature (*pūrṇa-svarūpa*). As a result of this voluntary self-limitation, he who always experiences himself as *pūrṇa Aham* ceases to have that kind of self-experience. The *pūrṇa Ahamtā*, the characteristic essence of his Absolute nature, disappears, as it were, with the imposition of self-limitation (*nigraha*). A cleavage appears in his self-experience as *Aham*, and he appears as having split himself spontaneously, as it were, into two sections—one which remains self-revealed as *Aham*, and the other which becomes "dark", as it were, with the imposition of limitation due to the cessation of self-revelatory power (*Vimarśa Śakti*). The portion that becomes "dark" consequent on the cessation of self-revelatory power and there, by suppression of *Ahaṁtā*, appears as a void (*akāśa*) or absolute negation (*śūnya*), as *Ahaṁtā* is negated from it. This is a necessary precondition for the emergence of the self-experience as *viśva*, symbolized by the term *Idam*.

47. *S.T.T.S.*, V–I, Comm., p. 1; *Sp. Nir,* III, 13, p. 66, App. V–2, p. 1.
48. The Supreme Lord even as a *saṁsārin* is said to perform five *kṛtyas;* for explanation. see *Pr. Hd.*, Sū 10., Comm. pp. 51ff.

The Supreme Lord then makes the *'Idam'* appear[49] in the background of "void" (*ākāśa*) created by his self-limitation or self-negation; and this function is technically called *sṛṣṭi.*[50] As *Idam* or not-Self is totally free from the characteristic feature of self-consciousness, which is the essential feature of *Ahaṁtā,* the *Idam* appears, as it were, as something distinct from and outside of *Ahaṁtā.* But, as a matter of fact, *Ahamtā* and *Idaṁtā* are not different from each other: they are only the polarized aspects of experience. Hence the duality does not appear in the manifestation of *Idaṁtā.*

In the beginning, the self-experience as *Ahaṁtā* prevails over the self-experience as *Idaṁtā,* the latter being indistinct. But the *Idaṁtā* does not remain so for long; it gradually develops and grows distinct, until at last it reaches a stage where both appear as perfectly balanced. This stage of development is reached due to the *kṛtya* that is technically called *sthiti.*

In the next moment, what had emerged from *Ahaṁtā* as *Idam* is made to disappear completely by the Supreme Lord. It is withdrawn and absorbed in the *Ahaṁtā;* this stage of development is known as *saṁhāra.*

With the *saṁhāra,* the cycle of outward manifestation, which had commenced with *sṛṣṭi,* is completed, but the cycle of functions as such does not end there. The first four *kṛtyas* (functions), beginning with *nigraha,* constitute the process of cosmic manifestation (*viśvaṣṛṭi*) lasting and repeating itself, as it does, from eternity to eternity. The cycle of outward self-absorption is technically called a *kalpa.*

The original self-limitation, which has started with *nigraha* carried through the successive stages, must also end before the cycles of functions close. Hence, it is said that *anugraha,* which puts an end to self-limitation, is the final function which completes the cycle. The *anugraha* as putting an end to original self-limitation lies on a different plane. It is the function by which the Supreme Lord, throwing aside his self-limited form, restores himself to his original nature (*svabhāva*). We shall discuss this function in greater detail later on.

49. The "*Idam*" is only a form of self-experience as object. See *Pr. Hd.,* Sū., Comm. p. 54.

50. *Sṛṣṭi* is only the Supreme Lord's act of making the "*Idam*" appear in his self-experience. For explanation, see *Pr. Hd.* p. 54.

Before we discuss the process of *Parama Śiva's* self-manifestation as universe as described in the texts of the Trika system, it is necessary to draw the attention of the reader to certain aspects and characteristic features of the process of self-manifestation that are peculiar to this system.

We have observed that from *Parama Śiva's* point of view, the process of universal manifestation is only a mode of self-experience. It appears, therefore, quite consistent that this process should resemble to a large extent the psychological process of our daily life. Indeed, it is for this reason that the Trika system describes this process as the process of *Parama Śiva's* experiencing himself outwardly, which has been technically called the *abhāsa*. It has often been described beautifully with the help of a metaphor, which is as follows: *Parama Śiva*, it is said, always "sees" himself reflected in a clear mirror which is nothing but his own Śakti. As he always "sees" (*paśyati*) himself as the one undifferentiated Principle without a second, the self-experience (*anubhava*) which he has from this process, is of the nature of *pūrṇa Aham*. But sometimes, i.e., during the period of creative activity, when he causes himself to appear as the universe, he "sees" (*paśyati*) himself as the universe.[51] The manifestation of the universe is, thus in reality, only the self-experience as the universe by *Parama Śiva*.

Thus we find that according to the Trika view, the process of universal manifestation is, in the first instance, purely "ideal" as it begins with the divine resolve (*saṅkalpa*) of becoming many, and then flowers and develops into "Divine Ideal," which is experienced by the Supreme Lord. The "Divine Ideal" later assumes gross form when it is expressed in and through the medium of matter. The "ideal" form of the universe, in which the Śakti retains its pristine purity remaining as *cit śakti*, is regarded to be pure[52] and undifferentiated from himself. But when it is manifested in matter, it assumes concrete form and becomes impure when duality (*dvaitabhāva*) appears.

In manifesting himself as the universe, the *Parama Śiva* plays the dual roles, both at the same time. On one hand, he remains

51. Cf. *Par. Sār.*, v–12–13, Comm. p. 39; *I.P.V.V.*, *I*, v–7, p. 144.

52. Technically called the *Śuddha Adhva*. *STTS.*, v–1, p. 2.

in the background as he ever is—as the Supreme Lord (*Parameś-vara*) when he is the Spectator (*sākṣī*), watching the play of his Śakti as the universe, but at the same time actually controlling and governing it as the Supreme Agent (*kartā*).[53] On the other hand, he, assuming the various roles of subjects (*pramātā*), objects (*prameya*), and the means of achieving them (*karaṇa*), appears on different levels of creation, and thus, actively participates in the play of Śakti (*līlā*). These two aspects of *Parama Śiva's* nature are inseparable.

In the following paragraphs we shall describe briefly how the *Parama Śiva* "opens himself out" (*unmīṣati*)[54] in the aspect of Śakti as universe, as it is technically called in the phraseology of the system, when the thirty-six *tattvas* constituting the different levels of creation come into being. Though we would describe the process of how different *tattvas* emerge from one another in the involutionary process, it should not be taken to mean that the actual process of universal manifestation also consists of gradual involution in which different *tattvas* unfold gradually from the Supreme Being.[55] The process of involution, technically called *unmeṣa,* is not a temporal process; it is instantaneous, so that the moment the *Parama Śiva* 'opens himself out' exercising the divine freedom, the same moment the entire creation, beginning from the *śiva tattva* down to the *pṛthvī tattva* comes to be,[56] and the moment he 'closes himself up' (*nimiṣati*), the entire creation is reabsorbed in him in a moment, as it were.

The gradual development of the universal manifestation that we shall trace here is only a logical description of the process. For it is known that during the period when the *cidaṇu* (self-limited aspect of *Caitanya*) that is the human soul, evolves and progresses towards his Ultimate Goal, i.e., the realization of *Śivatva* through his *sādhanā* he traverses certain levels, passes through certain stages which are actually the different levels of creation through which he must have passed during the process of his involution, i.e., the descent. These levels of creation represented by the dif-

53. Cf. *Par. Sār,* v–13, Comm. p. 36; *MM* v–18, Comm. p. 49.
54. *Pr. Hd..* Sū I Comm. p. 21
55. Cf. *T.S.* VIII, p. 79.
56. Cf. *STTS,* v–1 Comm. p. 1.

ferent *tattvas* must be there from the very beginning, that is, when the universe first came into being.

The term *tattva*,[57] literally meaning "thatness or whatness, namely, of everything that exists," signifies generally the fundamental factors or constituents that go to build up the creation. But according to the Trika system, *tattva* does not merely mean a category or a constituent of the universe; it means something more. Ontologically speaking, *tattva* is an evolved form of Śakti, since the universe itself is held to be an evolution of Śakti. The manifestation of the entire creation, consisting of different levels, each of which is represented by a *tattva*, takes place as the Śakti evolves and thus reveals the universe, lying absorbed and identified with itself, prior to manifestation. The different *tattvas* of creation thus symbolize different steps of the evolution of Śakti from the spiritual down to the material.

As all the *tattvas* are not equally pervasive and universal, they are arranged in a descending order of pervasion and universality so that they form a sort of hierarchy of *tattvas*. According to the Trika view, each higher *tattva*, representing a higher level of creation, pervades and permeates the successive ones, so that each lower *tattva* has its existence only in the higher one and so on to the highest *tattva*, which pervades and permeates the entire creation.[58] This, in other words, means that each higher *tattva* has in its bosom, as it were, the succession of *tattvas* in the seminal (*bīja*) form.

In the same way, each lower *tattva* implies and involves all the *tattvas* above it up to the highest *tattva*, so that the lowest of all implies and involves the whole range of *tattvas*. Thus it can be said that the process of universal manifestation is only a process of descent of the highest, the involution of the spiritual into the material and physical, each successive step of descent representing greater and greater restriction on the part of the highest Reality.

The manifestation of the universe, generally speaking, consists of three distinct stages—first is the germinal state (*bījāvasthā*)

---

57. For the nature of *tattva* see *I.P.V.*, (*Bhāskarī*). III, 1, 2 p. 219; also *T.S.* VIII p. 69. Cf. Author's article, "The concept of Tattva," a study in the Kaviraj Felicitation Volume, Lucknow.
58. Cf. *S.T.T.S.* Comm. V–21, p. 13.

when the Śakti that brings out the manifestation is pure in its spiritual form. Matter is completely absent and hence there is no appearance of duality (*dvaitādhāsa*) in this stage. The universe, which is epitomized by the '*Idam*' in this stage, does not appear as distinct from *Parama Śiva*, the Supreme Experiencer. The stage is represented by the five pure *tattvas*, viz., the *śiva tattva*, *śakti tattva*, *sadā śiva tattva*, *iśvara tattva*, and *śuddha-vidyā tattva*, which together constitute the Pure Order (śuddha-adhva).[59]

The second stage, representing the development of the previous one, is technically called the "sprouting stage" (*aṅkurāvasthā*). In this stage, matter makes its appearance along with the *Caitanya* aspect, although still in its subtle form. This stage is constituted by a mixed condition of matter and spirit (*Caitanya*), both of which are equally predominant. It is represented by the seven mixed *tattvas*, viz., *māyā* and its five *kañcukas* and the *puruṣa*.

Next is the 'flowering stage' (*pariṇatāvasthā*) when the involution is carried further so that the Śakti now appearing as material *śakti* (*jaḍa śakti*) assumes its grossest form of materiality. As a result, it becomes dense in material form as well as predominant, so much so that the *Caitanya* aspect is hidden completely by the overwhelming strong covering of matter. This stage is represented by a group of twenty-four *tattvas*, beginning from the *prakṛti* down to *pṛthvi*.

Logically speaking, the highest and the first at the top of the hierarchy of *tattvas* is the *Parama Śiva*. From him, the entire range of *tattvas* emanates as his self-formation or self-experience (*ābhāsa*). The *Parama Śiva* is not only the Supreme Lord (Maheśvara), but he is also the Ultimate Reality who holds (*bibharti*) within himself the entire range of the unmanifest (*avyakta*) universe as an idea (*āmarśa* or *parāmarśa*),[60] which later becomes expressible in the forms of discursive thought and speech[61] (*paśyanti*, *madhyamā*, and *vaikhari*) when it is manifested.

There is yet another aspect of *Parama Śiva*. As the Supreme Reality (*anuttara*) he transcends all, even the supremely ideal form of universe when it is unmanifest as 'idea'.

59. Cf. Ibid., Verse 4, Comm.

60. *Āmarśaḥ Paranādagarbhaḥ*.

61. *Vijñānabhairava Āgama*, v–3–4, Comm. p.5.

Parama Śiva is, by his nature, full-in-himself (*pūrṇa*) and self-centered (*Atma-viśrānta*). As long as he remains so, there is not even the slightest possibility of a universal manifestation. Hence, in order that there may be a universe, he first (this is only a logical first) limits his absolute (*anuttara*) nature by bringing into operation that aspect of Śakti which functions as the principle of negation (*niṣedha vyāpārarūpa*).[62] Thereby he allows, as it were, his *svarūpa*, as the transcendence and fullness, to disappear from his view so that he may feel a want (*abhāva*). Unless that want in the form of negation is created by this self-limitation, there is no scope for the manifestation of the universe which lies identified with his Essence prior to manifestation.

This is the first step toward the universal manifestation, which is technically called the *śiva tattva*. In this state he is what he was as *Parama Śiva*, in all his essentials and in every respect, with the only difference being that his experience of fullness (*pūrṇtva*) is eliminated. There is no change or mutation whatsoever when the *śiva tattva* comes into manifestation; in fact, the *Parama Śiva* remains as he ever was, and exists simultaneously with and including the *śiva tattva*.

Śiva tattva is only the pure light of *Caitanya*[63] without anything else to shine upon except himself as *Aham*—without even a trace of any other experience. It is the state when the self-experience (*svaparāmarśa*) of the *Parama Śiva* is only pure '*Aham*', without even the thought or feeling of *Aham asmi* (I am), for even *being* implies a relation of identity, however indistinct it might be.

Although said to be produced (*jātaḥ*)[64] or manifested in a sense from *Parama Śiva* inasmuch as it forms an experience distinct from the Supreme Experience, *pūrṇa Aham*, it is truly speaking, the first 'flutter' (*prathamo spandaḥ*) towards the manifestation

62. *Par. Sār.*, v–4, Comm., p.10.

63. *T.S.*, VIII p. 74. In this aspect it is said to resemble a clear mirror capable of reflecting the manifestation and maintenance and dissolution of Universe. Cf. *I.P.V.* (*Bhāskarī*), III, 1, 1, Comm. p. 216; also *S.T.T.S.*, verse I, p. 2.

64. For the cause and effect relationship between the different *tattvas*, see *I.P.V.*, II, 4.

of universe eternally existing in him as seed. In this stage the *cit* aspect of Śakti is held to be most manifest.[65]

The *śakti tattva,* though described as the second *tattva* in the hierarchy of *tattvas,* can scarcely be called the second *tattva.*[66] Because the manifestation of the *śakti tattva* is always simultaneous with the *śiva tattva,* the operation of *śakti tattva* makes the revelation of *śiva tattva* possible. It is, therefore, held to be existing eternally along with the *śiva tattva.* In some texts *śakti tattva* is not even separately enumerated as a *tattva;* it is counted as one with and included in the *śiva tattva.*

As observed above, the *Parama Śiva,* in order that he might experience himself as the universe, first (in the logical sense) negates and suppresses his Absolute (*viśvottīrṇa*) character, thereby allowing his supermost experience as *pūrṇāhaṁtā* to disappear, as it were, from his view. For so long as he continues to have *pūrṇāhaṁtā* as his self-experience, he cannot possibly experience himself as the universe. The stage in which the tremendous act of negation is achieved due to the operation of Śakti as the principle of negation (*niṣedha*) is technically called the *śakti tattva.*

The negation[67] or, precisely speaking, the suppression of the supermost experience does not, however, mean that *Parama Śiva's* self-experience becomes a total void (*śūnya*), or that he ceases to have any kind of self-experience. It only means that he no longer experiences himself as *pūrṇāhaṁtā,* the transcendent (*viśvottīrṇa*) aspect of his nature having been suppressed and having gone to the background. In its place he has the experience of himself as *Aham,* which is the same in every respect as the *pūrṇāhaṁtā,* minus its *viśvottiṙṇa* character.

65. *T.S.*, VIII, p. 74; also *S.T.T.S.*, verse 2 comm. p. 3. According to Utpala, however, *icchā śakti* predominates in this *tattva. Ś.D.* II, 1, Comm. p. 37.

66. In fact, the *śiva* and *śakti tattvas* are said to be outside the range of creation. Cf. *I.P.V.*, III, 1, 2, p. 218.

67. In the self-experience of *Parama Śiva* as *pūrṇahamtā,* both aspects of his nature, namely the transcendent and the immanent, are held in perfect equilibrium (*S.D.I.*, v–3–4 Comm. p. 7). The elimination of the former leaves the latter in the field of experience, which is but natural as a precondition to universal manifestation.

In other words, the only change brought about in his self-experience by the operation of Śakti as the principle of negation in this stage is in respect to the replacement of *pūrṇāhaṁtā* by pure *Ahaṁtā*, the transcendent aspect by the immanent aspect.

The elimination of the transcendent (*viśvottīrṇa*) aspect from his self-experience at this stage paves the way for unfoldment of the immanent aspect in successive stages, in which the universal manifestation takes place. It is for this reason that the *śakti tattva* is also described as the womb (*yoni*) and the seed of universal manifestation. The universe, though unmanifest (*avyakta*) in this stage, is implied in it as a potentiality (*bīja*).

In the *śakti tattva* the aspect of divine Śakti as *ānanda* is said to be most manifest.[68] The very nature of *ānanda*, or bliss, is the self-satisfaction and absolute rest within himself.[69] Hence in this stage there is no movement in the form of thoughts, no "flutter" (*spanda*)—the self-experience as *Aham* remains confined to its essential nature.

Though described as produced from the *Parama Śiva*, the *śakti tattva*, like the *śiva tattva*, is held to be eternally existent. It is said that the *śiva* and *śakti tattvas* do not disappear at the time of cosmic dissolution (*mahāpralaya*), but they remain in the bosom of *Parama Śiva*, as it were, as the seed of the universe to come.

The next step toward the universal manifestation is the manifestation of *sādākhya tattva*.[70] In this stage, the *Aham* in the self-experience develops to an extent that the notion of "being" makes its first appearance beside the *Aham*. That is, the *Parama Śiva* in this stage does not experience himself as merely *Aham*, but also as having a being over and above it. The self-experience as *Aham* thus no longer remains confined to himself but is extended to something appearing as not-Self, quite distinct and outside of himself.[71] That which appears as not-Self (*Idam*) is really and essentially not different from himself (*Aham*); it is only a self-extended aspect of himself, which, on account of appearing distinct and separate from himself, is experienced as being out-

---

68. *T.S.* VIII, p. 74: STTS., v–2, Comm. p. 3.
69. Cf. *T.S.*, VIII, p. 74.
70. *I.P.V.* (*Bhāskari*), III, 1, 2. p. 217.
71. Ibid., III, 1, 3, p. 223.

side of himself. The experience of this stage can be formulated as *ahameva Idam* (I am this).

The appearance of *Idam*, in this stage, not only aids in the realization by *Parama Śiva* of his 'being' as something different and apart from the *Aham*, it also marks the beginning of the appearance of the universe in its 'ideal form' when it is very subtle and indistinct.

The *Idam* in the initial stages of its manifestation appears as very vague and indistinct (*dhyāmala*), so that the *Ahamtā* prevails over it.[72]

In this state, the *icchā* aspect of divine Śakti is held to be the dominant feature.[73] The *icchā*, we have stated, is at the root of forming the divine resolve (*saṅkalpa*), and of all movements and activity (*kriyā*). As the *icchā śakti* precedes the manifestation of *kriyā* there is actually no movement or activity in this stage. There is only the will (*icchā*) to act (*kriyā*) following the stage of perfect bliss (*ānanda*) and rest (*viśrānti*), but no activity. This is logically an essential step, without which the activity of the kind that is going to follow, is not possible.

Although the *sādākhya tattva* is counted as the third in the hierarchy of *tattvas*, it is actually the first,[74] considering the facts that the universe in its ideal form appears for the first time in this stage, and that the *śiva* and *śakti tattvas* are eternally existent.

In the succeeding stage the *Idam*, which was appearing as very indistinct and subdued, being in the background of experience of 'being,' assumes importance as it emerges as the prominent element of experience.[75] The self-experience of *Parama Śiva*, in this stage, thus assumes the form of *Idameva Aham*.

The development of the *Idam* into the dominant element (*adhyāmala*), as is obvious from the self-experience formulated above, throws the *Aham* into the background,[76] as it were, in the experience, so that their relative position appears as reversed in this stage.

72. Ibid., III, I, 3, p. 224, Comm.; *STTS.*, v–3 Comm. p. 3.
73. *T.S.*, VIII, p. 74; *STTS*, v–3, Comm. p. 3.
74. *I.P.V.* (*Bhāskari*), III, 1, 2, Comm., p. 218.
75. Cf. Ibid., III, 1, 2, Comm. p, 218; *STTS*, v–4, Comm. p. 4
76. Ibid.

The development of *Idam* into prominence in experience enables the *Parama Śiva* to make a full survey, as it were, of the *Idam,* and know its real nature, since it has come into his clear view due to its prominence. This stage of making full survey of what constitutes the lordliness (*aiśvarya*) or the glory of his divine Being is technically called the *īśvara tattva* or *aiśvara tattva.*

In this stage, the *jñāna* aspect of his divine Śakti is held to be most manifest.[77] The prominence of the *jñāna śakti* appears very natural here, because the *Idam* in this stage appears in his full and clear view, when he makes a full "survey" of the "*Idam.*"

In the next stage, the two poles of his self-experience, the *Idam* and the *Aham* are fully equalized,[78] so much so that they are experienced as almost identified with each other, though they are separable in thought.

In this stage the *Aham* is not as dominant as in the *śiva tattva* stage, nor is it eclipsed as in the *īśvara tattva* stage. Likewise, the *Idam* is neither obscure as in the *śiva tattva* stage nor dominant as in the *īśvara tattva* stage; they are held in a perfect equilibrium like the two pans of a balance.[79] This means that both the *Aham* and *Idam* are equally clear so that their nature can be fully realized at one and the same time.

This stage of self-experience, consisting of the equalization of the two poles of experience, the *Aham* and the *Idam,* is technically called the *sad-vidyā* or *śuddha vidyā tattva.*[80]

The experience of equalizing the two factors, namely of *Aham* and *Idam,* implies and involves the knowledge of the fact that one belongs to the other. This can be formulated thus—*Aham-eva Idam, Sarvo mamayam vibhavaḥ* (I am all this, all this is mine as a part and parcel of myself). Thus it can be said that it is in this stage that there arises, for the first time, the realization of what may be termed *bhedābhedā* (diversity-in-unity-and identity).

Such an experience is possible only in this stage, and not in the previous ones. For unless both factors or elements of experience, the *Aham* and *Idam,* are fully brought out in experience,

77. *T.S.,* VIII, p. 74; *STTS,* v–4 Comm. p. 4.
78. *I.P.V.* (*Bhāskari*), III, 1, 2, Comm., p. 221, ff.
79. *STTS.* v–4, Comm. p. 4.
80. *I.P.V.* (*Bhāskari*), III, 1, 3, p. 221 ff.

and their nature fully realized, it is not possible to make a comparison between the two aspects, as is done in this stage, and thereby to realize both the contrast and identity subsisting between the two.

In this stage there is some "movement" implied in the thought, in the mental act of separating and thus realizing their relationship. Hence the *Kriyā* aspect of divine Śakti is held to be most dominant.[81]

With the manifestation of *śuddha vidyā tattva,* the first stage of universal manifestation comes to an end. The universe so far manifested is pure and 'ideal' as it lies within *Parama Śiva,* identified with him in his self-experience. As such, there is no blemish in it in the form of duality (*dvaita*). It is, therefore, technically called the Pure Order or the Perfect Way (*Śuddha Adhva*).[82] The *tattvas* are, it is said, realized in the true form and nature in this order.

In the next stage, technically described as the "sprouting stage" (*aṅkurāvasthā*) of the universal manifestation, the Śakti does not function in its pure form as *cit śakti.*[83] It assumes the form of *jaḍa śakti* (material power) and functions as the power of obscuration (*tirodhāna*), technically called the *maya śakti.* At the root of this development lies the emergence of *bheda saṅkalpa* of the *Parama Śiva,* the divine resolve of making multiplicity appear.

Operating his *māyā śakti,*[84] the *Parama Śiva* obscures, as it were, his own divine nature as the Supreme Experiencer (*Para pramātā*) and makes himself to appear as the innumerable limited experiencers (*mita pramātā*). As a limited experiencer, he does not experience the whole of the universe (*viśva*) as *Idam* but experiences only a fragment of it, and that, too, as existing apart from himself.[85] Thus, the obscuration of his *svarūpa* leads the *Aham* of *suddha vidyā* level to go to "sleep,"[86] and to be "covered up" by the function of *māyā.*

---

81. *T.S.*, VIII, p. 74: *STTS*, v–4, Comm. p. 4.
82. *STTS.*, v–5, Comm., p. 5.
83. *STTS.*, v–5, Comm. p. 5.
84. Ibid.
85. Ibid.
86. *I.P.V.* (*Bhāskarī*) III, 1, Comm. p. 336 ff.

With the obscuration of *Aham* by the *māyā*, the *Idam* rises up and splits up, as it were, to fill the vacuum created by the obscuration of pure Subject, and thus plays the dual role of limited subject and object. The experience of limited subject (*Aham bhāva*) is thus only a superimposition on the *Idam*. As limited subject, he feels himself to be one with the object so that the defects[87] of the object, such as discreteness and separateness, which are there due to limitation and obscuration of its true nature, come to infect him also. He also begins to feel his distinction and separateness from other limited subjects, with the result that his distinct individuality develops and makes its first appearance in him.

The obscuring power of *māyā* acts as veil upon the Supreme Experiencer's omnipotence (*sarva-kartṛtva*), omniscience (*sarva jñatrtva*), self-contentment (*pūrṇatva*), eternity (*nityatva*), and omnipresence (*vyāpakatva*), and transforms them into five snares (*pāśas*)[88] which bind him. These five forms of *pāśa*, which were originally, in their unlimited pure form, the embodiments of his divinity, are technically called *kañcukas*,[89] or principles of limitation. They are called *kalā* (limited authorship), *vidyā* (limited consciousness), *rāga* (limited interest), *kāla* (limitation with regard to time), and *niyati* (limitation with regard to space).[90] As these result from the obscuring activity of *māyā*, they are sometimes described as the five progeny of *māyā śakti*.

Obscured by *māyā*, and bound by those five kinds of snares, the Supreme Experiencer, deprived of his divinity, becomes a limited being: he forgets his essential nature, and he now appears in a different form altogether, viz., as an infinite number of *puruṣas*.[91]

We have observed that the *idam*, through the functioning of *māyā* as the power of obscuration, appears as having two forms side by side, viz., the subject and the object. The subject (*pramātā*)

---

87. *I.P.V.* (*Bhāskarī*) III, 1. Comm. p. 336.
88. *MM.*, v–18, p. 49.
89. *I.P.V.* (*Bhāskarī*), III, 1,9 p. 237; *STTS* v–6, 7 p. 5–6.
90. For the details of their nature as *tattvas*, see *STTS*, v–8 to 12; *T.S.*, VIII p.81 ff, *I.P.V.*, III, 1, 9, comm., p. 237 ff.
91. According to the Sāṅkhya system, *puruṣas* are independent beings from the very beginning of creation, but according to the Trika system they are only the self-manifestation of the Supreme Lord.

is what may be in its true form called the *puruṣa,* and the object as the *prakṛti.* The *puruṣa* and the *prakṛti* are thus brought into existence simultaneously by *māyā śakti's* operation.

Puruṣa is, as a matter of fact, the self-limited and impure form of the Divine Experiencer (*para pramātā*). By allowing himself to be enshrouded and ensnared by *māyā* and its five progeny, the Divine Experiencer comes to assume the form of *puruṣa.* But it must be remembered that in assuming that form he does not undergo any change in himself; he remains what he ever is, the Divine Experiencer in his essence.

The *māyā*[92] that enwraps and obscures him also implies a process of multiplication and differentiation along with obscuration,[93] so that when he allows himself to be enshrouded by *māyā,* he appears not as one *puruṣa* but as an infinity of *puruṣas,* all of whom experience themselves as differentiated and separated from one another.

Simultaneously with the manifestation of the *puruṣa* the *prakṛti* is manifested. As the number of *puruṣas* manifested by this process is unlimited, the number of *prakṛtis* is also unlimited, so that there is one *prakṛti* for every *purusa.*[94]

The experience of *prakṛti* on the part of *puruṣa* is one in which there is no specific feeling of any sort. The reason for such a view is that *puruṣa* in this stage under the obscuring power of *māyā* is in a state of deep "sleep".[95] He does not have the experience of 'I'. In the absence of any self-experience as 'I' he cannot have a clear and definite objective experience of anything. Hence he has only a vague and indefinite experience of *prakṛti* for which reason the *Prakṛti* is also called the *bhogasāmānya* for *puruṣa.*[96]

---

92. Like all *śuddha tattvas,* i.e., the *tattvas* of Pure Order, the *māyā* in the Trika system is said to be one and universal by nature. The impure *tattvas* below *māyā* are, however, held to be many and limited, as they are attached to limited experiencers.
93. Cf. *S.T.T.S.,* v–5.
94. This is contrary to what is held in the classical Sāṅkhya system, viz., one *prakṛti* for an infinite number of *purusas. T.A.,* X, Comm. p. 172; *T.S.,* VIII, p. 83.
95. *Śiv. Sū.,* I, 10, Comm. p. 25.
96. *T.S.* VIII p. 83.

In the next stage, when *prakṛti* is stirred by *ananta*[97] (the lord of the *prakṛti* region), it produces everything of specific experiences for *puruṣa*, either in the form of objects (*kārya*), or the means (*karaṇa*) whereby objects are experienced, or both. The process following which these means and the objects of experience come into manifestation from *prakṛti* is very much the same, as has been recognized by the Sāṅkhya system. There are, of course, slight differences in the details which are mainly due to Sāṅkhya's nonrecognition of a clear-cut distinction between the Universal Self and the limited self, but the process is substantially the same as in the classical Sāṅkhya system. Hence we do not propose here to enter into the details of the evolution of twenty-three *tattvas* from the *prakṛti.*

In this way we find the Supreme Lord, exercising his divine freedom, making the entire creation consisting of thirty-six *tattvas,* ranging from *sadāśiva tattva* down to *pṛthvi,* appear in himself. Thus he becomes, as it were, the universe, the totality of creation, out of his free and independent will.

---

97. Ibid. VIII p. 75; For reasons, see Ibid., VIII, p. 85.

CHAPTER 2

The Origin and Nature of Man

THE INDIVIDUAL BEING, who in his present form is called the human being, is said to be not only nondifferent from the Supreme Being, *Parama Śiva*,[1] but is also regarded in the Trika system as being a self-limited and self-contracted (*svasañkocita*) form[2] of him.

The reason for such a view is not difficult to find. In the foregoing chapter we have indicated that the *Parama Śiva* is, by his very nature, free and independent (*svatantraḥ*) as the Supreme Lord; and it is he who reveals himself to himself out of his free independent will as the universe (*viśva*). Since the manifestation of universe implies and involves also the manifestation of limited subjects and their objects of experience (*pramātā* and *prameya*) in the different levels of creation, it is said that the *Parama Śiva*, concealing his real nature, assumes diverse forms and makes himself appear as the countless number of *pramātās* and *prameyas*[3] in creation.

Thus, the countless number of *pramātās* and *prameyas* we come across in the different levels of existence are nothing but self-assumed forms of the Supreme Lord. It must be remem-

1. *Sp. Nir:*, II, 4, Comm. p. 48.
2. *JMV.* p. 2.
3. *Par. Sār.*, v–6, Comm. p. 18; Ibid., v–7, Comm, p. 23; PC., v–3.

bered, however, that the Supreme Lord, by making himself appear as the countless numbers of limited subjects and objects in creation, does not renounce his essential nature. He remains beyond his self-manifestation as the ever-transcendent Supreme Being and the Supreme Experiencer, experiencing the manifested universe as his self-projection (*sphāra*) and self-manifestation out of his free and independent will.[4]

From his point of view, the entire creation of the universe is only a manifestation of his divine glory, and as such, it is sometimes described as his divine sport (*krīḍā* or *līlā*),[5] proceeding from his own nature (*svabhāva*).

Strictly speaking, it is not possible, according to the Trika view, to describe how exactly the Supreme Lord conducts this *līlā* in the form of universal manifestation, that is, how he actually accomplishes the task of his self-concealment and thus makes himself appear (*abhāsayati*) as limited subjects (*pramātā*) and objects (*prameya*) in creation. The reason for holding this view is twofold. First, the act of self-concealment (*svarūpa-gopanam*), being an act of divine freedom *svātantrya*), is indescribable by its very nature. It cannot be described, for instance, from the standpoint of the *Parama Śiva* because, strictly speaking, he is not aware of its being accomplished, as it is actually accomplished in a moment.[6] Nor can it be described from the standpoint of the limited individual being who cannot even be aware of it. Second, the act of self-concealment is not a temporal process; it is an instantaneous and unitive act which has neither beginning in time nor stages or steps[7] involved in its actual accomplishment. It is a unique act of divine freedom (*svātantrya*).

But to explain logically how man made his first appearance in creation and how he assumed his present form by a process of logical involution, we have to assume a beginning in the process

---

4. *Par. Sār.*, Comm. p. 17.
5. Ibid., v–33, p. 72; *Śiv. Sū*. III, 9–10, Comm. pp. 89–90. Also see Sū III, 10 p. 90.
6. *Pr. Hd.*, Sū. 1 Comm. p. 21.
7. *T.S.*, Āh. VIII. p. 79.

of *Parama Śiva's* self-concealment by way of abstraction, and trace the course of its development up to his present form.

Now, since the functioning of the *tirodhāna* aspect of divine Śakti is held responsible for the negation of *Parama Śiva's* Absolute nature, we may assume that the imposition of self-limitation (*nigraha*), following directly from the functioning of *tirodhāna śakti,* is the first step in the process of *Parama Śiva's* self-concealment (*svarūpa-gopanam*).

That is to say, as the *Parama Śiva,* exercising his divine freedom (*svatantrva*), imposes limitation on himself, his limitless nature (*paripūrṇa avarūpa*) in the form of the Supreme Experiencer becomes immediately concealed and he assumes a finite form, in which he is technically called *cidaṇu* (spiritual nomad).[8] The form of *cidaṇu* is the original and principal form of limited individual being. And in fact, it is in this form that the individual being develops a distinct personality of his own when he is fit to be called an individual being.

As the imposition of the self-limitation by *Parama Śiva* results[9] in the veiling of his essential nature (*svarūpa*), characterized by such qualities as omnipotence (*sarvakartrtva*), omniscience (*sarvajñatva*), self-contentment (*purṇatva*), eternity (*nityatva*), and freedom (*svatantrya*), it has been technically called *āṇavamala.*[10]

The individual being in the form of *cidaṇu* is incorporal, i.e., devoid of any body-apparatus (*dehayantra*). As such, he is inactive in himself, incapable of participating in any activity in creation. He lies immersed, as it were, in *ajñāna* (ignorance) like an insentient piece of matter. Naturally such a state of his existence cannot be the final and the culminating stage of his involution.

In order that he might come in close contact with the objects and the universe as a whole, and enjoy the world through action (i.e., *karma*), it is essential that he should be associated

---

8. *JMV,* p. 2. The imposition of *nigraha* results in the manifestation of *cidaṇus.*
9. It is only after the imposition of self-limitation that the self-limited *Caitanya* becomes affected by the *māyā* and its different *kañcukas. Par Sār.,* v–16 Comm. p, 46 ff; also *Sp. Nir.,* I, 9, p. 23.
10. *Par. Sār.,* v–16, p. 45.

with a suitable body-apparatus (*deha*), as *karma* is impossible without its instrumentality.

But his association with a body-apparatus is not possible until and unless he develops within himself an intense "desire for enjoyment" (*bhogavāsanā*) to be fulfilled only through *karma*. The desire for enjoyment (*bhogavāsanā*)[11] is said to be generated by his association with what is technically called *karmabīja* (lit., the seeds of past actions). This, in other words, means that his prior association with *karmabīja* is indispensable for his association with a body-apparatus.

But again, the *karmabījas* are said to be lying in the level of *māyā*, and they cannot become attached to *cidaṇu* unless his real *svarūpa* is first fully obscured. This can be achieved only by his being enshrouded by *māyā* in the form of a veil (*ācchādana*). Hence, it is held in the Trika system that the imposition of *āṇavamala* on the individual being is followed by his veiling by *māyā*,[12] before he is ready to be associated with *karmabīja*.

The *māyā tattva* is said to be of the nature of obscuration. His being covered by the veil of *māyā* does not only result in the veiling of his true nature, as a consequence of which he becomes totally oblivious of his self as it were, but it also paves the way for the rise of the experience of duality (*dvaita*)[13] in the place of oneness and identity.

The task of obscuring his *svarūpa* having been achieved by *māyā*, the *karmabīja* lying dormant in *māyā tattva* automatically becomes attached to the *cidaṇu* and awakens the desire for enjoyment (*bhogavāsanā*) through *karma*. To satiate this desire, he is forced to assume a suitable body-apparatus (*deha*) constituted by *prakṛti* and her constituent elements (*tattvas*).[14] As his association with a body-apparatus results in the further concealment of his nature, the *karmabīja* responsible for this conjunction is technically called the *kārmamala*.

11. Cf. *MW*, p. 11. The *bhogvāsanā* arising in the *cidaṇus* in their disembodied state of existence is technically called *bhoga-lolikā;* this is said to be stirred up by the divine will of *Īśvara*. *Cf. T. A.*, IX, 61, p. 55 ff.
12. Cf. *Par. Sār.* v–57 p. 109; see also *Pr. Hd.*, Sū. 7.
13. *Sp. Nir.*, I, 9, Comm. p. 23; *Par. Sār.*, v24 Comm. p. 56.
14. *Par. Sār.*, v–24 Comm. p. 56.

His association with a suitable body-apparatus completes the tasks of his self-concealment, and he comes to be known as *sakala* (lit., with a *kalā* or *deha*).[15] This stage, therefore, marks the climax of his involution in creation.

We have stated that the individual being in the form of *sakala* is completely oblivious of his real Self. That being so, when he is associated with a body-apparatus, he identifies himself fully either with his body-apparatus or one of its constituent *tattvas*, so that his ego-experience (*ahaṁpratiti*) arises only from a false identification of not-Self with Self (*Aham*), the latter being only a superimposition on the former.[16] As such, his experience of self in that state is regarded as conceptual (*vaikalpika*) by nature, and is equated with arrogance (*ahamkāra*).

Thus, being in a state of ignorance (*ajñāna*) when he performs actions (*karma*) more to sustain himself in embodied form than to satiate his intense desire for enjoyment, he is bound more and more by the laws of *karma*. Every deed performed by him in that state produces results which he cannot escape. He must suffer the consequences of his own deeds, which are sometimes so powerful that they cause his transmigration from one level of existence to another.[17]

As his embodied existence is full of such transmigrations from one body-apparatus to another, and sometimes from one level of existence to another,[18] he is also known as *samsārī* (transmigratory being) in his embodied form.

Thus, according to the Trika system, every embodied individual being is covered by three kinds of self-imposed veils,[19] technically called *malas*, viz., the *āṇavamala*, the *māyīyamala*, and the *karmamala*. These *malas*, or defilements, are said to cover him exactly in the manner in which an ovule (*kaṇa*) is covered by nucleus (*kambuka*), integument (*kiṁśaruka*), and husk (*tuṣa*).[20] These

15. Cf. *Par. Sār.*, v–23 Comm. p. 55.
16. Ibid., v–32, Comm., p. 69; *I.P.V.*, IV, 1, 3 Comm. p. 282/283.
17. Ibid., v–66, Comm. p. 125.
18. Cf. *Śiv. Sū.*, III, 1. Comm. p. 73, ff.
19. The *malas* are self-imposed only from the Supreme Lord's point of view. See *T.S.*, *Āh.* VIII. p. 76.
20. *Par. Sār.*, V2-23/24, Comm. p. 54 ff., *T.A.*, IX, 212, p. 117.

malas, being self-imposed (*bandha*) in nature, are also described as fetters (*pāśa*).

In this connection, it may be pointed out that the analogy of an ovule covered by various kinds of 'shells', and of an individual being covered by different kinds of *malas* is true only in a restricted sense. It would be wrong to draw the conclusion from this analogy that the *malas* are of the nature of substance (*dravya*), having an independent existence of their own, just as the various covers have in the case of an ovule. In fact, according to Trika view, the *malas* are in essence the different modifications of the *tirodhāna* aspect of divine freedom (*svātantrya*)[21] and as such, they have no existence apart from the self-limited individual being.

In the foregoing paragraphs we have described the process of *Parama Śiva's* self-concealment from the highest point of view only to show the logical interconnection between the different steps of self-concealment, represented by the various *malas*. This should not be taken to mean that the *Parama Śiva* actually assumes the various *malas* in successive stages. For as we have already pointed out, the act of self-concealment, being a unique and instantaneous act of divine freedom, (*svātantrya*), has no scope for a real succession in it. As a matter of fact, the Trika system does not admit that the concealment by one *mala* will necessarily be followed by the imposition of other two *malas* in all the cases; there are cases in which the *cidaṇu* is enwrapped by one[22] or two[23] *malas* only.

What is actually sought to be conveyed by the causal interconnection is that one *mala* is related to the other *mala* in such a way that without the one the other cannot exist. The existence of each of the preceding *malas* is an indispensable condition for the existence of the subsequent one. For instance, the existence of *āṇavamala* is said to be an essential precondition for the existence of *māyīya*- and *kārmamalas*, so much so that when the former is completely destroyed by the operation of divine Śakti from above, the latter two also cease to exist.

---

21. Cf. *Sp. Nir.*, I, 9 Comm. p. 24; *T.S.*, VIII, p. 76; for their nature, see *T.A.*, IV, 70–71, Comm. p. 64 ff.
22. Such as the *vijñānākalas*.
23. Such as the *pralayākalas*.

Although all the *malas* in general are said to be the modifications of the act of self-concealment of the Supreme Lord, caused by the functioning of *nigraha śakti*, the *āṇavamala*, being the fundamental *mala* (*mūlamala*), is said to be directly caused by the act of self-limitation,[24] and as such, it has a unique position among the *malas*.

The imposition of self-limitation by the *Parama Śiva*, we have observed, results in the obscuration of his Absolute nature and he comes to imagine himself as a finite being. This leads to his appearance in the form of a spiritual monad, technically called the *cidaṇu*.[25] In that state, the *cidaṇu* is not able to experience his pure *svarūpa* due to his self-limited form; hence the *āṇavamala* is described to be of the nature of noncognition (*akhyāti*)[26].

It must, be remembered, however, that the veiling of *Parama Śiva* by the *āṇavamala* does not result in the manifestation of one spiritual monad (*cidaṇu*) only; it is said to result actually in the manifestation of a countless number of *cidaṇus*, each having a distinct individuality of his own owing to his limited nature.

Though the act of self-limitation is one and unique, the *āṇavamala* as associated with every individual is manifold in nature.[27] For this reason it is said that the destruction of *āṇavamala* in one does not lead to its destruction in all other individuals.

Like all other *malas*, *āṇavamala* is said to be beginningless (*anādi*),[28] though destructible. Its destruction, however, cannot be brought about by the individual being through his personal endeavor. As it comes into being by the functioning of the *nigraha* aspect of divine Śakti, its removal is said to be possible only by the functioning of a corresponding aspect of divine Śakti, viz., the *anugraha*.

The *āṇavamala* is said to be the fundamental *mala* (*mūlamala*), which is associated with the very being (*sattā*) of every individual

---

24. *Sp. Nir.*, I, 9, Comm. p. 23.
25. For the real nature of *cidaṇu*, see *T.A.*, IX, 144–45. Comm. p. 112 ff.
26. Ibid., I, 37–38. Comm. p. 73 ff.
27. Cf. *T.A.*, IX. 68 Comm. p. 61 ff.
28. In fact, the act of self-limitation itself is beginningless, hence all *malas* possess this characteristic. Ibid., IX, 67 Comm. p. 60.

being. As such it is described as innate in individual beings (*āntara*).[29] It is said to be the substratum for the existence of the other two *malas*, which are dependent on it for their existence. It is, however, said to be independent of the other two *malas* as it continues to exist in some cases even after they have been destroyed.

The concealment (*sañkoca*) of the real nature of *cidaṇu* by the *āṇavamala* gives rise to *ajñāna* in him, which is said to be of the nature of *akhyāti*, i.e., noncognition of Self in Pure Self (*Śuddha Aham*). The noncognition of Self in Pure Self leads to the rise of the experience of not-Self in Self,[30] which is technically called the *pauruṣa ajñāna* (lit., ignorance of Real Self).

Caused by the fundamental *mala*, the *pauruṣa ajñāna* is also called the fundamental *ajñāna*. This *ajñāna*, being an offshoot of the *cidaṇu's* limited nature, forms an essential aspect of his nature.

The *pauruṣa ajñāna* must be distinguished from the *bauddha ajñāna* (ignorance of the intellect), which is said to be conceptual (in ordinary sense of the term) in nature, caused by false identification of not-Self with Self.[31] As is obvious from the name itself, the *bauddha ajñāna* is an affection of intellect, and as such it cannot arise in the individual being until he is associated with a body-apparatus. It is thus said to be dependent upon the connection of the *cidaṇu* with a body-apparatus, with which it is said to exist. But, on the other hand, the *pauruṣa ajñāna*, being the *ajñāna* associated with the very being of individual being, is said to be independent of any such connection. It is there even in the disembodied beings (such as *vijñānākalas*), or beings in the state of disembodied existence (i.e., *pralayākalas*).[32]

The *bauddha ajñāna* is thus temporary, and it lasts only as long as there is an association with the body-apparatus. As compared to this, the *pauruṣa ajñāna* is permanent, as it exists until the end of his self-limitation, brought about by the descent of divine *anugraha*.[33]

---

29. *Par. Sār.* v–24, Comm. p. 55.
30. *T.A.* I, 36/37/38 Comm. p. 73 ff; *Par. Sār.* v–53 p. 105; *T.S.* I, p. 3.
31. Ibid.
32. The form of *ajñāna* in the *vijñanākalas* is, however, very much different from that of the *pralayākalas*.
33. *T.S.*, I, p. 3; Also *T.A.*, I, 46 Comm. p. 85.

As we have already indicated, the Supreme Being, *Parama Śiva*, according to the Trika system, is both the omniscient (*sarvajña*) and the omnipotent (*sarvakartā*) Supreme Lord (Maheśvara), so that the perfect knowledge (*pūrṇa jñāna*) and the freedom of action (*svātantrya*) constitute the two principal aspects of his Absolute nature (*svarūpa*). As long as he is not affected by the *aṇavamala*, these two essential aspects of his nature remain coalesced, as it were, in such a way that they are indistinguishable in his pure nature.

But, as he is covered by the self-imposed *āṇavamala*, these two aspects of his nature appear as differentiated and affected severally by limitation (*sañkoca*) in the individual *cidaṇus*. Thus, there appear two distinct types of *cidaṇus*, according to the aspects of their *svarūpa*, viz., knowledge (*jñāna*) and action (*kriyā*).

As this differentiation of *cidaṇus* into two classes is wholly due to *āṇavamala*, concealing one of the two principal aspects of his pure nature, it is said to be of two kinds.[34] In the case of some *cidaṇus*, the *āṇavamala* is said to affect only the *kriyā* aspect of their nature, and thereby deprive them of their freedom of action (*svātantrya*). In such cases, the *cidaṇus*, however, retain knowledge, i.e., the consciousness of their true selves (*bodha*). Hence they are technically called the *vijñānākalas* or the *vijñānakevalis*.[35]

These *vijñānakevalis* do not differ vastly from the Supreme Being inasmuch as they are conscious of their pure Self.[36] But because they are devoid of the freedom of action,[37] an essential aspect of pure nature, they are regarded as fettered beings (*pāśabaddha*), and are, therefore, included in the category of *paśupramātās* (fettered experiencers).

The *vijñānakevalis*, it may be pointed out, form a unique class of *paśupramātās* who stay above the level of *māyā*, and have no further involution in *māyā*, due to their being conscious of their pure Self.[38] They are, therefore, not affected by the *māyīya*

34. *I.P.V.*, III, 2, 4. p. 248.
35. Ibid., III, 2, 7. p. 251.
36. *T.A.*, IX, 91, Comm. p. 77 ff.
37. *I.P.V.*, III, 2, 6, p. 250.
38. *T.A.*, IX, 91 Comm. p. 77 ff.

or *karmamalas*,[39] and they remain immersed in *ajñāna*, as it were, in a disembodied condition (*ākalāvasthā*).

But in the case of other *cidaṇus*, the *āṇavamala* obscures the knowledge or the Self-consciousness (*bodha*)[40] aspect of their nature, and thereby makes them totally oblivious of their pure nature. The *kriyā* aspect of their nature is, however, not affected by the *āṇavamala*, and it is this which induces them to undergo further involution. With their freedom of action remaining intact, they cannot remain immobile in one state, as the disembodied beings (*akalas*). To give *kriyā śakti* an opportunity of expression through *karma*, they must undergo involution when they come under the influence of the *māyā*.

The *māyā*, we have observed, is the universal power of obscuration *tirodhānakārī*). As it enwraps the individual *cidaṇus*, whatever remains of their pure nature after the imposition of *āṇavamala* (i.e., the *kriyā* aspect of their nature) becomes covered by a veil (*āvaraṇa*), as it were, which has been technically referred to as *māyīyamala*[41] from the individual point of view.

But the *māyā* is not alone in accomplishing this task of obscuration. We have observed that when *māyā śakti* comes into operation, it brings into existence, along with it, five other forces of limitation, technically called the *kañcukas*. These *kañcukas* have particular spheres of operation, and they limit only particular aspects of the *cidaṇus'* pure Self. Thus when the imposition of *māyīyamala* results in the obscuration of *cidaṇu's* true nature, they also play their part by limiting the five powers of *cidaṇus'* pure Self.[42]

The obscuration by the *māyīyamala* is not, however, restricted to the hiding of the true Self of the *cidaṇus;* it also brings about other changes that follow as a logical corollary to obscuration. For this reason it is held that the *māyā* is also responsible for the rise of the experience of differentiation and discreteness (*dvaita*) in the *cidaṇu*. But this experience of differentiation and discreteness remains indistinct and hazy in that stage because

---

39. Ibid., IX, 94, 95, Comm., p. 79–80.
40. *I.P.V.*, III, 2, 8. p. 252.
41. *T.A.*, IX, 180, p. 139.
42. *Anuttara-prakāśa-pañcāśika*, verses 21–25; See also *T.S.*, VIII p. 82 ff.

the *cidaṇus* then lack distinct self-consciousness of "ego" (*aham-praitīti*).[43] But when they "get back" their sense of self-consciousness, or their identification with a suitable body-apparatus, they begin experiencing this discreteness and differentiation between the subject and object, Self and not-Self.

Like the *āṇavamala, māyīyamala* is also beginningless, though it is destructible. Its destruction can be brought about by the individual being, through his persistent and intense endeavor.

As indicated above, the task of concealing the pure Self of *cidaṇu,* having been accomplished by the *māyīyamala,* the *karmabījas* lying dormant in *māyā* become attached to *cidaṇu.* The *karmabījas* are the products of the subtle residual impressions of past actions (*karma saṁskāras*), performed by the individuals in their embodied form, and they remain eternally lying in *māyā.* As they are associated with the individual *cidaṇu,* they awaken the desire for action (*karmavāsanā*) in him. This desire, in its turn, impels the individual *cidaṇu* to associate himself with a body-apparatus, produced out of *prakṛti* and its constituent *tattvas.*

Since it is this awakened desire for *karma* that is the prime cause of his association with a body-apparatus resulting in the further obscuration of his pure Self, the associated *karmabīja* is regarded as being of the nature of a veil, and is technically called the *kārmamala.*

The *kārmamala* is thus the root cause of the conjunction of the individual being with a body-apparatus.[44] As such, it cannot be said to be associated with the body-apparatus of the individual being. It is always associated with the Self of the *cidaṇu.* Hence, it is not destroyed with the destruction of the individual beings' body-apparatus. It is the relatively permanent attachment of the *cidaṇu* that persists thorough the births and deaths and transmigrates with the individual self.

Like the *āṇava-* and *māyīyamalas,* the *kārmamala* is also said to be beginningless (*anādi*), though destructible. Its destruction can be achieved by the individual being through his intense personal efforts.

43. *Par. Sār.* v–32 Comm. p. 70.
44. Cf. *T.A.* IX, 88, Comm. p. 75; *I.P.V.* III, 2, 10, Comm. p. 254–255.

Associated with every embodied being (*sakala*), the *karmamala* is said to be manifold in nature so that it is unique in every individual being. The distinctness of *kārmamalas* associated with the individual being is largely responsible for the growth of his distinct personality, notwithstanding the fact that all the *sakalas* are bound by the same three *malas:* the *āṇava, māyīya* and *karma.*

Besides this, the *kārmamala* is also held responsible for determining the type of body, with which the individual *cidaṇu* is going to be associated.[45]

According to the Trika system there are three principal kinds of body-apparatuses, associated with three different categories of *sakalas,* viz., superhuman (*daiva*), human (*mānuṣa*), and subhuman (*tiryag*).[46] Of these, the body apparatuses of superhuman and subhuman beings are also called the *bhogāyatanas* (lit., vehicles for enjoyment) or *bhogadehas,* as they serve the purpose of enjoyment (*bhoga*), while the body-apparatuses of the human beings (*mānuṣa*), serving as the vehicle for performance of *karma,* are technically called *karmadehas* (lit., bodies suitable for performance of *karma*).

In so far as the constitution of these *dehas* is concerned, it appears that there is not much difference between them, except that in the case of individuals possessing *bhogadeha,* their egosense is latent.

As we in our present study are mainly concerned with human beings, we shall confine ourselves in the following paragraphs to the examination of the constitution of *karmadeha* only.

At the outset it must be made clear that when the Trika system speaks of the body-apparatus of the individual being, it does not mean only the outer, visible gross body which houses the individual self, but it also means the entire complex organism consisting of three kinds of bodies, one over the other. The three kinds of bodies, according to the Trika system, are the *kāraṇa śarīra, puryaṣṭaka śarīra,* and *sthūla śarīra,* broadly corresponding to the *kāraṇa, sthūla,* and *sukaṃa sarīras* as admitted in the Advaita Vedānta of Saṅkara.

45. *T.A.*, IX, 99–100 Comm. pp. 82–83.

46. From the point of view of *jāti, āyu,* and *bhoga,* the human and subhuman *sakalas* are again subdivided into four classes: the *jarāyuja, aṇḍaja, udbhija,* and *svedaja.* Cf. *JVM.*, p. 7.

The *kāraṇa sarīra,* also called the *para śarīra,*[47] is the subtlest form of body that is constituted by the *māyā tattva* and its five *kañcukas.* As it is produced from *māyā,* it is associated with the individual being the moment he is covered by *māyīyamala.* Being subtle in form, it is the innermost cover, which is said to be closely associated with him, and is also the substratum for the other two kinds of bodies. It is relatively permanent and stays with the individual being even when he is not liberated from the shackles of *mayīyamala.* It is said to migrate with the individual being from one gross body to another at the time of his physical death. It is not even destroyed by cosmic dissolution (*pralaya*), but remains associated with the individual being during that period.

Over the *kāraṇa śarīra,* there is another subtle body, technically called the *puryaṣṭaka*[48] (lit., the eightfold in the city). Though it is constituted by some *tattvas* of *prakṛti,* it is said to be associated with the individual being covered by *kārmamala.* Being subtle in form, it is said to serve as the substratum for the gross physical body.

There are two main views regarding its constitution. Vasugupta[49] and Kṣemarāja[50] are unanimous in holding that it is constituted of eight *tattvas,* viz., the *manas, buddhi, ahaṁkāra,* and the five *tanmātras.* But Abhinavagupta is of the opinion that the *puryaṣṭaka* is made of eleven *tattvas,*[51] viz., five vital airs (the *praṇa, apana, samāna, udāna,* and *vyāna*), the *buddhi,* and the five *karmendriyas.*

Like the *kāraṇa śarīra,* it is also relatively permanent as it comes into being in the beginning of a cycle of manifestation (*kalpa*) and lasts until the individual being is completely liberated from *karmamala.* It is that part of the individual being which, unlike the gross body, is not cast off at death but migrates from one existence to another, thus guaranteeing the continuity of personal identity throughout his existence in *saṁsāra.*[52]

---

47. *Śiva Sū.*, III, 4, Comm. p. 78.
48. For its definition, see *Sp. Ka,* IV, 20n Comm. p. 155–56.
49. *Sp. Nir.*, III, 17 p. 73; *Sp. Ka* IV, 19, Comm. p. 155 ff.
50. *Śiv. Sū.*, III, 2 Comm. p. 75.
51. *I.P.V.*, III, 2, 3, p. 264; also see the editor's note.
52. *Śiv. Sū.*, 10–11 Comm. p. 90–91.

The individual being's association with *puryaṣṭaka* gives him an opportunity, for the first time, to come into contact with the sense-objects of the world through his *manas, buddhi,* and *ahaṁkāra,* though he is then incapable of enjoying them directly in the absence of a gross physical body.

Besides this, the *manas, buddhi,* and *ahaṁkāra* of his *puryaṣṭaka* also serve the purpose of a storehouse for the residual impressions of *karma* (*karma-saṁskāras*) performed by him in his present bodily form. These stored-up (*karma-saṁskāras* awaken again the *karmavāsanā* in him, in order to satiate which he must assume and relinquish a number of gross physical bodies (*sthūla śarīras*) in succession.[53] Thus, his association with *puryaṣṭaka* initiates his career as *saṁsārin,* which lasts until he is fully liberated from the shackles of *kārmamala.*

The *sthūla śarīras,* sometimes called the *bhogāyatanas,*[54] are the outermost cover that are said to be brought into existence by *kārmamala.* It is constituted by such gross *prakṛta* elements as five *jnāñendriyas* (sense-organs), and five *karmendriyas.* The individual being's association with the gross body enables him to perform actions and come in closer contact with sense-objects, in accordance with his *karmavāsanā.* This also enables him to live and move in space and time.

The gross body is temporary. It lasts until the exhaustion of a particular *vāsanā,* which has induced him to assume this form. In the process of exhausting a particular *vāsanā,* he, however, accumulates fresh *vāsanās* from the residual impressions of the deeds he has been performing, and this again impels him to assume a fresh gross body in his next birth. This process continues *ad infinitum* until he is able, through his personal efforts, to liberate himself from the unending series of transmigrations.

---

53. *Sp. Nir.,* III, 18, Comm. p. 73.
54. Ibid.

CHAPTER 3

The Status of Man in Creation

IN THE FOREGOING chapter we observed that the creation of the universe, according to the Trika system, is only a process of *parama śiva's* self-revelation in the immanent aspect. Its revelation begins (in the logical sense) with the manifestation of *sadā śiva tattva,* which is held to be the highest stage of creation, and culminates with the manifestation of *pṛthvi tattva,* the lowest and grossest of all.

Broadly speaking, the entire creation (*sṛṣṭi*) is said to have two "planes" (*bhūmi*) of manifestation, technically called the *adhvas* (lit., ways or orders), viz., the *śuddha adhva* (Pure Order) *aśuddha adhva* (Impure Order).[1] The creation beyond the level of *māyā tattva,* instituted by five pure *tattvas* (*śiva tattva, śakti tattva, śadā śiva tattva, īśvara tattva,* and *śuddha vidhyā tattva*), forms this higher order, which is known as the *śuddha adhva.*[2] The manifestation of this *adhva* is said to be brought about directly by the Supreme Lord (*Parameśvara*) himself who is its controller and governor (*kartā*).[3] The experiencers or subjects (*pramātā*), who are none but diverse forms of *parama śiva* himself[4] residing in the dif-

1. *Sp Nir.*, II, Comm. p. 45, *STTS,* p. 3.
2. *T.S.*, VIII, p. 74.
3. *T.S.*, VIII, p. 75.
4. Cf. *Pr. Hd.* Sū. 3, Comm. p. 26–29; also *Par. Sār,* v–5, Comm. p. 15ff.

ferent levels of pure creation, are technically called the pure *pramātās* (pure experiencers).

The reason for their being called the pure *pramātās* is twofold—first, they are the denizens of pure creation, and as such they are not very much different from the highest experiencer (*parapramātā*). Like him, they are also "universal" by nature, and as such, they experience the entire universe as the '*Idam*,' not different from themselves.[5] Being free from limitation (*sañkoca*), they are always conscious of their pure Self (*Śuddha Aham*) and their essential divinity (*aiśvarya*). And second, which follows from the first as a logical corollary, they never experience duality (*dvaita*) in any form, as it is totally nonexistent on that level. They are always conscious of the fundamental unity and identity of all.

There are, according to the Trika system, four classes of *śuddha paramātās*,[6] viz., the *śiva*, the *mantramaheśa*, the *mantreśa*, and the *mantra*, belonging respectively to the levels of the *śiva śakti tattva*,[7] the *śadāśiva tattva*, the *iśvara tattva*, and the *śuddha vidyā tattva* of pure creation. Of these, excepting the *śiva* of the *śiva śakti tattvas*, of all other kinds of *śuddha pramātās* are said to be countless in number.[8] The *śiva pramātā* is regarded to be the highest *pramātā*, and is, therefore, considered as singular in number.

All the *śuddha pramātās* (pure experiences) are said to possess bodies made of the *bindu*, divine Śakti in potentialized form. They are therefore incapable of participating in worldly activity in the absence of a physical body made from material (*jada*) elements

---

5. *Par. Sār.*, v–14, Comm. p. 41–43.
6. *Pr. Hd.* Sū. 3, Comm. p. 27–29. Abhinavagupta, however, maintains that there are five classes of *śuddha pramātās*, viz., *sāmbhava*, *śaktija*, *mantramaheśa*, *mantreśa*, and *mantra pramātās* (*T.S.* VIII, p. 75). If Abhinavagupta's classification is accepted, the total classes of *pramātās* would amount to eight instead of the seven propounded by all other authorities. See *Pr. Hd.*, Sū. 7 Comm. p. 40. In *Āh.* IX of the *Tantrasāra* (p. 94) however, he appears supporting the classical theory of the seven *pramātās*.
7. The *śiva* and *śakti tattvas* are actually regarded as one *tattva*. Cf. J. C. Chatterji, *Kashmir Saivism*. Abhinavagupta, however, considers them as constituting the two separate levels of creation in which two distinct kinds of *śuddha pramātās* live. See *T.S.* VIII, p. 75.
8. Ibid., VIII, p. 74; also, IX, p. 98.

from *māyā* and *prakṛti*. They stay above the level of *māyā* and function in accordance with the divine will of the Supreme Lord.

Although all the four classes of experiencers are equally pure and "universal" by their nature, they are not all alike, nor do they occupy the same position in the hierarchy of *śuddha pramātās*. They are regarded as mutually distinct, though this distinction is only a nominal distinction, which for all practical purposes has no value. Their differences are said to be due to the predominance of any one of the *śaktis* of the *Parama Śiva*, viz., *cidānanda, icchā, jñāna,* and *kriyā*,[9] which is also reflected in the predominant *Aham* and *Idam* aspects of their pure nature.[10]

The creation below the level of *śuddha vidyā tattva*, constituted by all the *tattvas* beginning from *māyā tattva* down to the *pṛthvī tattva*, is technically called the *aśuddha adhya* (Impure Order). It is said to be brought into existence by *ananta*, the *aghoreśa* (presiding deity) of this order, in obedience to the will (*icchā*) of the Supreme Lord to provide the limited beings (*cidaṇus*) with an opportunity of satiating their "desire for enjoyment and *karma*" (technically called *bhogalolikā*) which are on the verge of fruition.[11]

The chief reason for this creation, labelled the "impure creation" (*aśuddha adhva*) is the dominance of *māyā śakti*, which is also regarded to be its material cause (*upādāna kāraṇa*). Hence, the distinguishing feature of this creation is the prominence of the power of obscuration or limitation, from which follows the preponderance of duality and discreteness in every sphere of creation.

The experiencers or subjects residing on the various levels of this creation are therefore characterized by limitation. They are therefore regarded as impure by nature and are technically called the *paśus* (lit., fettered beings).[12]

The *paśus* are broadly classified under three heads,[13] viz., the *vijñānākala*, the *pralayākala*, and the *sakala*.

9. *T.S.* VIII, p. 75; also IX, p. 93.
10. *I.P.V.* III, 1, 3–4 Comm. p. 221 ff.
11. *T.S.* VIII, p. 75; *T.A.* VI, 56.
12. For definition of *paśus*, see *I.P.V.*, III, 2, 2–3 Comm. pp. 246–47, *Sp. Ka.*, IV. 16 Comm. p. 136.
13. *Sp. Ka.* IV, 16 Comm. p. 127.

The *vijñānākalas,* we have observed, constitute a unique class of *paśu pramātās,* as they have nothing in common with the other kinds of *paśu pramātās,* except that they are also bound by the *āṇavamala,* which is a bond common to all *paśus.* Apart from this common feature, there is nothing else that can justify their inclusion in the category of *paśu pramātās.* For instance, unlike the other *paśu pramātās,* they are said to have consciousness of their Pure Self (*śuddha ahambodha*).[14] As such, they are not affected by *karma* and *mayīyamala,* which no doubt implies that they are not the creatures of impure creation (*aśuddha adhya*). They are, therefore, said to be existing outside the realm of *māyā,* i.e., the impure creation.[15]

However, that does not necessarily mean that they are the denizens of pure creation (*śuddha adhva*). The pure creation, we have observed, is exclusively inhabited by the pure *pramātās* who are "universal" in their nature. The *vijñānākalas,* being limited and impure by nature, have no room in the pure creation,[16] and as such, they are said to remain below the *śuddha vidyā* level.

From what has been stated above regarding the position of *vijñānākalas* in creation (*sṛṣṭi*), it would be wrong to assume that there exists some kind of transitional level of creation between the *śuddha vidyā tattva* and the *māyā tattva,* to which the *vijñānākalas* may be said to belong. The existence of any such intermediate level, whether in the pure creation or in the impure creation (*aśuddha adhva*), is not admitted by the Trika system.

But if we must specify the particular level where the *vijñānākalas* might be said to be existing, we have no alternative but to give a noncommittal reply, namely, that like all other kinds of *pramātās,* both *śuddha* and *aśuddha,* they rest in the highest *pramātā,* that is, the Supreme Being. As a matter of fact, the root cause of their anomolous position in creation is their peculiar nature, for which they cannot be grouped with the pure *pramātās* of *śuddha adhva.*

---

14. Cf. *I.P.V.* III, 2, 6–7, Comm, p. 250 ff.
15. *Par. Sār.*, v–14, Comm. p. 43.
16. Cf. Ibid.

As the *vijñānākalas* are said to be bound only by the *āṇavamala*, they are devoid of any body-apparatus (*deha*).[17] They are, therefore, incapable of performing any action. Hence, the question of their elevation to higher levels or degradation to lower levels through action (*karma*) does not arise; they remain as they are, submerged in the ignorance (*ajñāna*) arising out of *aṇavamala*. And for their emancipation from that state, they are totally at the mercy of the descent of divine grace from the Supreme Lord.

As their self-consciousness remains confined to the pure Self only, they do not have any objective experience, that is, the experience of something other than and outside of the Self. They are always conscious of the Pure Self (*śuddha Aham*) only.

The *vijñānākalas* are said to be infinite in number.[18] But owing to their being conscious of the Pure Self which is not subject to temporal or spatial limitations, they are not conscious of their mutual difference. Nevertheless, the fact remains that they are different from one another, because of the will of the Supreme Lord to manifest himself as the many.[19]

The remaining two kinds of *paśu pramātās*, the *pralayākala* and *sakala*, are both the creatures of impure creation, as they are said to exist in the region of *māyā*.

The *pralayākalas*, however, are disembodied (*akala*)[20] as their body-apparatuses (*deha*) lie dissolved (*pralina*) in *māyā*. As such, they do not have a distinct ego-consciousness. Their ego-consciousness is said to be identified with the *śūnya* (void),[21] and for this reason they are sometimes known as *śūnya pramātā*. Being devoid of ego-consciousness (*Aham*), they do not have any experience; hence they are sometimes described as subjects without knowledge (*jñāna*).[22] As they have neither ego-consciousness, nor the power of action or *kriyā*, they are said to exist like insentient objects (*jaḍavat*) immersed in the ocean of ignorance.

---

17. *I.P.V.*, III, 2, 7, Comm. p. 251.
18. Ibid., 2, 6, Comm. p. 250; *J.M.V.*, p. 5.
19. Ibid., 2, 7, Comm. p. 251.
20. Ibid., 2, 8, p. 252.
21. *I.P.V.*, III, 2, 8, p. 252.
22. Ibid.

They are said to be fettered by two kinds of *mala, āṇava* and *kārma,* the latter being only in the form of residual impressions (*saṁskāra*).[23] They are not associated with *mayīyamala* because their body-apparatuses are in a state of dissolution (*laya*).

The state of dissolution (*pralaya*),[24] however, is not a permanent state. For them, it lasts only for a limited period of time.

As soon as the state of dissolution is over, they are associated with appropriate body-apparatuses,[25] determined by their *kārmamala,* when they come to be known as *sakala* (lit., embodied being).

Utpalācārya and Abhinavagupta, however, mention two distinct types of *pralayākalas,*[26] which are as follows. First, are those who, identified with the *śūnya* (void) and made insentient, as it were, by extremely deep sleep, are said to be in *apavedya suṣupta,* i.e., a state in which there is no awareness of any object. They are not associated with the *māyīyamala.* But there are others who, by identifying themselves with the *buddhi,* etc., have the consciousness of separate objects in the form of pleasure and pain only. They are said to be in *savedya suṣupta,* i.e., deep sleep, which has objective reference. In them, the *māyīyamala* is present only in a subtle form, *pākṣika.* Both these kinds of *pralayākalas* are, however, disembodied beings.

The *sakalas* are the embodied creatures of impure creation (*aśuddha adhva*). As such, they occupy an important place in the hierarchy of beings. Unlike the *pralayākalas,* they are said to be associated with all the three kinds of *malas—the āṇava, māyīya,* and *kārma.*

Though all *sakalas* are embodied beings, they are not all alike. Their differences are primarily due to the type of the body-

23. Ibid., III, 3, 8 Comm. and *Bhaskarī,* pp. 252–53. The existence of *kārmamala* in them in the form of *saṁskāras* is an essential factor, because when the state of dissolution would be over, *kārmamala* would serve as the causal factor in bringing about their association with a body-apparatus. Cf. *T.A.,* IX, 138 Comm. p. 109 ff.
24. *Pralaya* here means the dissolution of the *tattvas* below the *māyā tattva* and not the cosmic *pralaya,* technically called *mahāpralaya.*
25. Cf. *I.P.V.,* III, 2, 10 Comm. p. 254.
26. Ibid., III, 2, 8 Comm. p. 252.

apparatus with which they are equipped, which is again conditioned by the particular *karmabīja* with which they are associated. But as the body-apparatuses (*deha*) are said to be of two kinds, the *sakalas* associated with them may also be broadly classified into two categories, viz., the *sakalas* possessing the first type of body-apparatuses, technically called the *karmadeha,* and the *sakalas* equipped with second type of body-apparatuses, called the *bhogadeha.*

The *karmadeha,* as we have observed, is that kind of body-apparatus which serves as the instrument in the performance of *karma.* Hence, the *sakalas,* possessing this type of body, not only have a distinct personality of their own, but they are also endowed with limited will (*icchā*) and restricted freedom of action (*kriyā*). They have, therefore, the unique privilege of exercising their will and of performing actions, of course within limitations. They have therefore to suffer the consequences of their own deeds, and this sometime causes their migration from one level of existence to another. Human beings alone are possessed of this privilege.

Since the *bhogadeha* is only a vehicle for passive enjoyment (*bhoga*), the *sakalas* associated with this kind of body do not have a distinct personality of their own. They are, therefore, either subordinate to the will (*icchā*) of some higher being or subservient to the collective will or instincts of their species. They have no freedom of action (*kriyā*), even in the restricted sense. Their activities are more or less mechanical, often blind responses to external or internal stimuli.

The *sakalas* possessing the *bhogadeha* can again be subdivided into two classes—the superhuman *sakalas* and the subhuman *sakalas,* the form occupying a somewhat higher position than the human beings and the latter occupying a lower position in the hierarchy of beings.

Thus all the *sakalas* can be broadly put under three principal categories, viz., the superhuman, technically called *devatās,* the human, or the *mānuṣa,* and the subhuman, or the *tiryag.*

The superhuman beings (*daiva-sakala*), having a higher position in the hierarchy of *sakalas* and being equipped with *bhogadeha,* are incapable of performing any *karma* of their own free will. They are merely the tools of the supreme will of the Supreme

Lord. They have, therefore, no transmigration; they stay in the level of which they are the presiding deities until the exhaustion of their *bhogavāsanā*. After their *bhogavāsanā* is exhausted, they assume the body-apparatuses of *mānuṣa sakalas*, i.e., *karmadeha*.

As the presiding deities of particular regions, their main function is to govern that region on behalf of the Supreme Lord. Governing here means merely operating the fundamental laws of *prakṛti* and dispensing the fruits of *karma* to the doer. It is through these functions that they enjoy and exhaust their *bhogavāsanā*. As there are said to be eight regions in the impure creation, the presiding deities are also said to be of eight kinds.[27]

Though the subhuman *tiryag* or *sakalas* also possess *bhogadeha*, they are said to occupy the lowest position in the hierarchy of embodied beings. There are mainly five varieties of *tiryags*,[28] viz., *paśu* (name used in the nontechnical sense to denote creatures not covered by any classification), *mṛga* (quadrupeds), *sarisṛpa* (reptile), *paksī* (birds), and *sthāvara* (stationary creation, i.e., trees, etc.). Like the superhuman *sakalas*, they do not have the privilege of performing *karma* out of their will (*icchā*). They have no ego-consciousness. Their actions are guided by their blind instincts.

But, unlike the superhuman *sakalas*, they do not remain imprisoned in one level of existence: they have evolution. Their evolution is, however, governed by the general laws of *prakṛti*.

In the hierarchy of *sakalas*, the human *sakalas* (*mānuṣa*) have a unique position on account of their association with *karmadeha*. They have the singular privilege of performing actions of their own and, as a consequence, of elevating and degrading themselves in the different levels of creation. They alone are possessed of distinct personality or ego-consciousness, and limited will and freedom of action. Being possessed of the ego-consciousness which is not a bane according to the Trika system but a blessing in disguise, they have the freedom of directing their efforts wherever they like. They can, if they so desire, elevate themselves to higher and higher levels of existence through their *karma* and reach the zenith of evolution in the impure creation, or even go

---

27. Cf. *I.P.V.* III, 2, 10. Comm. p. 254. See also the *Bhāskarī* thereon.
28. Ibid.

beyond the *māyā* level, a capacity that is not found in other kinds of embodied beings.

At the same time, they have also the capacity of degrading themselves to lower levels of existence, i.e., the subhuman levels, through their *karma*. In such cases, however, their stay in the subhuman level is not permanent; they remain there until they have exhausted the fruits of their deeds (*karmaphala*) which have forced them to go there. In the same way, if they develop the intense desire for enjoyment (*bhogavāsanā*) and perform suitable deeds, it is possible that they assume the *bhogadeha* of superhuman beings through their mercy and stay in the superhuman level of existence until the exhaustion of such *bhogavāsanā*. In both the cases, however, their stay is temporary and limited to shorter periods of time.

Unlike other kinds of *sakalas*, the human *sakala* is said to be existing in the different levels of impure creation, beginning from the *mahat* down to the *pṛthvā*.[29] His being on a particular level of creation is determined by his identification with a particular *tattva* which is a constituent of his body-apparatus. As we have observed, every individual human being identifies himself either with his body-apparatus or one of its constituent *tattvas* so that his ego-consciousness arises from this false identification of not-Self with Self.[30] He is said to be existing in that particular level of existence represented by the *tattva* with which his ego-consciousness is identified. To give a concrete example, if an individual being has his ego-consciousness identified with his *buddhi*, he would be regarded as existing on the *buddhi tattva* level and if he has his ego-consciousness arising from his identification with *pṛthvī tattva*, he would be said to be existing on the level of *pṛthī*, and so on.

But the human *sakalas'* existence on different levels of creation does not necessarily mean that they are different in their constitution; for all human *sakalas* are practically and essentially alike. Their existence on the different levels of creation does not make any difference, except that they have different starting points of evolution in creation. In other words, every human

---

29. Cf. *Pr. Hd.*, Sū. 3 Comm. p. 28.
30. Cf. *T.S.* I 192.

sakala normally evolves to higher levels of existence like the *sakalas* of the subhuman level, so that if he happens to be on the lowest rung of impure creation, his gradual evolution under normal circumstances would be a long-drawn process; he will have to traverse a number of stages or steps of creation before he is able to reach the highest level in impure creation entirely of his own.

CHAPTER 4

The Way to Ultimate Self-Realization

1. THE TRIKA VIEW

It has been observed in the previous chapter that *karma* is the most important factor in the individual being's existence as *sakala*, and that it is chiefly responsible for his transmigratory character in creation. But *karma*, according to the Trika system, is of two distinct kinds—one, which is intimately connected with his "earthly" existence, and is, therefore, responsible for his ceaseless transmigrations in the different levels of creation, popularly known as the *sāṁsārika karma*, and the other, diametrically opposed to the former in nature, which helps him in securing his release from bondage, and is therefore technically designated as the *ātma karma.*[1]

While the performance of the first kind of *karma* is deemed as essential to sustain him in his embodied form, the performance of the second kind is optional with the individual being as it has nothing to do with his earthly existence. The performance of *sāṁsārika karma* (worldly activity) by the individual being results in his increased entanglements in *saṁsāra* (the world) and his prolonged suffering, and the performance of *ātma karma*

1. The performance of such *karma* which brings about his release from the bondage, i.e., the *sādhanā*.

brings about the destruction of his bonds of ignorance (*ajñāna*), and thereby his liberation from the shackles of *saṁsāra*.

Thus, in the Trika view, the performance of *karma* as such is not a necessary evil or a curse of "earthly" existence from which the individual being, desiring liberation, should try to escape. It may also prove a blessing in disguise, provided he knows the right type of *karma* to be performed and acts[2] accordingly. If the individual beings were not endowed with this capacity, viz., the capacity of performing *karma* out of their individual independent will and thereby working out their liberation from *saṁsāra*, they would have been completely at the mercy of the laws of nature and the operation of divine *anugraha*, over which they have no control.

It is indeed for this reason that the Trika system, unlike some other Brahmanical systems of Indian philosophy, such as Vedānta and the Sāṁkhya, does not consider the performance of *karma* to be essentially a fruitless or harmful act, which, being a product of ignorance (*ajñāna*), is incapable of serving any useful purpose in the achievement of the Ultimate Goal. On the other hand, the Trika system acknowledges the real value of *karma* and gives it a proper place in the *sādhanā* of man. It maintains that performance of *karma* is an important tool in the hands of the human being in bondage, and this tool can effectively be utilized in bringing about his release from *saṁsāra*. Just as a thorn can prove to be a very useful instrument in removing another thorn from the affected part of the body, in the same way the performance of *ātma karma* can also prove very useful in getting rid of the afflictions of *saṁsāra* that are due to bondage.

In this connection, one may pertinently raise the question that if an individual being does not strive for his liberation by performing *ātma karma* what will be his ultimate fate? Will he continue to live eternally in that state, that is, the state of bondage, or is there even a remote possibility of his being released from bondage without making any personal effort? The reply according to the Trika system would be that it is logically unthinkable that man would remain forever in the state of bondage, because the human being is none other than a self-limited form

2. The quotation from the Āgama in MM. V–7, Comm. p. 24.

of the Supreme Being, the *Parama Śiva*.[3] As we have observed above, it is the Supreme Being who exercising his divine freedom imposes limitation on himself and assumes the form of limited beings (*cidaṇus*); on their being associated with a human form, they come to be known as human beings. Obviously, this self-limited state of man's existence cannot be the final and the perennial state of his being; he must be restored to his original status, viz., *śivatva*. Accordingly, it is held that since the Supreme Lord assumes the self-limited form of *paśu* (which includes the human beings) by exercising the *tirodhāna* aspect of his divine freedom, he is restored to his essential state[4] by exercising a corresponding aspect of his divine freedom technically called the *anugraha*.

Thus, if it be assumed that the human being in his present state of existence represents one fallen from his divine status, his restoration to his Essence then is only a logical corollary. It is, therefore, obvious that whether or not the individual being in *saṁsāra* strives for his liberation and carves out a path to his ultimate destiny, one day he is sure to realize it. The finale may come sooner or later, depending on a number of factors, but it is nonetheless inevitable.

In this connection, it will perhaps not be out of place to state that the Trika system does not attach much importance to the achievement of liberation from *saṁsāra*, since it falls far short of their ultimate Goal, which is the integral realization of Essence, the *śivatva*. For in their view, the achievement of mere liberation by the individual being from transmigrations does not lead him very far; at best it takes him beyond the province of ignorance and *māyā* (i.e., the *bauddha-ajñāna*) and secure his *videhamukti* (disembodied state of liberation from the shackles of body). But the freedom from ignorance is not the same as the awakening of the knowledge of one's divinity (*aiśvarya*), nor is the *videhamukti* the same as the realization of *śivatva*, one's Essence. As a matter of fact, the Trika system considers the achievement of this kind of liberation to be a sort of deviation from the individual's path of self-realization, a kind of impediment, because the individual being who achieves the state of

3. Cf. *T.V.* I, 24–25.
4. Cf. *T.S.* XI. p. 118.

videhamukti,[5] throws himself thereby completely at the mercy of divine *anugraha* from the highest Source. Owing to his dissociation with a body-apparatus, he cannot do anything of his own to create favorable conditions for the descent of divine grace on him. We shall revert to this point at a later stage.

Having come to the conclusion that the individual being, now in the state of *sakala*, is bound to regain his Essence one day, we shall endeavor in the following paragraphs to explain the preliminary difficulties and obstacles which he has to face in the very beginning of his journey to the ultimate destiny.

The obstacles, broadly speaking, are twofold—first, those that arise from his association with the *kārmamala*, and second, those that are due to his being covered by the fundamental *mala* (*mūlamala*), i.e., *āṇavmala*.

It has been stated that man's existence in the state of *sakala* is mainly due to his association with *kārmamala*. The *kārmamala* is said to be grounded on the *ajñāna* resulting from the self-limitation (*ātma-sañkoca*) due to the *āṇavamala*. The *kārmamala* is not only responsible for his existence as *sakala*, but is also instrumental in bringing about the existence of *saṁsāra* (i.e., the objective universe), since this provides him with the only outlet for the exhaustion of the accumulated fruits of all his past *karmas* (*sañcita karma*) through enjoyment.[6] In *saṁsāra* the human being is forced to pass successively through two states of existence (*avasthās*), technically known as the *vikṣepa* and *laya avasthās*. The *vikṣepa* is that state of man's existence in which he is endowed with an appropriate body-apparatus (*deha*) through which he enjoys the creation and performs actions in the world. All his actions performed in this state leave their residual impressions (*saṁskāra*), which are accumulated and carried forward for fruition in the next cycle. When he is in the *laya* state, his psychophysical organism (*deha*), including the sense organs, *manas*, *buddhi*, and *ahaṁkāra*, is in a state of dissolution (*līna*) in its material cause (*upādāna-kāraṇa*), which is the *māyā* together with the

5. This roughly corresponds to the state of *vijñānākala*. They have to depend on the Supreme Lord for direct transmission of divine grace (cf. *T.S.*, VIII., p. 80).

6. *Par. Sār.*, v–63, Comm, p. 121 ff.

prakṛti, and consequently he exists without a physical body, and is known as *akala*. When he is in this state, the accumulated residual-impressions of his *karmas* of the previous cycles grow mature due to the functioning of *kāla śakti* (time-force), and consequently he is forced to reappear in embodied form (i.e., in *vikṣepa avasthā*) in the next cycle, to suffer the fruits of his own deeds. In this way, the *kārmamala* forces him to pass through the successive stages of *vikṣepa* and *laya* without a break and this is what makes his existence in *saṁsāra* transmigratory.

Now, logically speaking, the *kārmamala* is the first hurdle in his way, which he must cross before he can begin his journey to the ultimate Goal. He should put an end to the endless series of his transmigrations by destroying the *kārmamala* which is associated with him. For until he succeeds in stopping the cycle of his transmigrations, he cannot hope to make any progress in his *sādhanā*. Though this appears to be the only plausible course open to all aspirants, curiously enough, it has not been advocated in clear terms at any place in the texts of the Trika system. As a matter of fact, the Trika system appears to be reticent in laying down a rigid and definite course of *sādhanā* applicable to all without an exception, in outlining what an aspirant should do or refrain from doing in the initial stages. Of course, their reticence in this respect is not without reason; it is in fact quite consistent with their line of approach.

Although it is stated that there are three kinds of *malas* enveloping every embodied being, it cannot be said with certainty that their annihilation in all cases will have a uniform pattern, or the destruction of one will entail the destruction of the other two in succession. Neither can it be said with certainty that the destruction of the *kārmamala* in the case of a particular individual will precede the destruction of the *āṇavamala*. The reason for such a view is not difficult to find. According to the Trika system, the destruction of the *āṇavamala* is totally independent of the destruction of other two kinds of *malas*, and as such, it does not necessarily presuppose or entail the annihilation of the other two kinds of *malas*. In the same way, it cannot be said with certainty that the prior annihilation of the *kārma-* and *māyīyamalas* in an individual, which can be achieved by him through his personal efforts (*puruṣakāra*), in any way hastens the destruction of the *āṇavamala.* For the *āṇavamala,* it is held, cannot be annihilated even by intense personal efforts; its destruction results directly from the descent of divine *anugraha* on the individual in the form of *śaktipāta.*[7] Since the destruction of *kārma-* and *māyiyamalas* is generally achieved by the aspirant through his personal efforts, and the destruction of the *āṇavamala* is effected by the descent of divine grace. The Trika system admits the possibilities of cases[8] where the *āṇavamala* has been fully annihilated following *śaktipāta* but the *kārma-* and *māyīyamalas* persist undisturbed, owing to the aspirant not striving for their destruction.

From the above account it is obvious that, in the case of a particular aspirant, it cannot be confidently foreseen whether the destruction of the *āṇavamala* will precede or follow the destruction of the other two kinds of *malas,* because of the fact that it cannot be known beforehand when the divine grace will descend on the individual being. As there are a number of possibilities depending on the particular individual being and his circumstances, the Trika system refrains from laying down a rigid formula.

In view of these facts, let us imagine the hypothetical case of an individual aspirant who has not been a recipient of divine *anugraha,* and explain how he will proceed on in his way to the ultimate Goal. The divine *anugraha* not having descended on him, the *āṇavamala* veiling him remains undisturbed. Now, his first task would be to emancipate himself from the endless cycles of transmigrations, from the state of *vikṣepa* to *laya* and *vice versa.* The only way to escape this endless transmigration (*saṁsāraṇa*), which is due to *kārmamala,* lies in the awakening of *viveka jñāna* in himself, the discriminatory knowledge of oneself as a principle of pure *caitanya* as distinct from the impure matter that is associated with him in the form of his body-apparatus. With the awakening of *viveka jñāna* in the aspirant, the aspect of *ajñāna* that veils him in the form of *kārmamala* is destroyed, and consequently he is liberated from the bonds of *karma* and *saṁsāra.* The aspirant's achievement of liberation from the shackles of *karma* (*karmaban-*

7. *T.S.,* XI., p. 118.
8. As in the case of *ādhikārins* of the *śambhavā, śakta,* and *ānava upāyas* (cf. *Śiv. Su.,* II H. and *T.S.* III, IV, V.).

dhana) also involves the achievement of liberation from the necessary corollary of *māyīyamala*, since the *kārma* and *māyīyamalas* are products of the same *ajñāna* (i.e., *anyathā-khyāti*).

But mere achievement of this kind of liberation is not the true aim of the aspirant's life—it is not the final end of man's journey. At best, it is a stepping-stone to his ultimate destiny which, as we have observed, is the integral realization of his essential divinity, the *śivatva*. The separation of Self from matter is essential as a preliminary step, because otherwise the knowledge of Self as distinct from not-Self having been lacking, the individual identifies himself with his body-apparatus, senses, etc.[9] He has, therefore, first to regain the knowledge of Self as the principle of *Caitanya* (Pure Consciousness) distinct from matter (*acaitanya*), before he can know his real nature (*svarūpa*) and then realize everything else as Pure Consciousness (*Caitanya*), which is the same as knowing everything as Self.

This stage of complete separation of Self from not-Self, which we have just described, corresponds to the state of the individual's existence that is technically known as *vijñāna kaivalya* in the Trika system. It is true that the aspirant in this state achieves complete liberation from the *kārma*- and *māyīyamalas*, but still he cannot be said to be absolutely free from *mala* because the fundamental *mala* (*mūlamala*) continues to veil him even in that stage. Unless this *āṇavamala* is fully destroyed and he is completely emancipated from the clutches of limitations, how can he hope to realize his Essence, the *śivatva* which is beyond all limitations? But since the *āṇavamala* is self-imposed by the Supreme Lord, it can be removed by him alone, exercising the corresponding aspect of his divine freedom, the *anugraha śakti*. Hence, the possibility of intense personal endeavor achieving this task does not arise at all.

In this connection it is interesting to note that almost all Brahmanical systems of Indian philosophy consider the achievement of freedom (*mukti*) from repeated transmigrations and the attendant misery to be the only aim of man's life. The Saṁkhya and the Yoga systems, for instance, are content with the achievement of liberation of *puruṣa* (the pure Self) from the clutches of

9. *Par. Sār.*, v–32, Comm., p. 69 ff.

prakṛti (matter) through *vivekajñāna* (the knowledge of discrimination of Self from not-Self). The complete eradication of all kinds of miseries is the Supreme Goal in their view. That this liberation of *puruṣa* implies also the realization of Self goes without saying. The Nyāyikas and the Vaiśeṣikas have as their Goal the absolute abolition of pain which is consequent on birth, caused by the desires (*vasānā*) produced through self-ignorance. Hence, their aim is achieved through the realization of *ātman* in its essence as free from the influence of ignorance (*ajñāna*) and its attendant forces, and beyond the possibility of contact with the mental organ (*manas*). In short, the liberation of the human being from the ill effects of his association with physical body is the purpose of his life. The Vedānta, on the other hand, considers that man's realization of the true nature of Self, i.e., his complete identity with *Brahman*, puts an end to all his misery.

In short, the accent of the different schools of Brahmanical philosophy in the conception of man's ultimate destiny is on securing freedom from *saṁsāra*. Of course, that this implies also the realization of the true nature of Self is admitted by all schools of Indian philosophy.

But it must also be taken into account that the conception of Self varies widely according to the differences of approach of the different systems of Indian philosophy. While in the Nyāya-Vaiśeṣika and Sāṃkhya-Yoga systems the individual self as such is emphasized, its innate relation to some Universal Self is positively denied. As a matter of fact, there is no conception of the Universal Self in these systems; that is why the emphasis is on the individual self in them. The Vedānta, on the other hand, emphasizes the identity of individual self with the Universal Self, the *Brahman*. But this Universal Self is conceived of only as being static (*niṣkriya*) in nature. Being devoid of the dynamic Principle (i.e., the Śakti), the Self (*Ātman*) of the Vedāntic system cannot be said to represent the true nature of the Absolute in its plenary form.

At this stage we do not wish to enter into a detailed discussion about the relative merits of the conception of Self according to different schools of Indian philosophy. We only wish to point out that there exists a wide gulf of difference on this issue and this can be attributed to the differences in the angles of vision and approach of different systems of philosophy. This is also precisely the reason for the fundamental difference in the means of realization of the ultimate destiny.

It has been stated above that the achievement of liberation by the embodied human being (*sakala*) from the bondage of *kārma-* and *māyīyamalas*, logically, is the first step in the direction of realization of the Ultimate Goal. The achievement of this kind of liberation, we have been told, is possible through the rise of discriminatory knowledge (*vivekajñāna*). Now, it remains to be seen here what are the conditions according to the Trika system that are conducive to its rise in the *buddhi* of the aspirant.

It may be observed here that the Trika system does not formulate its views distinctly on the subject nor does it criticize the general views accepted by almost all other systems of Indian philosophy; hence we may safely presume that it concurs with the conventional views. According to these views, the awakening of *vivekajñāna* in the *buddhi* of the aspirant is possible only after it has been cleansed of its impurities which are due to the predominance of *rājasika* and *tāmasika guṇas.* As the *buddhi* is gradually purged of impurities, the aspirant develops an intense feeling of nonattachment toward transient objects, the feeling of *vairāgya,* or *saṁvega* as it has been technically called. He also develops the feeling of insatiability (*tṛṣṇa*) and dissatisfaction with his present state, a sort of spiritual craving which forces him to abandon his present self-complacent attitude. As these symptoms become noticeable in him after he has had prolonged sufferings in the various states of his existence, we can safely conclude that the time for his deliverance from bondage is imminent. These symptoms are precursor to the rise of *viveka jñāna* in him and with its rise the bonds of *kārma-* and *māyīyamalas* are snapped in an instant, as it were. The task of cleansing the *buddhi* is not accomplished only by the aspirant through his personal efforts; it is also an automatic process which goes on with the passage of time (*kāla*). Of course, the aspirant can, if he so desires, aid and accelerate the process by following certain "aids."

Accordingly, it is held that the practice of fourfold aids[10] goes a long way in purging the *buddhi* of its impurities, and thus creating favorable conditions for the rise of *vivekajñāna.* They are:

---

10. *Ved. Sār.* p. 1.

(1) *nityānityavastuviveka,* the ability to discriminate between the transient and the eternal, (2) *ihāmutrārthabhogavirāga,* the absence of desire for securing happiness, or avoiding pain here or elsewhere, (3) *śamādisādhanasampad,* the development of sixfold qualities which are conducive to inward obstruction of sense organ and consequent spiritual elevation and, (4) *mumukṣatvam,* the burning desire for Self-realization. We shall explain these aids in the following paragraphs.

The development of the ability to discriminate between the transient and the eternal is, in the initial stages, a very important qualification for the aspirant because it is this which puts him on the right path. Though this ability fully develops when the aspirant is able to have Self-realization, it is possible even before such realization to feel convinced somewhat vaguely that there are things of eternal value, as opposed to those of provisional value,[11] and as such, to be attracted irresistibly toward the values eternal. In other words, the power of correct appraisal of values is an important qualification that the aspirant must develop.

The aspirant should also cultivate an attitude of detachment from all selfish ends—the absence of desire for self-gratification, or its contrary, self-mortification.[12] With the development of such an attitude, the outward movement of senses (*indriyas*) ceases and the aspirant is able to sever his intimate connections with the external world.

The development of sixfold qualities,[13] e.g., *śama, dama, uparati, titikṣā, samādhanā,* and *śraddhā* in the aspirant are universally acclaimed as helpful in training the various senses and disciplining the *manas.* Of these, the cultivation of *śama* and *dama* aims at controlling the *manas* and senses respectively. *Uparati* brings in the temperance of action, while *titikṣā* enables the aspirant to endure the opposites, such as pain and pleasure, heat and cold, etc. The cultivation of *samādhāna* develops mental concentration, while *śraddhā* aims at making the aspirant steadfastly loyal to the ideal. The development of all these qualities not only enables the aspirant to have effective control over his sense

11. Ibid., p. 1.
12. Ibid., p. 2.
13. Ibid.

organs and *manas*, but also minimizes the risk of his straying from the right path.

The growth of burning desire for Self-realization[14] is extremely important for the aspirant in the beginning and its value cannot be over emphasized, since it is this quality in the aspirant that provides the necessary impetus to begin the quest.

The cultivation of all these qualities by the individual aspirant through his incessant personal endeavors produces the desired result, namely the purgation of his *buddhi*, the seat of all knowledge (*jñāna*). The pronounced appearance of these traits is the unfailing sign of the aspirant's elevation which is conducive to the rise of *vivekajñāna* in the *buddhi*. It may, however, be stated here, by way of clarification, that though the development of these traits is considered as preparatory to the rise of *vivekajñāna* in the Advaita-Vedānta system of *Śaṅkara*, almost all other schools of Indian philosophy also subscribe to these views in principle.

As the *vivekajñāna* arises and illumines the *buddhi* of the aspirant, he is able to distinguish between the Self and not-Self associated with the form of the body-apparatus, and puts himself on the side of Self. Since the false identification of Self with not-Self through ignorance takes place in the *buddhi*, the rise of *vivekajñāna* in the *buddhi* removes this confusion between the Self and not-Self and enables him to experience his Self (*Aham*) as isolated from the not-Self (*Idam*). Thus, the aspirant succeeds through his personal endeavor in the initial task of separating *Caitanya*, his Self, from the insentient matter (*acaitanya*), and with it he accomplishes his part in the *sādhanā*.

When the separation of Self from not-Self is fully accomplished, the aspirant no longer exists as a *sakala* (embodied being); he dissociates himself from his body-apparatus, and later with the destruction of physical body in course of time he becomes disembodied (*akala*). He can exist in that state of disembodied existence, either as a *pralaya kevalin* or a *vijñāna kevalin* as the case may be; if he is able to traverse the region of *prakṛti*, he attains the state of *pralaya kevalin*, where he has to lie submerged (*līna*) in the *mūla prakṛti*, i.e., unevolved *prakṛti*, and if, on the

---

14. *Ved. Sār.*, p. 2.

other hand, he succeeds in crossing the region of *māyā*, he becomes a disembodied *cidaṇu*, such as a *vijñāna kevalin*, and lies nascent in *māhāmāyā*.

But by merely achieving the state of disembodied existence, he cannot be said to be nearer his Ultimate Goal, because he is still not absolutely free from limitation. For when he is a *pralaya kevalin* lying nascent in the *māyā*, he is associated with the *āṇava-* and *māyīya malas;* and when he is a *vijñāna kevalin* he has the *āṇavamala* still veiling him. In any case, the *āṇavamala*, being the fundamental *mala*, continues to affect him and unless this is removed or destroyed he cannot hope to realize his true Essence.

As we have observed, the destruction of *āṇavamala* is possible only when the divine *anugraha* in the form of *śaktipāta* descends on him. He will have to wait for it after having achieved this much through his personal endeavor.

In this connection it may be pointed out that the descent of divine *anugraha* on the individual has no relation to the state of his existence. Therefore all aspirants, irrespective of their state of existence, such as *sakala*, *pralayākala*, or *vijñanākala*, or the position which they might be holding in creation, must wait for the descent of *śaktipāta* from above before they enter into the pure realm of Spirit, technically called the *śuddha adhva*. And in a sense, the existence of the individual, as we have seen, in any of the disembodied states, is disadvantageous to him because, as we shall later observe, he must remain completely at the mercy of the divine *anugraha* from above for his emancipation.

As soon as the divine *anugraha* descends on the individual, the *āṇavamala* is immediately destroyed and his latent divinity awakens, which in the technical language of the Trika system is called 'the awakening of *suddha vidyā*' (*śuddhavidyodaya*). With the awakening of *śuddha vidyā*, he is said to be restored to his pure *svarūpa*, the *śuddha ahaṁta*. This paves the way to his realization of his Ultimate Goal, the *śivatva*.

It is now obvious from this account that the descent of divine *anugraha* on the individual being is not merely a crucial step towards his 'divinization'; it in fact marks the beginning of that process. And it is for this reason that the Trika system is of the view that the real journey of man to his Ultimate Goal commences only after he is a recipient of divine grace.

As the problem of *śaktipāta* is of great importance and has been emphasized in almost all the texts of the Trika system, we shall devote a separate section to its critical examination.

2. THE DESCENT OF DIVINE GRACE (*ŚAKTIPĀTA*)

In the foregoing section we have indicated that the Trika system regards the descent of divine *anugraha* on the individual aspirant (*sādhaka*) from the highest planes of Reality, i.e., the *Parama Śiva*, as indispensable for the achievement of his supreme destiny, i.e., the *śivatva*. In that connection we have also observed that the descent of divine grace, in the Trika view, marks the beginning of the process of divinization of the aspirant. It is interesting to note here that this issue of divine grace (*anugraha*), though appearing altogether new to the students of Orthodox Indian philosophy, figures prominently not only in the Trika system but also in many other systems of Indian philosophy, which draw their inspiration from the Āgamas. For instance, in all the different branches of the Śaiva, Śākta, and Vaiṣṇava systems, we find that the descent of divine grace (*anugraha*) on the aspirant from the highest Reality is considered to be an essential prerequisite for his realization of the supreme goal. Hence, in all these systems of philosophy, divine grace occupies a unique place in the field of *sādhanā*. Even in the Mahāyāna school of Buddhism, it is said that the aspirants cannot realize the highest state of perfection, i.e., the Buddhahood, without the help of grace[15] from above. Christian mystics of medieval age in the West have also recognized the importance of divine grace[16] in the practical field of Self-

---

15. The development of *bodhicitta*, according to the Mahāyāna Buddhists, is an essential precondition for the achievement of Buddhahood. The development of *bodhicitta*, which makes him the Elect to proceed along the stream of sanctification, is dependent on certain factors which includes help by *kalyānamitras* (spiritual guides) and *pāramitās*. Cf. *AMBHS* pp. 247 and 257. For the nature of *kalyānamitras* see ibid., pp. 312–13.
16. According to St. Augustine, the eternal life can be won by merit only, and the merit is established by good works. The ability to perform good works, in its turn, comes from the descent of divine grace.

realization, and have accordingly assigned it its due place in their *sādhanā*. According to them, the stage of the soul's divine illumination is always preceded by a purgatory stage, in which the descent of divine grace from above is implied. Though they do not always specifically mention divine grace as the essential precondition for Self-realization, it is clear from what they say in this connection that the full purgation is not possible without the descent of divine grace on the individual. Here we do not propose to make a comparative study of the concept of divine grace (*anugraha*) from the standpoints of different systems of philosophy, as it falls outside the scope of present study, but we only wish to point out that the importance of *śaktipāta* as a factor essential for Self-realization has been recognized not only by the Trika system but also by many other systems of philosophy which are in no way allied to the Trika system.

For the proper evaluation of the unique place that the descent of divine grace (*anugraha*) occupies in the field of *sādhanā*, it appears proper here to discuss, according to the Trika view, how far the individual aspirant can go on his way to the ultimate goal of integral Self-realization, i.e., *Śivatva,* on his own, or how much he can achieve through his personal efforts. This question can be examined from two standpoints: first, from the standpoint of his status as an embodied being in creation, and second, from the point of view of his constitution.

As we have already observed, the entire creation (*sṛṣṭi*), according to the Trika view, is made up of two strata or planes (*bhūmi*) of existence, technically called the *adhvas* (lit., ways). They are the impure domain of world-order commonly known as the Impure Order (*aśuddha adhva*) and the pure domain of spiritual order, ordinarily called the Pure Order (*śuddha adhva*). They broadly correspond to the material (*jaḍātmaka*) and spiritual planes (*caitanyātmaka*) of existence respectively. These orders (*adhvas*), it may be pointed out here, do not exist somewhere in "outer space," apart from the individual; they are, as a matter of

---

Hence, even the merits of men are really the gifts of God. The medieval schoolmen also recognized the importance of baptismal grace, which alone is said to be capable of putting men on the right path.

fact, within every individual being[17] who is comprised of all the thirty-six *tattvas*. Of course, it is a fact that these very thirty-six *tattvas* also go to make the entire field of creation, so that what is true of the microcosm, i.e., the individual being, is also equally true of the macrocosm, i.e., the cosmos.

Normally, the individual being is said to be a denizen of impure world order (*aśuddha adhva*). Being associated with a material body-apparatus (*deha*), he is very intimately, inseparably connected with the external material world. His Ultimate goal, the integral realization of his Essence, *śivatva*, however, lies on the spiritual planes. Hence obviously, the first step toward the achievement of his Goal would be his attempt to disentangle himself from the web of matter by cultivating nonattachment (*vairāgya*) toward the transient. The process of disentanglement implies his withdrawal from the outside world to the core of his being, his pure Self (*śuddha svarūpa*), through the process of introversion. The process of introversion is generally described with the help of the analogy of his journey through the various levels of existence or *tattvas* of impure creation.

The embodied human being is said to be capable of traversing or evolving through the extensive regions of *prakṛti* and *māyā*[18] through his incessant endeavor. He is even said to be potentially capable of transcending the levels of *prakṛti* and *māyā*,[19] thereby achieving liberation from the shackles of bondage that

---

17. The Trika conception of the individual human being, being a composite of material and spiritual elements, is not a new idea; even the Upaniṣads speak of two stratas or planes of the Self. The first is the material or phenomenal self, generally called the *bhūtātman*, which is subject to the stress and strain of the ever-changing and ever-moving material world; the second is the spiritual, or noumenal, Self (the *antarātman*) which is immutable, the Seer, the subject, and the agent (*jñatā* and *kaṛtā*). Cf. *Ma. Up.*, II, 9; IV, 2.
18. The evolution of individual being is actually said to take place with the "shifting" of his identification with one of the higher *tattvas* which constitutes his body substratum.
19. Cf. *T.S.*, VIII, pp. 80–81. The grace of Īśvara, referred to here, is available to individual beings only when they have performed appropriate *karma* and thus earned the eligibility for it.

are due to his association with matter. But that is the farthest limit to which he can go on his own, the highest point to which he can evolve through his efforts. Though he is said to be capable of transcending the regions of *prakṛti* and *māyā*[20] through his own efforts, he is held to be incapable, by his very nature, of entering into the pure realm of spirit (i.e., the *śuddha adhva*). The moment he crosses *prakṛti*, he falls, as it were, in an ocean of ignorance, which is due to *māyā*, and becomes completely submerged in it (*līna*). His body-apparatus is dissolved in *māyā*, resulting in the loss of his distinct individuality or ego-consciousness, as his ego-consciousness arises out of a false identification of Self with not-Self. Such a state of his disembodied existence is technically called *pralayākala*, a state already described in the foregoing pages. Once he achieves that state, the question of his making any progress does not arise until he is once more associated with a body-apparatus and his ego-consciousness is again reawakened in him. Even the awakening of his ego-consciousness consequent on his association with a body-apparatus is of little help to him, because it does not enable him to cross the abyss of ignorance due to the fundamental self-limitation (*ātma-saṅkoca*). The awakened ego-consciousness is as false as the earlier one (*aśuddha-aham*), it is not the real Self of the aspirant. It is only a conceptual (*vaikalpika*) prototype of the real Self (*śuddha Aham*) of the aspirant, which remains hidden behind the veil of ignorance. Hence, like all others, he has to wait for the descent of divine grace (*anugraha*) from the highest level, without which he cannot move out of the impure creation. With the descent of divine grace (*anugraha*), his latent *svarūpa*, i.e., the consciousness of real Self (*svarūpa Aham* or *śuddha Aham*) is awakened, and this enables him to enter into the pure realm of spirit (*Caitanya*) i.e., the *śuddha adhva*.

Again, the whole problem can be looked at from the point of view of the constitution of the individual aspirant. Every em-

20. Normally, individual beings' evolution is confined to the region of *prakṛti*, i.e., the *tattvas* beginning from prakṛti down to the earth. In exceptional cases, when the feeling of nonattachment is very intense, the aspirant might evolve beyond *māyā*, i.e., cross the region of *Aśuddha adhva* and thus attain the state of *vijñānākala*. Such cases are, however, very rare. Cf. ibid., pp. 80–81.

bodied being, according to the Trika view, is covered by two kinds of veils (*āvaraṇa*) of self-ignorance—the primary veil of self-ignorance (*mūla-ajñāna*), and the secondary veil of self-ignorance (*bauddha ajñāna*). The primary veil of self-ignorance is the innermost veil, which arises directly from the individual being's self-limited atomic nature (*svasañkocita aṇurūpa*). As it is connected with the very being of the individual, it has been technically designated as the *pauruṣa ajñāna* (lit., the ignorance of real Self).[21] Being the basic self-ignorance, it is innate in all individual beings and lies at the root of the secondary self-ignorance. It has been described as conceptual by nature, in the sense that it is only a cover concealing the pure *svarūpa* of the individual, and as such, it has no existence apart from him.

The secondary veil of self-ignorance, on the other hand, is said to be consequent on his association with a body-apparatus as it arises from the false identification of Self with not-Self (*i.e.*, the *deha*, etc.) As this false identification takes place in the *buddhi*, it has been technically called the *bauddha ajñāna* (lit., the intellectual ignorance).[22] As such, it is said to be conceptual by nature, and is regarded as the outer shell of ignorance.

Of the two kinds of self-ignorance enveloping every individual being, the aspirant can only accomplish the annihilation of the outermost cover of self-ignorance, i.e., the *bauddha ajñāna*, through his intense personal efforts, by dissociating himself from the not-Self (*Idam*, i.e., the *deha*), and thereby destroying the false identification taking place in his *buddhi*. But he cannot achieve the destruction of the innermost cover of self-ignorance, the *pauruṣa ajñāna*, in spite of his best and concerted efforts, because he cannot put an end to his atomic nature (*aṇurūpa*) which has been imposed on him by the operation of the *nigraha* aspect of divine Śakti from above. Since the destruction of the self-imposed limitation (*sañkoca*) is said to be affected only by the operation of the *anugraha* aspect of divine Śakti, the *pauruṣa ajñāna* in the aspirant is held to be destroyed in an instant with the descent of divine *anugraha* on him.

---

21. *T.S.* I. pp. 2–3.
22. Cf. *T.S.* p. 2.

With the destruction of *pauruṣa ajñāna* through the descent of divine grace, the greatest impediment in the way of the rise of *pauruṣa jñāna* (lit., the knowledge of Self) is removed. The *pauruṣa jñāna* is the knowledge[23] of one's divine nature (*svarūpa*) (i.e., the *śuddha Aham*), and it lies latent in every individual being. With the destruction of *pauruṣa ajñāna*, this knowledge normally shines forth and illumines the being of the individual. Though the destruction of the *pauruṣa ajñāna* and the rise of *pauruṣa jñāna* are said to be simultaneously brought about in the aspirant by the *śaktipāta*,[24] the destruction of the *bauddha ajñāna* in all cases is not instantaneous with the destruction of the *paurụsa ajñāna*, or more precisely, the rise of *paurụsa jñāna*. In such cases, as we shall observe in the following section, the destruction of the *bauddha ajñāna* has be be accomplished by the aspirant through his *sādhanā*, in order that he might experience the *pauruṣa jñāna* in his *buddhi*[25] in the form of *bauddha jñāna* (lit., intellectual knowledge).

As we critically examine *śaktipata* and the process of divinization following it, we find that it consists of three distinct phases or stages of divinization, all of which are implicit in the very act of *śaktipāta*. It is true that the texts of the Trika system do not specifically mention these three stages, but when we examine *śaktipāta* and the transformation brought about by it in the aspirant, they become obvious. These three stages are (1) *pāśakṣaya* (lit., the destruction of bonds in the form of *malas*), (2) *śivatvayojana* or *pratibhā jñānodaya* (lit., the awakening of *pratibhā* (knowledge) as is accomplished in the process of *dikṣā*), and (3) *śivatvaprāpti* (lit., the integral realization of the Essence), corresponding to the three stages of the purgation, illumination, and the divine union generally spoken of by the Christian mystics of the medieval age.[26]

Of the three stages of *śaktipāta*, the first stage of *pāśakṣaya* is extremely important from the individual aspirant's point of view.

23. This knowledge is said to be nonconceptual by nature. Cf. *T.A.*, I, 41., p. 78.

24. Cf. *T.A.*, I, 46, Comm. p. 85.

25. Ibid., I, 44, Comm. p. 82; ibid. I, 50, p. 88.

26. E. Underhill, in her well-known book *Mysticism*, mentions five great stages leading to divine union, Viz., the awakening or conversion, purgation or self-knowledge, illumination, self-surrender or dark

It achieves the important task of purging the *ādhāra* (body-substratum) of the aspirant of the *mūlamala*, which is the *āṇavamala*, and thereby makes him a fit vehicle for receiving the divine knowledge, i.e., the knowledge of the divine *svarūpa* that lies latent in him. In this connection, it may be pointed out here that the term *pāśakṣaya* in the Trika system refers to the destruction of *āṇavamala* only, and not to the other *malas*. The reason for this is that while the *āṇavamala*, being the fundamental *mala*, cannot otherwise be destroyed, other kinds of *malas*, *māyīya* and *kārma*, being only the secondary *malas* based on the fundamental *mala*, can be destroyed by the aspirant through his own effort.

In the next stage, when the aspirant's *ādhāra* is free from the bond of fundamental self-limitation, the divine knowledge, technically designated the *pratibhā jñāna*, shines forth from within and illumines his being. The *pratibhā jñāna*, knowledge of one's Essence, lies latent in every individual being, and it requires only a spark of divine Śakti in the form of *śaktipāta*[27] to rouse or awaken it.

The rise of *pratibhā jñāna* is, however, not uniform in all aspirants; in some it is immediate and instantaneous with the *śaktipāta*, while in others it must be awakened through the mediation of an external agent, depending on the intensity of *śaktipāta* on the individual aspirant as well as the degree of purity of his *ādhāra*. The aid of an external agent is indispensable in the cases where the descent of divine *anugraha* is not sufficiently intense. The agent's task, as we shall later observe, is to awaken the latent *pratibhā jñāna* in the aspirant through a process that is technically called *dīkṣā* (lit., initiation). Among the external agents mentioned by Abhinavagupta, the hearing of *upadeśa* (spiritual instruction) directly from the *guru's* lips and the study of *śāstras* (scriptures) are the common ones.[28]

In the final stage, the *pratibhā jñāna* consummates in the *pūrna jñāna* (the supreme knowledge), the integral realization of

---

night, and the divine union (cf. *Mysticism*, part II, Ch. I, p. 165 ff.). These five stages can, however, be subsumed under the three principal heads mentioned above.

27. The spark of divine *Śakti* is transmitted to the *sādhaka's ādhāra* through *dīkṣā*. For the nature of *dikṣā* see *T.A.* I, 43, Comm. p. 80.

28. Cf. *T.A. Āh*, I, 44, p. 82; ibid. XIII, 174, Comm. p. 110.

the Essence, the *śivatva*. This, therefore, marks the culmination of all his aspiration, the end of his journey or pilgrimage, corresponding to the stage of divine union spoken of by the Christian mystics.

In this connection it may be pointed out that though the stage of purgation of *pāśakṣaya* is said to be followed immediately and almost simultaneously by the rise of *pratibhā jñāna* in the aspirants, the culminating stage of integral Self-realization is not reached immediately by them in all cases. This is mainly because the persisting *māyīya-* and *karmamalas* are not eliminated from their *ādhāra* with the destruction of the *āṇavamala*, due to their receiving the divine *anugraha* in less intense form. In such cases, the aspirants must endeavor to remove the last vestiges of *malas* from their *ādhāra* and thereby make them perfectly pure in order that they might have the integral Self-realization of *śivatva* within their lifetime, i.e., during the period in which they are associated with a physical body-apparatus. If, on the other hand, they do not make any effort to purify their *ādhāra* and thus destroy the *bauddha ajñāna,* they are unable to have the awakened *pratibhā jñāna,* illumine their *buddhi*[29] and thus be conscious of their Essence, *śivatva.* But in any case, their self-realization is inevitable[30] after their dissociation with the physical body-apparatus, i.e., the physical death.

After having examined the nature of *śaktipāta* and evaluated its place in the *sādhanā* of human aspirants as we come to the practical field of *sādhanā,* we are, in the very beginning, confronted with the task of determining the conditions or causal factors (*nimitta*)[31] which, according to the Trika system, lead to the actual descent of divine grace (*anugraha*) on the individual aspirants. This problem, by its very nature, is complex, and can be studied from at least two different standpoints, viz., from that of the individual aspirant, and from that of the Supreme Reality, *Parama Śiva,* the dispenser of divine grace.

While discussing this problem from the individual aspirant's point of view, Abhinavagupta advances a good number of

29. Cf. *T.A.* I, 50–51, Comm. pp. 88–89.
30. Cf. ibid., p. 79.
31. *T.S.*, XI, p. 118ff.

plausible causes or conditions for the descent of divine *anugraha*, and examines their admissibility, one by one, on logical grounds,[32] a summary of which is given below.

If it is assumed, observes Abhinavagupta, that the descent of divine grace on an individual being is conditioned by his appropriate meritorious *karma* (deed) or *karmas*,[33] the question will then naturally arise: What are those *karmas* due to? For it is generally held that the present *karma* of the individual being is caused and governed by *karmas* performed in the past, inasmuch as the residual impressions (*saṁskāra*) of past *karmas* merely motivate the present *karmas*. This, in other words, means that every *karma* performed in the present, meritorious or otherwise, is related to some other antecedent *karma*, and that *karma*, in its turn, is again related to some other *karma*, and so on *ad infinitum*. In these circumstances, when we try to find out the ultimate cause of a particular *karma*, we are confronted by an unending series of *karmas*, each linked with the other by a causal chain so that we have ultimately to give up our search in despair. Hence, this explanation, involving the fallacy of *regressus ad infinitum*, is logically untenable.

Abhinavagupta in the *Tantrāloka*[34] refers to the view of his predecessors who postulate the equipoise of mutually opposite kinds of *karmas*, technically called *karmasāmya*, to be conducive to the awakening of spiritual knowledge (*prātibha jñāna*) from within, which implies the descent of divine grace as a precondition. Explaining the concept of *karmasāmya* put forward by his opponents, he observes that there are mainly two kinds of *karma*, meritorious deeds or *śukla karma*, and demeritorious deeds, or *kṛṣṇa karma*. If the residual impressions of two mutually opposite kinds of *karma* producing opposite results are perfectly balanced, they would cancel one another, leaving the individual doer absolutely free from the bondage caused by his actions (*karmabandhana*). The attainment of such a state is obviously an ideal one for the individual aspirant, in whom the spiritual knowledge (*prātibha jñāna*) can arise freely from within without any obstruc-

32. Ibid. For details see *M.V.V.*, I, v–689–93, p. 65.
33. *T.S.*, XI, p. 118 ff.
34. *Op. cit. Āh;.* XII, Pp. 49 f.

tion, illumining his mind. Abhinavagupta observes that this is not correct due to the fact that annihilation of all residual impressions of past actions would entail his dissociation with the body-apparatus, since continuance of the physical body in man is dependent on the continued existence of the residual impressions of his past *karma*. If an individual aspirant becomes disembodied on account of total absence of the residual impressions of past *karma* in him, there is no room for the awakening of spiritual knowledge (*pratibha jñāna*) in him. Hence the theory of *karmasāmya* advanced by some opponents is not tenable.

Some orthodox theistic schools, such as the Yoga system of Patañjali, the Advaita Vedānta of Śaṅkara, Rāmānuja, etc., hold that the spiritual knowledge (*pratibha jñāna*) arises in the aspirant from within following the descent of divine grace, which actually is the outcome of the divine will of the Supreme Lord (*parameśvarecchā*). Abhinavagupta points out two major flaws in this view. First, it is impossible for man existing on the mundane levels of creation to know and talk about the divine will of the Supreme Lord.[35] The operation of the will of God also cannot be inferred in the absence of reason (*hetu*) and the relation of invariable concomitance (*vyāpti*) between minor and major terms. Hence the very assumption of the existence of the divine will for the descent of divine grace from above does not have any known basis. Secondly, if it is granted for the sake of satisfying the opponents (*durjana-tosa-nyāya*) that the aspirants can somehow know the operation of divine will by the Supreme Lord, there arises another difficulty. One cannot then overlook the possibility of someone ascribing the motive of partiality (*rāga-dveṣa*) to the Supreme Lord while dispensing his grace to the individual aspirants.

Similarly, the causal factors (*nimitta*)—such as the development of an intense feeling of nonattachment (*vairāgya*) towards all the worldly objects;[36] or the achievement of self-purification by the aspirant through his personal endeavor, which might usher the rise of discriminatory wisdom in him; or worship of a particular deity (*devatā*) that might be adduced to explain the descent of

35. Cf *T.S.* XI, p. 118.
36. *MVV* I, V. 689 p. 65.

divine grace on the aspirants—are open to serious objections.[37] As such they cannot be sustained on logical grounds.

But the rational instinct of man cannot remain satisfied with this explanation: it always demands reason for every happening. It falls beyond his mental comprehension how the descent of divine grace could be unconditional and totally unrelated to the recipient. As a matter of fact, man being a rational creature cannot remain satisfied until he finds some cogent explanation for the descent of grace.

Abhinavagupta points out the paradox involved in our asking for the causal condition for the descent of divine grace when it is, according to the Trika system, essentially an act of divine freedom on the part of the Supreme Lord.[38] He refers to the theory of *malaparipāka* advanced by the Śaiva Siddhāntins in this context which might appear as plausible, and critically examines it. He says that this theory no doubt offers the best possible explanation from the point of view of the aspirant for the descent of divine grace, which might satisfy his rational instinct. But he says that this is not acceptable to him. He mentions a number of defects in this theory. Before rejecting their theory on logical and doctrinal grounds, he first elucidates their view in this regard and then points out his difficulty in accepting the theory of *malaparipāka* as a plausible explanation for the descent of divine grace.

He says that the Śaiva Siddhāntins or the dualist Śaivas consider the *malas* enveloping the individual beings, viz., the *ānava-*, *māyīya-* and *kārmamalas,* to be of the nature of substance (*dravya*). These *malas* shackle the individual being when the Supreme Lord so desires.

From the point of view of fettered beings, these *malas* have no beginning (*anādi*), though they are said to terminate (*santa*) in course of time. Since they are said to be of the nature of substance, and, as such, have existence only on the mundane level, they are believed to be subject to the influence of time (*kala*) like any other worldly object. It is said that the *malas* "ripen" under the influence of time, and the Supreme Lord, finding that the

---

37. Cf. *T.S.* XI, p. 118.
38. *T.S.* XI, p. 117; *T.A.* XIII, V.279f., pp. 171 ff.

malas have ripened and are about to fall away, removes them from the body-apparatus of aspirants, and thereafter bestows grace on them. In the garb of spiritual teacher (guru) He is said to appear before disciples, and accomplishes this task through the act of initiation (*dīksā*), which essentially is a kind of *kriyā* (action).[39] Thus the process of maturation of *malas* under the influence of time, technically called *malaparipāka,* is said to hasten the process of the descent of divine grace according to the dualist Śaiva Siddhāntins.

In this connection it must be pointed out that though the term *mala paripāka* signifies the maturation of all the three kinds of *malas* (defilements), in the restricted sense it refers to the maturation of only the *ānavamala,* which is the basic defilement responsible for his manifestation as a fettered being (*paśu*). This *mala,* as we have already seen, is common to all kinds of fettered beings, viz., *sakala, pralayākala, vijñānākala.* All these kinds of fettered beings (*paśus*) exist on different levels of creation of the Impure Order constituted by *māyā* and *prakṛti.*

As indicated above, Abhinavagupta rejects the theory of *mala paripāka* adduced by the dualist Śaiva Siddhāntins as an essential precondition for the descent of divine grace on the following grounds: first, the *malas,* according to the Trika system, are not of the nature of substance (*dravya*) as they come into being as a result of the act of self-limitation (*ātmanigraha*) exercised by the Supreme Lord out of his free will to manifest himself as the universe. In these circumstances how can the *malas,* which owe their existence to supramundane cause (the will of the Supreme Lord), be subject to the influence of a mundane force such as time, which exists and operates only on the level of *māyā?* The maturation of *kārma* and *mayīya mala* might be subject to the influence of time, which is a progeny of *māyā,* but the *ānavamala,* which follows as a consequence of the free will of the Supreme Lord, cannot be subject to influence of time (*kāla*). Secondly, the Trika system recognizes the possibility of the descent of divine grace on all three kinds of fettered beings, viz., *sakala, pralāyākala,* and *vijñānākala.* Of these three kinds of fettered beings, *vijñānākalas* and *pralayākalas* are unembodied and disembodied beings respec-

39. *T.A.* XIII. 88 p.60.

tively. How can the maturation of *malas* take place under the influence of time in their case? Lastly, if the theory of *mala paripāka* is accepted as conducive to the descent of divine grace then it will militate against their doctrine of divine freedom (*svātantrya*) of the Supreme Lord, which incidentally is their cardinal doctrine.[40] The very function of divine *anugraha*, being only an expression of divine freedom of the Supreme Lord, must be unrestricted and unconditional.[41] Hence, Abhinavagupta asserts that the Trika system cannot accept any causal condition for the descent of divine grace even for the sake of logical abstraction, for it would virtually amount to the crippling or narrowing down of the unrestricted scope of the operation of divine freedom by the Supreme Lord.[42]

After having examined critically the implications of all probable explanations for the descent of divine grace from the point of view of the Supreme Lord as well as of the aspirants, and dismissing them all as unsatisfactory and logically untenable, Abhinavagupta at last comes to the conclusion that it is not possible to offer a single valid explanation that might hold good in all cases. Such a conclusion is inevitable, and it can also be justified as being in strict conformity with the fundamental doctrine of *svātantrya* (divine freedom) of the Trika system.

However, some explanation from the point of view of the individual aspirant must be given for the descent of divine grace for the satisfaction of the rational intellect of man, who cannot appreciate the full significance of the unconditional nature of

40. *MVV* I, V.688–89, pp. 65–66, *T.A.* XIII, 99 Comm. p. 67.
41. *T.A.* XIII, 100 Comm. p.68.
42. By divine grace we mean here the grace of the Supreme Lord which is capable of accomplishing the aspirant's divine union (*T.A.* XIII, 279, p. 171). There is still another kind of grace available to the aspirants from the presiding deities of different regions, such as Rudra, Viṣṇu, Brahmā, etc. This grace is considered to be inferior in quality to the divine grace from the Supreme Lord as it is capable only of fulfilling the aspirant's desire for enjoyment (cf. *T.A.* XIII 270–75, pp. 166 ff). Sometimes the presiding deities of different regions are required to function as the medium for the transmission of the divine grace, which would then be of the same quality as that coming from the Supreme Lord.

divine *anugraha*. Hence, despite all objections put forward by Abhinavagupta against the Śaiva Siddhāntin's theory of *malaparipāka*, this theory seems to be the best and most satisfactory explanation for the descent of divine grace from the point of view of the individual aspirant. While it is true that the theory of *malaparipāka* in the aspirant cannot be directly linked to the descent of divine grace, it describes the state of the body-apparatus of the aspirant if it is fit enough to receive the divine grace from above.

Also, the assumption of *malaparipāka* in the individual being as a condition conducive to the descent of divine grace makes it easy for us to explain the difference in the intensity of *śaktipāta* received by the different individuals. It is said that the maturation of *malas* is not uniform in all individuals; it has quantitative difference, i.e. difference in respect to its degree in different individuals. The Trika system seems to justify the variety in the intensity of divine grace as it is received by the different aspirants on the basis of their capacity. The maturation of *malas* in the different aspirants generally indicates on the one hand the imminence of the moment when divine grace will actually descend on them, and, on the other, an index of the development of their capacity to receive it in appropriately intense form.

Though the *śaktipāta*, as an act of divine freedom, is essentially a unitive act, it has been classified in the Trika system under three principal heads, in accordance with the degree of intensity in which it is received by the individual beings. They are the *tīvra śaktipāta*, the *madhya śaktipāta* and the *manda śaktipāta*.[43] In *Tantrāloka*,[44] however, Abhinavagupta gives an elaborate classification, dividing each of the above kinds of *śaktipāta* into three more subdivisions, thus making a total of nine kinds of *śaktipāta* in all. Arranged in the descending order of intensity, they are: (1) *tīvra-utkṛṣṭa*, (2) *tīvra-madhyasta*, (3) *tīvra-nikṛṣṭa*, (4) *madhya-utkṛṣṭa*, (5) *madhya-madhyasta*, (6) *madhya-nikṛṣṭa*, (7) *manda-utkṛṣṭa*, (8) *manala-madhasta*, and (9) *manda-nikṛṣṭa śaktipāta*.[45]

---

43. They are said to receive the divine *anugrahā* directly from the Supreme Lord.
44. Cf. *MVV.*, I, v–658 p. 62.
45. *MVV.*, I, v. 687, p. 65. For details about the condition of *sādhakas* after receiving the divine grace in different degrees of intensity, see *T.S.*, XI, pp. 119–20 *M.V.T.*

Abhinavagupta has also mentioned there the different consequences to which the infusion of divine grace leads, due to differentiation in intensity. He says that as soon as a spiritual aspirant receives divine grace of the extremely intense (*utkṛṣṭa-tīvra*) variety, he is immediately restored to his divine status, i.e., *Śivatva*. The residual impressions of his *prārabdha karma* (past actions having started bearing fruit) 'burn off,' resulting in the instantaneous destruction of his body. Such a fortunate aspirant is not required to make any effort whatsoever; he achieves the Ultimate Goal immediately through *śaktipāta* alone.

But that aspirant who receives divine grace of extremely intense (*madhya tivra*) variety experiences within himself the rise of the highest spiritual knowledge, or *sattarka*. With the infusion of divine grace in a very intense form, his intellect is fully purged of impurities including the residual traces of *malas* of various kinds; hence it serves as a perfect medium for the awakening of the spiritual wisdom automatically from within, without the intervention of any external agency such as a spiritual teacher or the study of *śāstras* (scriptures) etc. The pure spiritual knowledge which fully illumines his intellect is known as *nirbhittika prātibha jñāna* (spiritual knowledge independent of causative factor). In some aspirants, the infusion of divine grace may be slightly milder in intensity, and therefore it might not result in cleansing the intellect fully. Such aspirants might need help from a spiritual teacher or feel the necessity of study of *śāstras*, etc., to remove the veil completely. The *prātibha jñāna* in such aspirants is called *sabhittika prātibha jñāna* (spiritual knowledge depending on causative factors).

If some spiritual aspirants receive the divine grace in very intense (*mandativra*) form, there arises a keen desire to approach a *sadguru* for spiritual knowledge. Abhinavagupta has distinguished a *sadguru* from an *asadguru*, saying that the former is one who, after obtaining highest spiritual knowledge from the Supreme Lord himself, has succeeded in uniting himself fully with the Supreme Lord. Such a *guru* is regarded as *Bhairava Bhaṭṭāraka* (a form of Supreme Lord) incarnate. An *asadguru* is only a spiritual teacher (*āchārya*) who is said to have gained intellectually the knowledge of his essence; hence he is incapable of leading his disciple to the realization of the Supreme Goal. On the other hand, the aspirant initiated by a *sadguru* is able to reach the ultimate destiny, even enjoy *jīvanmukti* (liberation while remaining in embodied state), but he has to perform certain rites externally as directed by a *sadguru* to cleanse his intellect and make it a fit receptacle for the awakening of the spiritual knowledge.

The aspirant receiving divine grace in *utkṛṣṭa madhya* (intense) form, when initiated by a *sadguru*, does not develop faith in the efficiency of the *śaktipāta*. Such aspirant (*sādhaka*) has to strive hard to cultivate faith in spiritual achievement and perform the rites advised by his *guru*. This accelerates the pace of purgation and enables him to reach the ultimate goal.

If a *sādhaka* is a recipient of *śaktipāta* of *madhya madhyasta* (less intense) variety, he merely develops within an inclination to move towards the achievement of *Śivatva*. Such a *sādhaka* has a lurking desire for pure enjoyment, hence he is unable to move at a faster pace toward the achievement of *Śivatva*. It is only after satiating his longing for enjoyment and performing appropriate rituals that he achieves the Supreme Goal.

A *sādhaka* infused with *saktipāta* of *nikṛṣṭa madhya* (very less intense) variety has a keen desire for enjoyment. He is not motivated towards striving for the achievement of the Ultimate Goal soon after the infusion of grace . Such a *sādhaka* has first to satiate his keen desire for enjoyment, then strive for reaching the Goal.

The recipients of *śaktipata* in *utkṛṣṭa manda* (mild), *madhya manda* (milder), *manda manda* (mildest), too, are observed with the desire for pure enjoyment in the same proportion as that of *śaktipāta*. Hence their spiritual journey to the Ultimate Goal is delayed and they are required to put in greater efforts to make up the deficiency in the intensity of *śaktipāta* to reach the ultimate destiny.

That this elaborate classification of *śaktipāta* on the basis of its intensity presupposes the existence of a corresponding difference in the degree of maturation of *malas* in different individual beings is very obvious, though no author, including Abhinavagupta, has explicitly made any mention of it.[46]

Very often the divine grace received by the aspirants is very mild in intensity. The *Mālinīvijayottara Tantra* enumerates a num-

46. This is in conformity with the Trika doctrine of *svātantrya*, to which they subscribe.

ber of signs indicating infusion of divine grace which it calls *Rudraśaktisamāveśa* (lit., infusion of the divine Śakti of Rudra or Śiva). The signs are (i) development of a firm sense of devotion towards Rudra or Śiva; (ii) success of *mantra* noticeable, yielding the desired result immediately after it is uttered, (iii) achievement of control over all creatures in the world; (iv) successful completion of all undertakings by the aspirant; (v) development of poetic faculty without any conscious effort on the part of the aspirant which culminates in a sudden rise of knowledge of all scriptures from within.[47] These signs indicate that spiritual transformation has already begun in aspirants who might not be aware of it, owing to the mildness of *śaktipāta*.[48]

In this connection it must be made clear that when the Trika system speaks of the intensity of *śaktipāta* and classifies it on this basis, it does so only from the point of view of the individual aspirants. As a matter of fact, the question of intensity of divine grace as such does not arise at all, when we look at it from the Supreme Lord's point of view. For divine grace, being an aspect of divine freedom, cannot have any qualitative adjunct. As all the aspirants do not have the capacity to receive divine grace in uniform measure due to their inherent deficiency, we have to admit a sort of gradation in the intensity of *saktipāta*, from the point of view of their receptivity.

Thus, when the Trika system speaks of the intensity of *śaktipāta*, it indicates only the difference (*tāratamya*) in the receptivity of the individual aspirants, which varies from person to person. Otherwise, *śaktipāta* as such is never strained. It is one and the same for all individuals.

3. THE INITIATION (*DĪKṢĀ*)

As has been indicated in the foregoing pages, the descent of divine grace resulting from the operation of the *anugraha* aspect of the divine Śakti is an eternal and independent process of the Su-

47. *Op. Cit*, II, v. 12–18 p. 8.

48. This roughly corresponds to the state of *śrotāpanna* (lit., aspirants who have fallen into the stream of spirituality), *sādhakas* mentioned by the Mahāyāna Buddhists. Cf. AMBH, p. 92.

preme Lord's (*Parameśvara's*) divine freedom, and as such it is considered as being one of his ever-operating five-fold functions (*kritya*).[49] Although as an aspect of the Supreme Lord's divine freedom, it is said to be flowing eternally and freely from the original Source, that is, the Supreme Lord; it is not directly accessible to all. As a rule it is said to act freely and directly[50] on the receptive vehicles (i.e., the aspirants) that are absolutely free from impure matter (*mala*), that is, the unembodied souls in their precreational state. It is also said to flow directly and freely to such disembodied beings who are not enwrapped by any kind of material vestment, viz., the *vijñānākalas*.[51] In both these cases, the divine grace flows freely and directly without any external support, because the recipient souls are not associated with any kind of impurity in the form of matter (*jaḍa*).

But when the individual beings, existing in creation (i.e. *sṛṣṭi*) take on bodies of impure matter, and thus manifest themselves as embodied beings, they are no longer capable of receiving grace directly from the original Source. Their association with impure matter in the form of *māyic* bodies does not permit direct transmission of grace from the highest Source, as they cannot stand the strain involved in it. Hence, the divine grace has to come to them through some mediating factor or a medium (*ādhāra*). This medium is normally an embodied being whose body might be made up of exclusively pure matter or pure matter mixed with impure. This medium functions not only as a relay center for transmitting grace from the Supreme Lord to the individual being, but also as the agent of the divine will of the Supreme Lord on a lower level of existence, performing the task of imparting divine knowledge to uninitiated seekers. Such persons are technically called *ācāryas* or *gurus*.

---

49. *STTS.* V–1, Comm. p. 1.

50. The grace coming directly to aspirants is technically called *sāṁsiddhika jñāna*. Cf. *T.S.* XI p. 120 (footnotes); for the nature of *sāṁsiddhika jñāna* see *T.A.* IV, 40 Comm. p. 44 ff.

51. Among the disembodied beings the *vijñānākalas* alone have no connection with matter. The *pralayākalas* possess material vestment, though they too are disembodied like the *vijñānākalas*. From this point of view, the *vijñānākalas* are superior to and purer than the *pralayākalas*.

Generally speaking, three classes of divine teachers are recognized in the Āgamas. They are the *daiva* (celestial teachers), the *siddha* (superhuman teachers) and the *puruṣa* (human teachers).

First are the celestial teachers who dispense grace to those aspirants who have attained the highest degree of perfection by dissociating themselves from the impure matter through their personal efforts and are absorbed in contemplation. Such aspirants need not necessarily be disembodied beings, as the human being is capable of dissociating himself from his body by destroying fully the *bauddha ajñāna*. The celestial teachers (*daiva guru*) are generally the presiding deities (*ādhikārika devatā*) of different regions, such as Rudra, Visnu, Brahmā, Mantra, Mantreśvara etc.,[52] whose normal function is to govern the region concerned and dispense the fruits of the deeds performed by the denizens of that region. But when they function as dispensers of divine grace, as celestial *gurus,* they suspend their independent will (*icchā*), and act only as instruments of the divine will of the Supreme Lord. The grace coming from celestial teachers is very often unconsciously received by the aspirants, though the possibility of its conscious reception cannot altogether be ruled out.

Again there are aspirants possessing only a lesser degree of purity in their receptive vehicles, i.e. the bodies. To such aspirants, grace generally comes through the superhuman teachers (*siddha*) who are perfect and embodied beings. Though the superhuman teachers are embodied beings, they occupy an elevated position in comparison to ordinary human aspirants, owing to their pure *ādhāra* and their connection with the will of the Supreme Lord. Their position in the hierarchy of divine teachers is, however, considered as one below the celestial teachers, but above the human teachers, owing to persistence of faint traces of impurities in their *ādhāra.*

In the third category, there are a large number of aspirants whose receptive vehicles are chiefly dominated by impure matter, owing to their close association with the body-apparatus.

---

52. Generally the *sādhakas* possessing pure *bhogavāsanā* (desire for enjoyment) receive the divine grace through the presiding deities, whereby they are said to secure sometimes elevated *ādhikārika* position. (Cf. *T.S.* XI p. 118, *T.A.* XIII, 270–75 p. 166 ff).

They cannot, therefore, receive the divine grace through any supranormal channel. They have to depend upon the human teacher for transmission of grace. The human teacher outwardly appears as though existing on the same level as the human aspirants, but as a matter of fact, the human teacher also occupies a superior position in comparison to the human disciple in view of his connection with the divine Being whom he is also said to represent on the ordinary level of existence. It is, therefore, enjoined in the *śāstras* that the human disciple should always look upon his *guru* as being the Supreme Lord incarnate. The transmission of grace from human teachers may be either conscious or unconscious; if conscious, it may be gross (*sthūla*), subtle (*sūkṣma*), more subtle (*sūkṣmatara*) or subtlest (*sukṣaṁatama*), according to whether it is transmitted through touch (*sparśa*), speech (*vāṇī*), vision (*darśana*), or mere thought. But it must be remembered that the mode of transmission does not produce any qualitative difference in divine grace, though it might have some connection with its intensity (*tīvratā*).

Again, the human *gurus* are said to be of four kinds, technically called *akalpita guru, akalpita-kalpaka guru, kalpita guru,* and *kalpita kalpaka guru*. The *kalpita gurus* are those human *gurus* who possess absolutely pure bodies, and therefore the supreme knowledge (*sattarka or prātibha jñāna*) has awakened in them from within automatically without their making any effort. Such *gurus* do not need initiation, nor are they required to perform spiritual discipline, for everything is automatically achieved from within. The divinc *anugraha* achieves everything in them. Such *gurus* are undoubtedly the most perfect among the human *gurus* who are also known as *sāmsiddhika guru*. They are said to possess the capacity to arouse the supreme spiritual knowledge in the human disciples without their performing any rite externally.

The *akalpita-kalpaka gurus* are those human *gurus* who also obtain the highest spiritual knowledge automatically from within, owing to their having a perfect body. But they have to concentrate on the spiritual knowledge in order to discover correspondence between their realization and what is written in the scriptures. They are required to perform certain rites as prescribed in the scriptures in order to obtain full spiritual vision. Such *gurus* are obviously relatively inferior to *akalpita gurus* who are held to be the highest kind of human *gurus*.[53]

The *kalpita* human *gurus* are those *yogins* in whom the highest spiritual knowledge (*sattarka*) does not arise automatically from within. They have approached other *gurus* for guidance and have followed instructions for performing spiritual discipline, primarily for cleansing their body-apparatus. After they obtain the highest knowledge, they develop the capacity for serving as a medium for the flow of divine grace, as they have the inclination for doing good to others.

The *kalpita-kalpaka* human *gurus* too have to depend on other *gurus* for instructions and guidance for performing spiritual discipline. But they are not required to perform rigorous spiritual discipline after undergoing initiatory rite and spiritual coronation under the guidance of a *guru*. As they are said to possess perfect body-apparatuses, fully purged of defilements, the spiritual knowledge awakens in them, as if in a flash, on being coronated by the *guru*.[54]

From what has been observed above, it is clear that there are two possible ways in which divine grace can descend on the individual beings from the highest Source—either it may come directly to the individual aspirant without the intervention of any mediating factor, as in the case of unembodied and some disembodied beings, or it might be made available through some pure bodies acting as mediums for its transmission. These ways meet and actually appear to be the two aspects of one and the same way. In both these ways, all the steps beginning from the descent of divine grace leading to the integral Self-realization by the aspirant are one and the same in principle. Beside this, both ways admit the principle of *guru* as being the only source of divine grace to aspirants[55] and assign an important place to him accordingly. In the former way, the abstract principle of divine grace itself is regarded as the *guru* while in the latter the principle of divine grace, acting through a concrete medium in one of the forms mentioned above, is said to function as the *guru*.

53. *T.A.* XIII, V. 142–43 Comm. p. 93.
54. Cf *T.A.* XIII, V. 144–45 p. 94–95.
55. Cf. *T.A.* XIII, 168–69 p. 107.

Thus the *guru* is, in theory, an abstract principle representing the supreme principle of compassion of the Supreme Lord. But since the Supreme Lord pervades all and is one with all, and by virtue of his omnipresence occupies every manifestation without abjuring his transcendent character and uniqueness, he sometimes adopts a concrete medium of his own choice to perform the function of dispensing grace to individual beings.[56] Then that embodied being comes to be known as the *guru* to the particular individual. An ordinary embodied being may also, by virtue of his spiritual elevation and inner disposition, as well as the will of the Supreme Lord, occupy the position of *guru* for some time, discharging the functions connected with this position. But his elevation to this position is temporary, and lasts only until the merits of his deeds are exhausted, whereupon he retires, giving place to another individual of the same kind who continues the function keeping the chain unbroken.

This shows that the *guru* in his embodied form may be both human and divine—human in view of the transitional character of the medium adopted by the Supreme Lord for its own purpose, and divine in consideration of the principle of divine compassion (*anugraha*) which functions in and through the medium concerned. It is for this reason that it is enjoined in the *śāstras* that even a secondary *guru*, i.e., *guru* in any of the forms of human (*pauruṣa*), superhuman (*siddha*) and celestial (*daiva*) teachers should be treated by the human disciple as divine and an object of veneration.

In this connection it might be pointed out that there are two distinct types of *sādhakas* even among the embodied beings. First are those *sādhakas* to whom the infusion of divine grace not only awakens instantaneously the latent knowledge of divinity but also spontaneously transforms their personality fully from human to divine so that they have full and integral Self-realization in a moment. Such aspirants do not have to depend on any external aid for their perfect Self-realization, which follows automatically from the descent of divine grace. They are therefore said to be masters of every phase of spiritual evolution, possessing the capacity of imparting knowledge to others when they are called upon to do so. They never feel the necessity of approach-

56. *T.A.* XIII, 171–72, Comm. p. 108; ibid. IV, 70–71, Comm. p. 78.

ing any external teacher (*guru*) for interpreting and understanding the intuitive experience of Self, which they have within themselves following the descent of grace and *dīkṣā*. Such persons are the highest type of aspirant.

But all aspirants do not possess the capacity of having full and integral Self-realization from within. Such aspirants have a lesser degree of perfection and, hence, they have to depend on an external *guru* for awakening the latent knowledge of divinity in themselves. They resort to external aid to bring the awakened Self-illumination into perfection, by removing from their *ādhāra* the imperfection in the form of *malas*. It is true that the divine knowledge is awakened in them as in all others through *dīkṣā*, but mere awakening of the divine knowledge is not the same as integral Self-realization. To have integral Self-realization, they have to exert themselves and take recourse to such means as *japa, dhyāna, prāṇāyama,* etc. Obviously such type of aspirants are of inferior kind.

As has already been observed, when divine grace is transmitted to the receptive vehicle of an aspirant by the *guru*, the veil of impurities covering his real *svarūpa* is lifted up in him, and the latent knowledge of his divinity is automatically aroused from within. The operation by which the *guru* actually accomplishes the twofold task is technically designated as the *dīkṣā*. This has been defined by Abhinavagupta as a process by which *śuddha jñāna* is infused in the *sādhaka* and his limited nature is destroyed. (*Dīyate jñānasadbhāvaḥ kṣīyate paśuvāsanā*).[57]

The *dīkṣā*, it is obvious, is an essential step in the path of integral Self-realization.[58] It is essential and inevitable in all cases of infusion of divine grace—even in those cases where the infusion has been direct from the divine Source. As such it does not merely signify external ceremonials which might be consciously experienced by the recipient souls or witnessed by all others. It is, in fact, a subtle and inner process by which the *guru* seeks to remove the *mūla ajñāna* from the *ādhāra* of the aspirant and awaken the latent knowledge of divinity in him,[59] and thus open the way to his integral Self-realization.

---

57. Quoted in the footnotes of *T.S.* I, p. 3.
58. Cf. *T.A.* XIII, 166–68, Comm. p. 106 ff.
59. Ibid. XIII, 174–75. Comm. p. 110 ff.

Looking from the external, ceremonial point of view, *dīkṣā*, according to the Āgamas, is of two kinds, viz., *sāmayī dīkṣā*, performed in the initial stages of *sādhanā*, aiming at preparing the aspirant (*sādhaka*) for spiritual discipline, and the *putraka dīkṣā*, performed later, which leads the aspirant to his Ultimate goal.

Sāmayī dīkṣā is a purificatory *dīkṣā*,[60] which seeks to achieve purification and perfection of the receptive vehicle of the aspirant. The task of purification is achieved through the performance of certain purification ceremonies (*saṁskāras*) at fixed periods of life. The number of purificatory ceremonies as listed in the Āgamas is forty-eight,[61] and they have been described there in detail.[62] The performance of these ceremonies, it is said, gives the aspirant a new "life" and thereby prepares him to enter into the path of spiritual discipline (*sādhanā*) as laid down in the Āgamas.[63] It also arouses within him a desire for his integral Self-realization. This is thus a preliminary but very important step in his way to the Ultimate Goal.

Putraka dīkṣā is generally performed after the *sāmayī dīkṣā*,[64] when the *ādhāra* (i.e., the body) of the aspirant is pure and in a fit condition to receive the divine Illumination from the *guru*.[65] In performing this *dīkṣā*, what the *guru* actually does is awaken the latent *svarūpa* of his disciple by transmitting the grace (*anugraha*) of his *ādhāra* from the highest Source. As a result of this, the aspirant is at once lifted to a higher[66] spiritual level (i.e., *śuddha adhva*, the realm of spirit) as it were, so that he no longer remains a *paśu* and a denizen of Impure Order (*aśuddha adhva*), although outwardly he might be moving about and living in the impure world like an ordinary embodied individual for some time to come.

Before performing *putraka dīkṣā*, it is enjoined in the *śāstras* that the *guru* should take into consideration the inclination of his

60. *Sva. Tan.* IV, 78, p. 36; also see *T.A.* XIII, 297, p. 179.
61. *T.S.* XIII p. 148; Kṣemarāja in his commentary on *Sva. Tan.* speaks of twenty-four *saṁskāras* only. See *Sva. Tan.* IV, 76, p. 36.
62. Ibid. XIII, p. 148; see also the footnotes.
63. *Sva. Tan.* IV, 76, p. 36. Comm.
64. *Sva. Tan.* IV, 79, p. 37 Comm.
65. Ibid. IV, 80 p. 39 Comm.
66. Ibid.; *T.A.* XIII, 297, p. 180.

disciple.[67] The inclination differs from individual to individual, and all aspirants do not desire to achieve *śivatva* straightaway. Generally speaking, two distinct kinds of inclinations are noticed in the aspirants—some have *bhogavāsanā* (the desire for enjoyment) predominant and are therefore more attracted towards enjoyment (*bhoga*), while others are so self-centered that they care only for their personal salvation. Accordingly, there are two distinct types of *sādhakas*, the former are technically called the *bubhukṣus* (lit., who desire enjoyment), and the latter known as the *mumukṣūs*[68] (lit., who desire salvation). In view of this divergence of aspirants' inclinations, it is laid down in the *śāstras* that the *guru* should "give" an appropriate *mantra*[69] to his disciple, so that he might achieve his cherished goal.

The *bubhukṣu sādhakas* can be classified under two heads, viz., the *śivadharmī bubhukṣus* and the *lokadharmī bubhukṣus*, according to the difference in their *bhogavāsanā*.[70] The *śivadharmī bubhukṣu sādhakas*, it is said, aspire to attain the elevated position of a presiding deity (*ādhikārika-pada;* lit. functional post) of some order, such as *mantra*, *mantramaheśa*[71] etc., wherefrom they can govern and enjoy (*bhoga*) as well.[72] To such *sādhakas*, the *guru* "gives the appropriate *mantra* and performs the appropriate form of *putraka dīkṣā*"[73] whereby the accumulated fruits of their past, present, and future *karmas* are automatically destroyed, *śodhayati*, lit. are purified.[74] This enables them to have uninterrupted en-

---

67. *Sva. Tan.* IV, 80 p. 39. The inclination of the disciple often remains hidden to the disciple himself, but the *guru* with his "searching eyes" can look into his mind.
68. *Bubhukṣu Sādhakas* are technically called *sādhakas*, while those aspiring for personal salvation are called *putrakā-cāryas*. *Sva Tan.* IV. 79, Comm. p. 39.
69. *Sva. Tan.* IV, 81–82. p. 40–41.
70. Ibid. IV. 82. p. 41.
71. Ibid. IV, 143–44, Comm. p. 89–90.
72. In fact, the attainment of a position of glory (*aiśvaryapada*), as involved in it, is another kind of *mukti* (*aparāmukti*). Ibid. IV, 78, Comm. p. 38.
73. This is technically called *bhoga-pratyayī-dīkṣā*.
74. This is necessary for their uninterrupted *bhoga*. *Sva Tan.* IV, 142, p. 89.

joyment of their *ādhikārika* (elevated) position, as well as to satiate their *vāsanā* (desire). The aspirants can continue to remain in this elevated position until the satiation of their *bhogavāsanā* or cosmic dissolution, *mahāpralava,* whichever is earlier, after which they attain their Supreme Goal, *śivatva.*[75]

The *loka-dharmi bubhukṣu sādhakas,* on the other hand, do not desire elevation, they prefer to remain in this world as the *jñānins* (enlightened beings), and move about like any other ordinary mortal.[76] Hence, the *guru* "gives" them appropriate *mantra* and performs appropriate form of *putraka dīkṣā* so accumulated fruits of their past and present *karmas* are automatically destroyed.[77] But the seeds of their *karmas* (*karmabīja*), which are at the root of future karma, are allowed to remain as they were, so that they might continue to live in this world performing meritorious deeds[78] until their physical body is automatically destroyed in course of time, after which they realize their Supreme Goal, *Śivatva.*

Even in the case of *mumukṣu sādhakas,* the *śāstras* prescribe two different kinds of *putraka dīkṣā*—the *sabīja mumukṣu dikṣā* and the *nirbīja mumukṣu dīkṣā.*[79] The *mumukṣu sādhakas,* who are given the *sabīja putraka dikṣā,* are able to remain in embodied form for some time, as their *karmabījas* are not totally destroyed in *dīkṣā.* They remain in the world like any other ordinary mortal, performing essential *karma* to sustain themselves in embodied form. It must be noted here that in performing *karma* they have, unlike *lokadharmī bubhhukṣu sādhakas,* no *bhogavāsanā* at all. Existing in the world (*saṁsāra*) like ordinary individuals, they are always conscious of their real Self, though they do not have integral Self-realization in that stage. Their existence in the world (*saṁsāra*)

75. Ibid. IV, 143–44, Comm. pp. 89–90.
76. Ibid. IV, 84, p. 42.
77. Ibid. IV, 144, Comm. p. 91.
78. Such as the visiting of holy places, donating food to the poor and needy, etc. Impelled by *bhogavāsanā,* they perform such deeds, in order that they might enjoy the fruits of their deeds in *saṁsāra.* Ibid. IV. 85. p. 42.
79. In the technical language of this system, this is known as purification of *samayācara-pāśa.* Ibid. IV, 147, p. 93.

roughly corresponds to that of the *jīvanmuktas*. When their physical body is destroyed in the course of time, they are automatically established in their *svarūpa*, the *śivatva*.

The *mumukṣu sādhakas* receiving the *nirbījaputraka dīkṣā*, on the other hand, realize their Supreme Goal instantaneously with the *dīkṣā*[80] by virtue of the fact that their *karmabījas* are totally destroyed in *dīkṣā*. Their dissociation from physical body and integral Self-realization happens simultaneously with the *dikṣā*.

This classification of *dikṣā* is based on the external ceremonies performed during the process of *dīkṣā*. *Dīkṣā*, it has been observed, has another aspect also. It is not merely an external ceremonial, it is an inner process in which the *guru* transmits the divine grace to the aspirant in intense form, commensurate with his capacity to receive it. Accordingly, four distinct forms of *dīkṣā* are recognized by the Trika system, viz., the *anupāya dīkṣā*, the *śāmbhavī dikṣā*, the *śakti dīkṣa*, and the *āṇavī dīkṣa*.[81]

When the descending divine grace is extremely powerful, the *anupāya dīkṣā* follows as a natural sequence. When this *dīkṣā* is performed, the *sādhaka* realizes his Goal at once. But where the descending grace is relatively less powerful, the *śāmbhavī dīkṣā* is performed. In case of descending grace being still less powerful, the *śakti dīkṣā* is prescribed. In both these forms of *dīkṣā* the necessity for external *krityas* to supplement the grace is not recognized. But where grace is very weak, as in the case of *sādhakas* receiving *āṇavī dīkṣā*, the resort to external rites (*krityas*) as an aid to self-purification is imperative.

---

80. *Sva. Tan.* IV, 148, p. 93.

81. Though Abhinavagupta does not clearly refer to these four types of *dīkṣā*, his description of four distinct forms of *samāveśa* (lit., divine union) in the four *upāyas* is clearly indicative of the fact that there exist four corresponding forms of *dīksā* also. (Cf. *T.S.* II, III, IV, V. pp. 9, 19, 31, and 37.) See also *T.A.* I, 168–70, pp. 202–03.

CHAPTER 5

The Ways of Spiritual Discipline

1. INTRODUCTORY REMARKS

In the foregoing pages we have observed that when divine grace descends on aspirants from the highest Source, i.e., the Supreme Lord, the aspirants are incapable of receiving it in uniform measure due to the lack of capacity in their receptive vehicle (*ādhāra*), i.e., the body, hence the divine grace received by them differs in intensity from individual to individual. On the basis of this difference, the aspirants are classified under three principal groups according to whether they receive the grace in mild (*manda*), intense (*madhya*), or most intense (*tīvra*) forms.[1] This classification of aspirants based on the intensity of divine grace received by them is a most important factor in the field of *sādhanā* as it not only reveals the capacity of aspirants but also broadly indicates the path they would have to follow to realize the Supreme Goal in their lifetime. When the capacity of the aspirants is different, the degree of perfection through purgation achieved by them is varied. It is natural that the ways of *sādhanā* leading to their inte-

1. *T.S.* XI, p. 120. Though Abhinavagupta speaks of nine kinds of *śaktipāta*, he classifies the *sādhakas* into three groups according to which of the three kinds of unification with the Supreme Lord (*samāveśa*) is achieved by them at the end. (Cf. *T.S.*, I, p. 7.)

gral Self-realization should also be different. They cannot adopt a uniform way of *sādhanā,* as the amount of effort which they would have to put in to achieve complete perfection of their *ādhāra* and thereafter realize their Supreme Goal, would be different in each case. In view of these differences, the Trika system lays down three different ways (*upāyas*) of *sādhanā* leading to integral Self-realization, each suiting a class of aspirants. The ways are known as the *śāṁbhava upāya, sākta upāya,* and *āṇavopāya*. . . .[2]

In this context, it would perhaps not be out of place to mention that the Trika system does not only believe in the different ways of *sādhanā (upāya)* being different to suit the *sādhakas* of different classes and capacities, it also simultaneously holds that the aim of all individuals, in the interim stage, is not necessarily the same. For instance, it recognizes that all *sādhakas* do not directly realize their Supreme Goal; there are *sādhakas* who are destined to function as the *gurus,*[3] while there are others who are destined to attain *ādhikārika* position and function as the presiding deities *(devatā)*[4] of different regions. But all *sādhakas* cannot attain these functionary offices merely by aspiring for them. Such attainments of certain *sādhakas* are not permanent, they are only for the interim period,[5] because the Trika system holds that the ultimate destiny of all beings is the attainment of *Śivatva*. And this *Śivatva,* the Trika system concedes, is the birthright of all beings and can be achieved by all individuals without any exception.

But the very fact that all aspirants cannot attain these functionary offices *(ādhikārikapada)* and that they are the privileged few singled out for the purpose by the divine will of the Supreme Lord, shows that every individual possesses a distinct individuality of his own, not only in the sense of his outer form, but also in a spiritual sense, i.e., as the *cidannu*. This view is not an exclusive one advocated only by the Trika system, but it is one

2. *T.S.* I, p. 7.
3. The fact that only the 'coronated' *(abhiṣikta) sādhakas* have the power to function as the agent of the Supreme Lord and dispense the divine grace indicates that the privilege of functioning as the *guru* is restricted to a few, chosen for the purpose. (Cf. *T.S.* XVIII, p. 173.)
4. Ibid.
5. Ibid.

shared by many other systems of Indian philosophy, such as Mahāyānā Buddhism, Vaiṣṇavism,[6] etc. Normally speaking, the innate individuality of aspirants does not makes its existence felt in ordinary life,[7] and is therefore not given any importance in other systems of philosopy. Nevertheless, its existence cannot be ignored. As a matter of fact, in the systems of philosopy which gives more emphasis on the *sādhanā* aspect, it finds prominent treatment.

If an attempt is made to trace the ultimate source of the innate individuality in men, it will be seen that its roots lie in the beginning of creation. In the beginning of universal manifestation *(sṛṣṭi)*—when the Supreme Lord, in exercising his divine freedom *(svātantrya),* imposes limitation *(saṅkoca)* on himself and thus manifests himself as the countless number of *cidaṇus,*[8]—variety creeps in due to the very act of self-limitation *(ātma-saṅkoca);* hence in *āṇavamala* the individual is covered due to the influence

---

6. Mahāyāna Buddhists hold that the Supreme Goal of all aspirants is the achievement of Buddhahood with the help of the functioning of Prajñāpārāmitā, whereby they may become *Bodhisattvas,* while the Hīnayāna Buddhists remain content with the attainment of *nirvāṇa* and becoming *Arhats.* Mahāyāna Buddhists as a matter of fact consider the achievement of *Nirvāṇa* to be a lesser achievement (Cf. Aspects of Mahāyāna Buddhism and its Relation to *Hinayana* Thought: *N. Dutt.* pp. 82 ff.) Taking an integral view of the various ideals put forward by the different schools of Buddhism, and bearing in mind the condemnation of Hinayānins' ideals by the Mahāyānins, we feel that various ideals are really meant for *sādhakas* of different categories who cannot follow one path, though all of them agree that the *Nirvāṇa* is the minimum that can be achieved by one and all without exception. The Vaiṣṇava philosophers have the same view in mind when they speak of different kinds of realizations (divine union) such as *sārupya, sāyujya,* etc.
7. The Śaṅkara Vedānta, for instance, does not recognize the need for admitting the innate individuality in men. It explains the plurality of *jīvas* with the help of *ajñāna.* But this raises certain difficulties in the field of morality, such as the performance of deeds and suffering their results, which have not been satisfactorily explained on the basis of its views.
8. Cf. Supra. Ch. II, p. 52 ff.

of the moment *(kṣaṇa)*.[9] This variety is at the root of the distinct individuality of all the aspirants, which is transmitted as an inherent quality from the point of their first appearance. The *cidaṇus* are later enwrapped by material vestment. The individuality thus becomes a permanent character[10] inherent in every individual and stays permanently in him until he is completely freed from the *āṇavamala*.

Though the Trika system prescribes three different ways of *sādhanā* suited to three different types of *(sādhakas)* aspirants, the end sought to be realized by every one of them is one and the same. Every path is said to lead to the achievement of the same Goal[11] viz., the *Śivatva*, so that the question of any path being superior or inferior to the rest does not arise at all. The chief point of distinction lies only in the mode of *sādhanā*—the amount of effort an aspirant *(sādhaka)* is required to put forth to realize the Supreme End. Otherwise, there is no intrinsic difference in them.

It has been observed that the aspirants whose *malas* are fully mature receive the divine grace in relatively intense form as their capacity of reception is said to be increased with the maturation of the *malas (mala-paripāka)*. It is no doubt true that with the descent of divine grace, however feeble it might be,

9. By *kṣaṇa* we mean here the *kṣaṇa* of *sūkṣmakāla*, which is an offshoot of the vibration of Śakti. The *sūkṣmakāla* must be distinguished from the ordinary *māyickakāla*, i.e., the *kāla-tattva*. (Cf. S.D. I, 8 Comm, p. 10–11.)
10. It is a fact that the maturation of *malas* is neither simultaneous in time nor in character. (Cf. *T.S.* XI, p. 117.)
11. Though all *upāyas* ultimately lead the *sādhakas* (aspirants) to divine union *(samāveśa)* which is of the nature of Śiva in essence, there are still some subtle differences between them in the content of final Self-realization, which is evident from the different names given to the divine union in different *upāyas*. This distinction is mainly due to the content of divine knowledge that the *sādhakas* have following different *upāyas*, and which varies from *nirvikalpa* to *savikalpa*. (Cf. *T.A.* 142–43, pp. 182–83 & v. 168–70 Comm. p. 203) The *upāyas* are, however, held to be independent of one another so that an aspirant following one *upāya* need not go through and repeat the *sādhanā* of the preceding *upāna*.

āṇavamala, the fundamental *(mūla) mala* enveloping every finite being, is totally destroyed. If the descending grace is extremely intense, *kārma-* and *māyīyamalas* might be immediately destroyed with the *āṇavamala*; but if it is relatively less intense, the remaining *malas* are affected only partially. Thus, in fact, the intensity of divine grace determines the extent to which the remaining *malas* are destroyed.

To put it in other words, the degree of intensity of divine grace descending on the individual aspirant depends logically on the development of his capacity to receive it, and this, in its turn, conditions the destruction of *malas* enveloping the individual in the form of self-ignorance *(ajñāna)* in consonance with its intensity. Just as one cannot see his reflection in a mirror covered with dirt, in the same way the aspirants *(sādhakas)* whose *buddhi* is veiled by the persisting *kārma-* and *māyīyamalas* cannot 'visualize' his Self-effulgent real *Svarūpa* unless the veils are completely removed. The destruction of *kārma-* and *māyīyamalas* is an essential prerequisite for his integral Self-realization while he is an embodied being.

To destroy the remnants of *malas* enveloping him and thereby remove the veil of self-ignorance, an aspirant *(sādhaka)* has to put in his own efforts, the amount of which is strictly in conformity with the grossness of this veil. Different courses of *sādhanā*, as prescribed by the Trika system, in fact, embody his efforts in different degrees; the particular course of *sādhanā* which an individual *sādhaka* will have to follow depends on the grossness of the veil of his self-ignorance. That is to say, if the veil of self-ignorance is relatively gross the amount of endeavor which the individual would have to put forth would be relatively greater, and so also the period of time for his achievement of the Supreme Goal; but if the veil is thin due to the intensity of divine grace, the *sādhaka* will have to strive less and the achievement of his Goal will be quicker in time.

In a nutshell, the maturation of an aspirant's *(sādhaka's) malas* indicating the development of his capacity for reception is related to the intensity of divine grace which, in its turn, conditions the destruction of different *malas*, the grossness of which practically determines the course of *sādhanā* which the *sādhaka* would have to adopt for the realization of his Essence. There is thus hardly any room for free choice;[12] everything is practically predetermined, as it were, by the intensity of divine grace descending on the individual.

So far we have discussed the problems of choice of the way of *sādhanā* on the assumption that everything in the field of *sādhanā* is rigidly fixed and that there are inflexible laws *(niyata krama)* governing every phase of it. But, as a matter of fact, the Trika system does not believe in principle in the existence of any such inviolable laws in the field of *sādhanā,* where the operation of *svātantrya śakti* in the form of divine grace is the most predominant factor. Even when the Trika system speaks of the *niyata krama* (fixed order) in *sādhanā,* and lays down more or less definite way of *sādhanā,* it believes in the possibility of divine intervention so that in the background of *niyata krama* (fixed order) there exists the *aniyata krama,* about which nothing can be spoken and, as such, is outside the scope of philosophy. In fact, there are infinite number of possibilities in the field of *sādhanā* due to individual peculiarities, hence a generalization is strictly impossible. The Trika system therefore remains content in indicating in a general way the direction in which the *sādhaka* should proceed to realize his Supreme Goal, leaving the minute details to the *sādhaka* to work out for himself.

Although it is said that the divine Śakti forms the basis of all the *upāyas,* as the operation of the divine Śakti and its utilization by the *sādhaka* forms an essential part in every step of his *sādhanā* it is still held that only one of the aspects of divine Śakti is predominant in each of the *upāyas*. Accordingly, it is held that

---

12. This is where the Trika system differs fundamentally from the classical view, viz., the different ways of *sādhanā* suggested by different temperaments and inclinations of different *sādhakas.* Cf. Puśpadanta's famous verse from the *Mahimna Stotra,* which states, "The triple Veda, Sāṁkhya, Yoga, *Paśupati* doctrine, *Vaiṣṇava* doctrine—in these differing paths one is as good and beneficial as any of the others. For men resort to different paths, some straight, others zigzag, on account of the difference in individual temperaments. Thou alone (O Lord) art the Goal, in the same way as the ocean is only resort of all the rivers."

the *icchā, jñāna* and *kriyā* aspects of divine Śakti are the dominating *śaktis* of *śāṁbhava, śākta* and *āṇava upāyas.*[13] In the practical field of *sādhanā* this actually signifies that the *sādhaka* following a particular course of *sādhanā* has to take the help of that aspect of Śakti which is held to be the dominating factor in that *upāya.* To illustrate, the *sādhaka* who is fit to follow *śāṁbhava upāya,* owing to the descent of divine grace in the required intensity, has a thin veil of self-ignorance over his *buddhi,* and it is this which prevents him from having instantaneous integral Self-realization. Following the *śāmbhava upāya,* all that he has to do is remove the veil of self-ignorance with the help of *icchā śakti,*[14] which also is said to form the basis of *śāmbhava upāya,* and realize his real *Svarūpa.* Thus, in the achievement of his Goal, other conventional expedients such as *japa, dhyāna, prāṇayāma,* etc. are found unnecessary. Similarly, in the case of the *sādhaka* who is qualified to follow the *śākta upāya,* the veil of self-ignorance left over on his *buddhi,* owing to the descent of divine grace in less intense form, is relatively gross *(sthūla).* It is due to this grossness of the veil of *ajñāna* covering his *buddhi* that he continues to experience duality *(dvaita jñāna)* and fails to experience the all-embracing knowledge of *advaita* (oneness) through his *buddhi,* despite the fact that it has awakened within him through the divine grace and *dīkṣā.* In order to root out the persisting *dvaita* experience from his *buddhi* he has to follow the mode of *sādhanā* prescribed in the *śākta upāya* that is based on *jñāna śakti.*[15] With the help of this *śakti,* he has to purify his *dvaita jñāna* or *dvaita vikalpa,* as it is called in the technical phraseology of the system, a process which actually means transformation of the *dvaita vikalpa* into *advaita vikalpa.*[16] When he accomplishes the process of purification or transformation, he realizes his Essence. On the other hand, there are *sādhakas* in whom the veil of self-ignorance persisting after the descent of di-

---

13. *T.S.,* I, p. 7.
14. *T.A.* I, 146, Comm. pp. 185–186.
15. *T.A.* I, 148, Comm. p. 187.
16. The development of the *śuddha-advaita vikalpa* into the *nirvikalpa jñāna* of the integral *svarūpa* does not require any effort on the part of the *sādhakas;* it follows as a natural sequence. (Cf. Ibid. I, 148, Comm. p. 187.)

vine grace in mild form is so gross that they cannot even take the assistance of *jñāna śakti*. Such *sādhakas* are *ādhikarins* for *āṇavopava*, and as such they have to base their *sādhanā* on the *Kriyā śakti*.[17] The grossness of the veil of self-ignorance prevents them from even getting a glimpse of their *Svarūpa*, hence the experience of duality is so deep-rooted and extensive in their *buddhi* that they have no other option but to follow the prescribed form of *kriyā (sādhanā)* and take the help of *kriyā śakti* to eradicate and destroy the deep-rooted *ajñāna*. When the *sādhakas*, following the mode of *sādhanā* laid down under the *āṇavopāya*, accomplish this task of destroying the deep-rooted *ajñāna*, the knowledge of their real *Svarūpa* arises automatically from within, and they realize their integral *Svarūpa*.

2. THE ANUPĀYA

The early exponents[18] of the Trika system speak of three *upāyas* only, the *śāṃbhava*, *śakta* and the *āṇava upāyas*. But Abhinavagupta who has discussed this problem in a very elaborate and lucid manner, maintains that the *upāyas*, in the first instance, can be classified under two principal heads, viz., *upāya par excellence* and the ordinary *upāyas*.[19] Under the first head he mentions the *anupāya* which, as we shall presently observe, is not an *upāya* in the conventional sense of the term. It is in fact an extraordinary *upāya*, meant for extraordinary class of *sādhakas* who have been recipients of an extremely intense form of divine grace.[20] He has put the remaining three *upāyas*, the *sāmbhava*, the *sākta*, and the *āṇava* in the second category as they have been prescribed for the ordinary *sādhakas*.

The *anupāya* (lit., the pathless path) is an extraordinary *upāya* in the true sense of the term, since all the accredited means

17. *T.A.* I, 149, Comm. pp. 187–188. For the relation of identity between *kriyā śakti* and *jñāna śakti*, see Ibid. 1, 151–55 pp. 189–91.
18. For instance, the founder of the system, Vasugupta, has divided the *Śiva Sūtras* into three sections, viz., the *śāmbhavopāya*, the *śāktopāya*, and the *āṇavopāya* corresponding to the three *upāyas* mentioned above. Other *ācāryas* like Siddha Somānanda, Utpala, Kṣemarāja, etc. support the three-*Upāya* view.
19. *T.S.* I., p. 7.
20. Ibid., II, p. 8.

of spiritual discipline that are generally held to be indispensable for the *sādhaka's* integral Self-realization are dismissed as being futile under this *upāya*, and yet the realization by the *sādhakas* following this path is said to be perfectly accomplished.[21] Hence, *anupāya* as a way of spiritual discipline cannot be compared with any other ordinary *upāya* meant for aspirants of ordinary calibre, and as such it stands unique in the field of *sādhanā*. Abhinavagupta's description of the final Self-realization achieved under it as *upāya-virahitaḥ asya samāveśaḥ*[22] (lit., divine union achieved with following any *upāya*) clearly demonstrates its extraordinary character.

Anticipating a possible objection that calling *anupāya* an *upāya* involves an apparent contradiction in terms, the commentator tries to explain the real meaning of the prefix *'nañ'* in *anupāya*. He tells us that the prefix *'nañ'* should not be interpreted in a negative sense; it has been used to denote the sense of *alpatva* (smallness) as in the case of the word *anudarā kanyā* (lit., girl with a lanky constitution).[23] What he actually seeks to convey here is that in *anupāya* the *upāya* portion or the portion of *sādhanā* embodying the efforts of the *sādhaka* in the form of *kriyā* (which is the real part of *sādhanā*) is negligible, as the major and most important task of freeing the body-apparatus *(ādhāra)* of the *sādhaka* from various *malas* enwrapping him is accomplished instantaneously and automatically by the descent of divine grace in extremely intense form. The *sādhanā* of the aspirant, it is said, is generally concerned with the achievement of complete purgation of his *ādhāra* (psycho-physical body-apparatus) so that he might realize his Essence in his pure *buddhi* immediately as it is aroused within him by the descent of divine *anugraha*. When this task of purgation has already been accomplished in the extraordinary class of *sādhakas* by the descent of divine grace in extremely intense form, nothing remains to be achieved by them through their personal efforts. Their integral Self-realization follows automatically and simultaneously as a natural sequence.

From what has been observed, it is clear that only those aspirants are considered to be *adhikārins* for this *upāya* who have

21. Ibid., II, p. 9; *T.A.*, II, 36–38, pp. 30–32.
22. *T.S.* II, p. 8.
23. Ibid., II, p. 8; *T.A.* II, 2 Comm. p. 3.

received divine grace in the extremely intense form of *śaktipāta*, which brings about total annihilation of *āṇavamala*. Therefore no trace of it is left in them. The absolute destruction of *āṇavamala* effects also the destruction of the other two kinds of *malas, kārma* and *māyīya*, which also veil their *buddhi*, along with the *Āṇavamala* as the latter are based on the former. The net result of the destruction of all the three *malas* is that both forms of *ajñāna* (ignorance)[24]—the superimposed *ajñāna* in the form of experience of not-Self in Self *(ātmani anātmajñāna)* arising from self-contraction *(svasaṅkoca)* and the *ājñāna* in the form of false identification of Self with not-Self *(anātmani ātmābodha)*, are completely liquidated, leaving the field clear of all obstructions to the rise of *svarūpa jñāna* following the *dikṣā*.[25]

The moment the *sādhaka* hears the sacred word embodying the Truth *(guruvacanam)* from the lips of the *guru*,[26] he has his integral Self-realization almost immediately, and he firmly rests in integral divine *svarūpa (akhaṇḍa-svarūpa)*. With his firm establishment in the divine *svarūpa*, he has the supreme experience as the *pūrṇa-ahamta*. The manifested universe does not disappear from his view, he continues to have its experience, not as distinct from him or existing outside himself (in which form it is the cause of bondage), but as reflected within himself *(antarmayi)* as nondistinct from him.[27] All this is accomplished automatically in a moment as it were; he does not have to make any effort worth the name. Hence it is said that he has his integral Self-realization (technically called the *pārameśvara samāveśa*) without following any *upāya*.

---

24. *T.A.* II, Comm. p. 7. These are technically called *pauruṣa ajñāna* and the *buddha ajnāna* respectively; they are of the nature of *vikalpa* (intellectual). For description of their nature see *T.S.*, Āh. I.
25. It may be noted here that Abhinavagupta does not specifically mention *dikṣā* as one of the steps necessary for integral Self-realization in this *upāya*. But in view of what we have observed about the indispensability of *dikṣā* and the dependence of *adhikārins* of this *upāya* on the sacred word from the *guru's* mouth, we may safely presume that the *adhikārins* of *anupāya* cannot do without it. However, it is possible that there is no need for external ceremonials in *dikṣā* in their case.
26. *T.S.* II, p, 8.
27. Ibid., p. 9; Cf. *T.A.* II, 35, Comm., p. 27.

3. THE ŚĀMBHAVA UPĀYA

In the arrangement of ordinary *upāyas* prescribed for the ordinary aspirants of different levels, the *śāmbhava upāya* may be considered to be the chief and best of all ordinary *upāyas* for the realization of the ultimate destiny, the *śivatva*. But if *anupāya* is also included in the general list of *upāyas* notwithstanding the fact that it is an *upāya par excellence*, the *śāmbhava upāya* in that case should be considered as the next best *upāya*, next only to the *anupāya*.

Before discussing the *śāmbhava upāya* it would be worthwhile to explain why the *śāmbhava upāya* has been called the chief and the best of all *upāyas*. As has already been indicated, the various *upāyas* are meant for aspirants with varying capacities and therefore, belonging to different levels of spiritual evolution. But this arrangement of *upāyas* according to the intrinsic difference in their mode of *sādhanā* should not be taken to mean that one *upāya* is relatively better than or superior to another in any way for an individual aspirant. In fact, all the *upāyas* lead to the same goal so that the ultimate realization in all the *upāyas* is one and the same. The *upāyas* are different because the starting point for the individual aspirants in their way to the Ultimate goal is different in accordance with their level of spiritual evolution, considering the point of view of the individual aspirant. The question, therefore, of superiority or inferiority of *upāyas* does not arise.

Thus, when the *śāmbhava upāya* is described as the best and the foremost among ordinary *upāyas*, the implication is that the *adhikārins* for *śāmbhava upāya* belong to the highest level of spiritual evolution,[28] and as such, they have already developed the power within themselves to realize their Essence in a very short time. How they have reached the peak of spiritual evolution is a different question altogether which has been answered in connection with the discussion on intensity of divine grace. It will suffice here to repeat that the Trika system considers the intensity of divine grace descending on the individual aspirants to be responsible for their spiritual elevation.

---

28. Barring, of course, the extraordinary class of *sādhakas*, the *adhikārins* of *anupāya*. Such *sādhakas* are extremely rare.

Outwardly, both the *śāmbhava upāya* and the *anupāya* seem very much alike, since in both of them we find that the conventional expedients of spiritual discipline such as, *japa, tapas, praṇāyāma* etc., are dispensed with, as they are found to be superfluous there.[29] But a careful examination of the two *upāyas* reveals that there exists a subtle distinction in the process of Self-realization in the two *upāyas* on the basis of which the superiority of *anupāya* over the *śāmbhava upāya* as a mode of spiritual discipline has to be recognized. To explain, it has been observed that the aspirant possessing the innate capacity of following *anupāya-marga* directly realizes his integral Essence *(akhaṇḍa Svarūpa)*, the *Śivatva*, the process of realization being instantaneous with the descent of extremely intense form of divine grace. In his Self-realization he does not have to do anything or depend on anything, as everything is immediately accomplished by the descent of grace, as it were. This, no doubt, indicates that the *adhikārin* for *anupāya* belongs to the highest level of spiritual evolution, having attained complete perfection of his body-apparatus, and also being the recipient of an extremely intense form of *śaktipāta*. On the other hand, the *adhikārin* for *śāmbhava upāya*, in spite of having reached the peak of individual perfection, receives divine grace in relatively milder intensity. This subtle differentiation in respect to the intensity of grace received by him affects his career and entirely changes the course of his journey. As a result of which he is unable to realize his Essence directly as his counterpart does in *anupāya*.[30] Due to this difference in the intensity of *śaktipāta* received by him, he is forced to seek the help of *śakti*,[31] the Essence of his divinity, to ultimately realize his integral nature.

Thus we find that the distinction in the two *upāyas* lies mainly in the approach and not in the way of *sādhanā* or the process of Self-realization, which is undoubtedly due to the difference in the intensity of *śaktipāta* in the two cases.

As soon as divine grace descends on the aspirant in very intense form, he is at once liberated from the shackles of various

29. *T.S.* III, p. 19.
30. Cf. *T.S.* III, p. 10.
31. The *icchā śakti*. Cf. *T.A.* I, 146 pp. 185–186.

kinds of *malas*, and his body-substratum *(ādhāra)* is rid of impurities. The *mala* due to self-limitation *(ātma-saṅkoca)* and self-ignorance *(ajñāna)* no longer clings to his *citta*, which becomes fully purified. But his emancipation from bondage or the purification of his *ādhāra* is not enough to kindle the latent knowledge of his divinity. It merely prepares him to have the knowledge of his divinity aroused within him. In the case of *adhikārins* for *anupāya* who are recipients of *śaktipāta* in the most intense form, the *śaktipāta* is so intense that it functions in two ways: it purges and purifies the *ādhāra* of the aspirants as well as simultaneously arousing the latent knowledge of divinity in them with the result that they have their integral Self-realization instantaneously. But in the case of *adhikārins* for *śāmbhava upāya*, the *śāktipāta* is relatively weaker; hence it cannot simultaneously accomplish the dual tasks of purgation and illumination, and it appears to exhaust itself in accomplishing the task of purgation. Hence, the *adhikārin* for *śāmbhava upāya* needs the help of a *guru* to arouse the latent knowledge of divinity in him.[32] The *guru*, it has been observed, represents the principle of grace in concrete form. As the *guru* transmits the spark of divine knowledge to his pure *ādhāra* in *dīkṣā*, there being no residue of *malas* left in him, the spark blazes forth into the fire of spiritual illumination, the light of which not only illumines his pure *citta* but also dispels at the same time every trace of ignorance *(ajñāna)* from him, including his false ego-sense arising out of the super-imposition of Self on not-Self *(idamtā)*. The awakening of spiritual knowledge *(pauruṣa jñāna)* within thus enables him to get a glimpse of his real *svarūpa*, the *Śuddha Ahamta*.

But merely getting a glimpse of real nature is not all; it is not the Supreme Realization. The *sādhaka* has not only to know his real *svarūpa* (nature), the *Aham*, he has also to realize the divinity of his *svarūpa*, viz., the *pūrṇa Ahamtā*, the integral Self. In short, he has to have the integral Self-realization, the *Śivatva*. This he can have only when the glory of his divine Self is revealed to him—the glory *(aiśvarya)* which is also his fullness *(pūrṇutva)*. In other words, the *sādhaka* has to realize himself not only as the pure *Ahamtā* but also as the *pūrṇa Ahamtā*.

32. *T.A.* I, 216, Comm. p. 240.

It must be noted here that the glory of the divine Self is revealed automatically to *sādhakas,* though it is not instantaneously revealed to all. To some who are the recipients of the extremely intense form of divine grace, such as the *adhikārins* of *anupāya,* the glory of divine Self is revealed instantaneously so that they are able to realize their integral divine nature, i.e., *nirvikalpa ādhaṇda svarūpa,* in a moment, as it were. In the case of others, e.g., the *adhikārins* of *sāmbhava upāya,* who have received the divine grace in less intense form, the glory of pure Self is not revealed to them instantaneously, so that they are unable to realize their integral nature, *nirvikalpa svarūpa,* immediately.[33] It is, however, revealed to them automatically in gradual steps following a logical order. Below we give a description of the logical order in which it is revealed to the *adhikārin* of the *śambhava upāya.*

In the beginning, immediately after his initiation *(dīkṣā),* the *sādhaka* experiences in his *pure citta*[34] (the reflecting medium of experiences) the supreme expression of Śakti as supreme light *(mahāprākasa)* in an intuitive flash, as it were. The supreme light, in the beginning, is undifferentiated. In the next moment, the supreme light appears to him to unfold the infinite variety of its self-expression that are merged in the unity of supreme light.[35] The infinite variety of self-expression of the supreme light is nothing but the countless number of self-expressions *(parāmarśa)* of the divine Śakti, which are technically called the *kalās,* (lit., aspects).

The divine Śakti, it has been observed, has twofold self-expressions at one and the same time. Held in identity with the Supreme Reality, the *Parama Śiva,* it expresses itself as the eternally immutable and ineffable divine Śakti when it is transcendent and indefinable, and is, therefore, technically known as the Indescribable[36] *(A varṇa).* At the same time, it expresses itself im-

33. *T.S.,* III, p. 11.
34. Technically called the *bodhagagana* or *cidākāśa.* Cf. ibid., III, p. 11. For explanation of the term *gagana* see *T.A.,* III, 3, Comm. p. 3 ff.
35. The entire universal manifestation is said to be of the nature of *Saṁvid* (Cf. *T.S., Āh.* III p, 11), which is again of the nature of divine light, the *Prakāśa* (Cf. *T.A., Āh.* III, 2, p. 2.)
36. *T.A., Āh.* III, 67, Comm. p. 75.

manently in infinite ways and forms as the universe. The two modes of its self-expressions are simultaneous. While expressing itself in infinite ways and forms, it retains its essential transcendent nature in which form it is technically called the Parāśakti.[37] But as the infinite forms emerge and finally merge in it, it is considered to be the mother of *kalās*, the infinite forms, technically designated as the *kula*, and the śakti, being the mother, as Kaulikī Śakti.[38]

The *sādhaka* experiences the supreme light as expressing itself, in the first instance, as the *Anuttara cit*, which is symbolized by the first vowel letter *'A' varṇa*[39] in the Trika system. The act of self-expression *(āmarśana)* of the supreme light as *'A' varṇa*, really speaking, involves a sort of "ejection" or "emergence" (technically called *visarga*) of its *kalā*-form *(kalātmaka rūpa)*, from its *Paraparāmarśa rūpa*,(lit., that which is of the nature of Supreme Self-expression), that is, Indescribable. But the process of "ejection" *(visarga)* is so subtle that it cannot be noticed by the *sādhaka*. Hence, the *anuttara-cit* appears to him to be the highest and the fundamental *(mūla)* Self-expression of Śakti, from which all movements in the form of further self-expressions follow. It is, in fact, on account of this that the *'A' varṇa* is considered to be the *mūla varṇa*[40] symbolizing the highest self-expression of Śakti.

The *'A' varṇa*, in the next movement, appears to him to express itself in the form of *ānanda*, which is symbolized by the second vowel, *'Ā'*. The *'Ā' varṇa*, as is well known, is biune by nature *(yāmala rūpa)* as it is made up of two *'A'*s, said to be held in identity.[41] The second *'A'*, it is held, is an emanation from the first *'A'*, the *anuttara cit*, so that in *'Ā'* the two *'A'*s are said to be facing each other *(abhimūkha)* like the divine Couple *(yugala)*. Hence an eternal interplay goes on in this self-created dichotomy, paving the way for further emanations.[42] The movement from *'A'*

---

37. Ibid.
38. Ibid. p. 67.
39. Ibid. Comm., p. 75 ff.
40. *T A, Āh.* III, 75.
41. Ibid. *Āh.* III, 68 p. 81.
42. *T A.* III, 68 Comm. p; 81; cf. also the quotation from the Āgama in ibid. p. 80.

to *'Ā'* is considered to be a state of restful poise *(viśrānti)* for *'A'*, the *anuttara cit.*

As the *anuttara cit* moves further, it expresses itself as the *icchā,* which is represented by the third vowel, *'I'.*[43] *Icchā* functions simultaneously in two directions: it negates, on one hand, the transcendent aspect of the *svarūpa-śakti,* the *anuttara cit* creating thereby a void as it were, and on the other, it causes further emanations to fill up the void so created. The *icchā śakti* is thus at the root of further movements of the *anuttara cit,* and may be taken to the responsible for emanations of more *kalās* (or aspects of *śakti*).

The *anuttara cit,* in the next movement, expresses itself as the *'īsanam',* which is nothing but a restful poise *(viśrānti)* of the *icchā (śakti).* It is symbolized by the fourth *'Ī'* vowel.[44]

In the following movement, the *anuttara cit* appears to him to express itself as the *'unmeṣa' (śakti),* which symbolizes the *jñāna śakti.*[45] It is represented by the vowel 'U'. The expression of Śakti as the *unmeṣa* represents that stage of development when the *anuttara cit* is about to take a form *(ākara);* hence it is too subtle to be experienced by the *sādhaka.* In fact, it represents the transitional stage in which the divine Śakti takes on a subtle ideal form before it can really become manifest to experience.[46]

In the next movement, which is nothing but a restful poise of *unmeṣa śakti,* the *anuttara cit* expresses itself as *'ūrmi'.*[47] In this stage, the *unmeṣa (śakti)* or *jñāna śakti* takes on a form *(ākāra)* for the first time, but this form is only an ideal form which can be experienced within by the *sādhaka,*[48] but not objectively perceived.

The vowels *'A', 'I'* and *'U'* symbolizing the three principal Śaktis—*anuttara, icchā,* and *unmeṣa* respectively, it is held, constitute the Primal Triangle *(trikoṇa)* with *'A' (anuttara cit)* at the vortex. *'I'* and *'U'* of the Primal Triangle *(trikoṇa)* are only two different self-expressions of the vortex *anuttara cit.*

---

43. Ibid. III, 71–72 Comm. p. 83 ff.
44. *T.A.*, III, 72–73 Comm. p. 8; *T.S*, III, p. 12.
45. *T.A.*, III, 73–74 p. 85.
46. Cf. *T.A.*, III, 74, p. 85.
47. T.S., III, p. 13.
48. Cf. *T.S.* III, p. 12; also called the *tripurā śakti.*

In the self-expressions of divine Śakti described above, it is held that the *kriyā śakti* does not operate in them or influence their manifestation.[49] But, when after expressing itself as *unmeṣa* the *anuttara cit* takes on a subtle ideal form, the *kriyā śakti* starts functioning and influencing the further movements of *anuttara cit.*[50] It becomes conjoined with the *icchā* and *īśana śaktis* as a result of which there appear four distinct self-expressions of the *anuttara,* symbolized by four vowels—*'ṛ', 'ṛl', 'lṛ'* and *ḻṛ.*[51] As these self-expressions *(āmarśa)* appear under the influence of *kriyā śakti's* operation, they are said to partake of the nature of both *kalā* and *kalā*-products (technically called *yoni*), and are, therefore, regarded to be neuter *(napuṁsaka).*[52]

In the next movement, the *anuttara* appears to express itself in conjunction with the *icchā (śakti),* which is symbolized by the vowel *'E'*. In the same way, the *ānanda śakti* appears to express itself in conjunction with the *icchā,* and this is represented by the vowel *'AI'*. Again, as the *anuttara cit* and *ānanda śaktis* express themselves in conjunction with the *unmeṣa śakti,* they give rise to two self-expressions, symbolized respectively by two vowels, *'O'* and *'AU'.*[53]

In this way, the *anuttara cit,* having expressed itself in different forms symbolized by different vowels, at last reaches a stage when all its self-expressions have emerged from the *'A' varṇa* appear once again to merge and coalesce in the *'A' varṇa.* Now this *'A' varṇa,* holding within itself in identity with itself all its self-expressions manifested *(abhivyakta)* so far, is a different *'A' varṇa* from the former one, the first self-expression of *śakti;* hence this is symbolized by a different vowel, *'AṀ'.*[54] The *bindu* (lit., the point) in the *'AṀ'* represents the *kalās* or the forms or self-expressions of śakti held in identity in the *bindu.*[55] Hence the

---

49. *T.S.* III, p. 13.
50. Ibid.
51. *T.S.* III, p. 14; *T.A.* III, 78–79 Comm. pp. 88–90.
52. Ibid; T.A. III, 79 Comm. pp. 89–90.
53. *T.S.* III; *T.A.* III, 92–93, Comm. pp. 101–02.
54. Ibid., *Āh.* III, pp. 14–15. It is described as of the nature of *trikoṇa.* Cf. *T.A.* III, 94, Comm. p. 102 ff.
55. Ibid., *Āh.* III, p. 15. For the nature of *bindu* see *T.A.*, III, 110 Comm. p. 117.

'AṀ' is regarded to be the most 'potential' self-expression of *anuttara cit* from which further emanations follow on a different plane.

In the next movement, the *anuttara cit* expresses itself as the *visarga (AḤ)*, the final stage of the *kalātmaka* self-expressions. This is symbolized by the vowel *'AḤ'*. The *visarga* in *'AḤ'* indicates that there would follow further emanations following further movements of the *anuttara cit*, and that they would be on a somewhat lower plane.[56]

The sixteen movements of the *anuttara cit* resulting in the manifestation of sixteen *kalās*, including the four neuter ones, represented by the sixteen vowels are technically called the "seeds" *(bījaḥ)*.[57] They are described as the "seeds" because they are regarded to be intrinsic by nature, and as such, relatively more subtle and pure in character. Moreover, it is from them that a series of further emanations follow, and as such, they inhere and constitute the very essence (*prāṇa*, life)[58] of the following self-expressions of Śakti.

In the following movements,[59] the *anuttara cit* appears to express itself in five principal groups of self-expressions representing five principal groups of *tattvas*,[60] in conjunction with itself, *śraddhā* and *icchā*, *kriyā* and *icchā*, and *unmeṣa śaktis*.[61] Each of the twenty-five *tattvas* is represented by one of the consonants, such that the *pañca mahābhūtas* are said to be represented by the consonant group *'ka'*, the five *tanmātrās, karmendriyas, jñānandriyas, manas, ahaṃkāra, buddhi, prakṛti* and *puruṣa* by the consonant groups *'ca'*, *'ṭa'*, *'ta'* and *'pa'* respectively.[62] The consonants *'ya'*, *'ra'*, *'la'* and *'va'* are said to symbolize the *rāga, vidyā, kala*, and *māyā tatt*

---

56. Lower in the sense that these self-expressions are regarded to be extrinsic by nature. Cf. *T.A., Āh*. III, v. 141, Comm, p, 144.
57. *T.S.*, III, p. 15, cf. *T.A.*, III, 82, Comm. p. 92.
58. Cf. *T.A.*, III, 83, p. 93.
59. Technically described as the *yoni*. Cf. *T.S*, III, p. 17.
60. The Trika system regards the *tattvas* to be not only modifications of *prakṛti*, but also to be self-expressions of the divine Śakti in their Essence. In fact, the *māyā* and *prakṛti* are essentially spiritual in nature.
61. *T.S.* III, pp. 15–16.
62. Ibid. p. 16; *Parā. Trim.* p. 112.

vas respectively.[63] The *icchā śakti,* we have observed, has two forms in which it manifests itself, viz., the undisturbed *(akṣubhita)* pure *icchā,* in which there is slight movement just before the beginning of *unmeṣa.* When the former combines with *anuttara* which is said to be 'ready to come out' *(pronmukhī),* it gives rise to the self-expression of Śakti symbolized by the vowel letter *'ya'.* In the same way, when the letter for *Īśana śakti* combines with the *anuttara,* it gives rise to two distinct kinds of self-expressions symbolized by the vowels *'ra'* and *'la'.* Likewise, when the *unmeṣa śakti* (which is also said to be of two kinds) conjoins with *anuttara,* it gives rise to the self-expression of Śakti symbolized by the vowel 'va'.[64]

Again, the pure *icchā śakti,* when 'untouched' *(aspṛṣṭa)* by *kriyā śakti,* is said to have three distinct forms of self-manifestations, viz., (1) the *anunmilita icchā,* in which form it retains its intrinsic purity, and therefore, is not clearly manifest, (2) the *unmilita icchā,* in which form it looses its pure character, and gradually manifests itself, and (3) the *pronmilita icchā,* in which form it loses completely, as it were, its pure nature and becomes fully manifest.[65] When these three forms of *icchā śakti* come under the influence of its ever-functioning *svātantrya,* they manifest themselves in three different forms of self-expressions, symbolized by the sibilants *'SA', 'ŚA',* and *'ṢA'.*[66]

In the next movement, *'KA',* the first self-expression of Śakti on the lower plane (i.e., the *kṣobha*) combines with the last self-expression, *'ṢA',* giving rise to an enigmatic self-expression which is symbolized by a joint letter of vowel or diphthong *'KṢA'.*[67]

The vowel letters from *'SA'* to *'KṢA'* are said to represent respectively *mahāmāyā,* (i.e., the Śakti) *śuddha vidyā,* Īśvara, Sadāśiva, and Śakti.

In this way, all the self-expressions of Śakti beginning from *'A' varṇa* and ending in *'HA' varṇa,* technically called the *kalās*

---

63. Ibid. pp. 16–17.
64. *T.A.,* III, 154–56, Comm. p. 156 ff.
65. *T.A.,* III, 163 p. 162. Cf. for its symbolic form ibid., III, 159, Comm. p. 160.
66. Ibid., III, 162–65, Comm. pp. 162–64.
67. Ibid., III, 166, p. 164.

and also the *mātrikās,* are revealed one by one to the *adhikārins* of *śāmbhava upāya* in their pure *citta.* They then begin to realize that the entire creation *(sṛṣṭi)* is nothing but a series of vibrations *(spandana)* of the ever-operating divine Śakti; the vibrations which are revealed to them as so many self-expressions of Śakti. In the beginning, the *sādhakas* get only a diffused view of the vibrations of divine Śakti when they intuitively experience them as *kalās.* But soon they complete the survey of the entire field of the ever-vibrating and ever-expressing *kalās* of Śakti, said to be consisting of fifty different self-expressions of Śakti,[68] as described above, or eighty-one *kalās*[69] when their *ardhmātrās* are also counted as distinct self-expressions *(parāmarśa).*

In the next movement they begin to have an integral view. The integral view reveals to them that there are only six fundamental self-expressions of Śakti,[70] or twelve self-expressions when the *pratisañcaraṇas* are also included,[71] ever-vibrating and ever revealing the totality of creation. He, then, realizes that the ever-vibrating divine Śakti is nothing but an aspect of his own pure Self *(Aham)* which holds within itself all the phases of the self-expression of Śakti.[72] This realization leads him to experience the entire creation to be only his self-expansion *(prasāra)* in exercise of his divine freedom. In this way, he divinizes every phase of his existence,[73] and begins to feel that the entire creation is his divine glory.[74] This experience leads him to the Supreme Realiza-

68. Of these, the twenty-five self-expressions of Śakti, beginning from *'KA' varṇa* and ending in *'HA' varṇa,* are said to constitute eight groups of *kalātmaka* self-expressions, or nine when *'KṢA' varṇa* is also included (cf. *T.S.,* III, p. 17).
69. *T.S.,* III, p. 17.
70. Ibid. p. 18.
71. *T.S.,* III, p. 18. In the mystic language of the Trika system they are sometimes described as constituting the "twelve rays" of the Parameśvara's divine nature.
72. In fact, the word *Aham* is said to be formed by the *'A',* the *anuttara,* combined with the penultimate vowel, *'AM',* and the last consonant, *'HA',* in the order of *'A' 'HA' 'M'.*
73. *T.S.,* III, p. 19.
74. Ibid.

tion *(Pūrṇa Ahamtā)*,[75] the integral realization of his pure *(nirvikalpa) svarūpa*, the *Śivatva*. This is the Goal, the Supreme End of his journey.

4. THE ŚĀKTA UPĀYA

As has been indicated above, all those aspirants who have received the divine grace in less intense form and are therefore possessed of relatively less perfect body-apparatuses *(ādhāra)* are incapable of following the *śāmbhava upāya*, which is meant for the *sādhakas* of higher order. Such aspirants are forced to follow the *śakta upāya* and perform arduous spiritual discipline prescribed thereunder for their integral Self-realization. It is true that both the *śāmbhava* and the *śākta upāyas* are prescribed for an ordinary class of *sādhakas*, the *adhikārins* of *anupaya* being the extraordinary ones, and they lead aspirants to the realization of same Goal—the achievement of *Śivatva*. Yet the path laid down in *śākta upāya* is considered to be more rigorous and difficult in comparison to that of the *śāmbhava upāya*, as it involves more rigorous spiritual discipline in which the aspirant has to contribute a significant amount of personal endeavor as a recompense for the deficiencies and shortcomings in his psychophysical apparatus *(ādhāra)*. The *śākta upāya* is said to be based on *jñāna śakti*, an aspect of divine Śakti, which, in the context of *sādhanā*, implies that the aspirants have to rely on and take the help of *jñāna śakti* in their journey to the ultimate Goal. In other words, *jñāna śakti* plays a prominent role in their spiritual ascent.

A word of explanation is necessary to explain the nature of deficiency in the aspirant's body-apparatus which serves as a vehicle in his integral Self-realization, and the causes thereof. In the foregoing pages it has been observed that the intensity of divine grace received by aspirants varies from individual to individual to such an extent that there are no two aspirants who have received

75. See author's article on the concept of *pūrṇahamtā*, a study in the 'Corpus of Indian Studies,' Calcutta, 1980.

grace in exactly the same measure.[76] This non-uniformity of divine grace has its repercussions reflected in the state of the individual's body-apparatus insofar as it is said to be the controlling factor in the purgation of *malas*. It is, therefore, held that in cases of aspirants where the *śaktipāta* has been relatively milder in intensity, as in the case of *adhikārins* for the *śakta upāya*, the process of purgation remains unaccomplished so that the remnants of *malas* continue to exist in their body-apparatuses.[77] It is, no doubt, a universally acknowledged principle of the Trika system that the moment divine *anugraha* is transmitted to the aspirant's body-apparatus, the thick crust of *āṇavamala* is broken immediately, irrespective of the degrees of its intensity. But this does not necessarily mean that *aṇavamala* absolutely ceases to exist or its influence is totally eradicated from the body. As a matter of fact, *āṇavamala* is supposed to be destroyed instantaneously in the body of the recipient of divine grace,[78] but its residual impressions in the form of a taint may continue to exist for some time, depending on the intensity of grace received by the individual aspirant, as is the case with the *adhikārins* for the *śākta upāya*. And based on this taint, the *kārma-* and *māyīyamalas* may also continue to exist for some time, causing the veil of *ajñāna* (ignorance) covering the *buddhi* to remain as it was prior to the descent of grace.

Obviously, with *kārma-* and *māyīyamalas* remaining intact in the body-apparatus of an aspirant and the veil of *ajñāna* (ignorance) continuing to cloud his *buddhi*, he cannot be said to have a perfect body-apparatus, i.e., without a taint or blemish of any sort. In order that the aspirant might have integral Self-realization, i.e., the *Śivatva*, during his existence as an embodied being, it is absolutely essential that his body-apparatus must be

76. The classification of *sādhakas* into nine categories according as they have received the divine grace in varying intensity is only a broad classification. It generally indicates the infinite variety of *sādhakas* and their individual lines of approach to the ultimate destiny.
77. The remnants of *malas* mean the *māyīya-* and *kārmamalas* and the residual impressions of the *āṇavamala*.
78. The *āṇavamala*, being a product of self-imposed limitation *(saṅkoca)*, cannot remain in the aspirant once he has received divine grace from the Supreme Lord.

made free from all *malas* so that it might serve as a perfect vehicle in the integral Self-realization, *Śivatva.*

To achieve this, it is obvious that the *sādhakas* having imperfect body-apparatuses, such as the *adhikārins* for the *śākta upāya,* have to resort to *sādhanā* and perform such disciplines as might be necessary to remove the remnants of *malas* from their body. The spiritual discipline *(sādhanā)* embodying their personal endeavor is not only an imperative in their case, but also essential as it has two obvious tasks to perform—first purifying their *ādhāra* by destroying the remnants of *malas,* and second, supplementing the mildness of the grace received by them.

The continued existence of *āṇavamala* in the form of residual impressions and the continuance of the *kārma-* and *māyīyamalas,* as they were (i.e., in impure form) in the body-apparatus of the *adhikārin* for the *śākta upāya,* are said to be responsible for the continuance of the *aśuddha vikalpa* (false experience of Self in the not-Self) in him even after the transmission of the divine grace from above. The *aśuddha vikalpa* is a product of ignorance and it is said to cloud only the *buddhi* of the aspirant until it is dispelled by its opposite *vikalpa—śuddha vikalpa—* the experience of his *svarūpa* (nature) as *Aham.*

Aśuddha vikalpa, also called *dvaita vikalpa,* as has already been explained, is a kind of conceptual knowledge *(vikalpa),*[79] or rather ignorance that arises from the false experience of Self *(Aham-abhimāna)* in not-Self (i.e., *Idam*)—the identification of ego with not-ego. Due to the veil of *ajñāna* (ignorance) covering his *buddhi,* the individual ordinarily has his sense of ego *(Aham-abhimāna)* superimposed on any one of the *tattvas* constituting his body-apparatus, such as different *indriyas, manas,* vital airs, *śūnya* (vacuity) etc., or the aggregation of *tattvas* e.g., *deha,* with which he also identifies himself.[80] As all these *tattvas* serving severally

79. Because its seat is in the *buddhi,* (cf. *T.S.,* IV p. 21), it corresponds to the *bauddha ajñāna.*

80. It may be pointed out here that according to the Trika system the superimposition of Self on not-Self precedes the Identification of Self with not-Self, though both of them are equally false. (Ct. *Par. Sār.* v-39 Comm. p. 86 ff.) This has been referred to as the "knot of ignorance" *(ajñāna-granthi)* in the Upanisads. Cf. *Katha Upaniṣad.*

as substratum *(āśraya)* for his ego-sense to rise are alike insofar as they all belong to the category of not-Self *(Idam)*, his sense of ego based on *(pariniṣṭhita)* any one of them is equally false and impure *(aśuddha)*,[81] and as such, it must be eradicated through personal endeavor.

In the *adhikārins* for *śākta upāya*, the transmission of divine grace in milder intensity does not produce any tangible effect on the *aśuddha vikalpa*, owing to its mild intensity. Consequently, aspirants do not feel a significant change in any sphere of their experience. They continue to have the experience of duality and discreteness in this world. Indeed, very often they are not even aware of great change having taken place in themselves, viz., the destruction of the veil of self-ignorance in the form of *āṇavamala* and the simultaneous awakening of "spiritual knowledge" *(śuddha vidyā)* from within, following the *dīkṣā*.

But the aspirants qualified to follow *anupāya* and *śāmbhava upāya* notice revolutionary changes immediately after the transmission of divine grace to their *ādhāra*. The reason for their noticing overwhelming change in every field of their experience is the extreme intensity of divine grace, which does not only cause immediate and absolute eradication of *āśuddha vikalpa* in them, but also, at the same time, brings about the rise of *śuddha vikalpa* in their *buddhi*.[82] The awakening of *śuddha vikalpa*, it is said, is not possible until the *buddhi* is purged of all impurities and thus attains to a state of intrinsic purity as a reflecting medium. In the *adhikārins* of *anupāya* and *śāmbhava upāya*, the *buddhi* is free from

81. It is indeed for this reason the Trika system calls the common ego-sense the *aśuddha Aham*.

82. The *śuddha vikalpa* is the intuitive pure knowledge of the real self, i.e., of the nature of the self-experience, *Aham* (cf. *T.A.*, IV, III–113, Comm. pp. 116–17.) It should be noted here that in the case of *adhikārins* of *anupāya*, the *śuddha vikalpo*, i.e., the self-experience as *Aham*, immediately develops into the *nirvikalpa jñāna* of the divine *Svarūpa*, the *Pūrṇa Aham*, so that they directly realize and rest in their integral divine *Svarūpa* (cf. *T.S.*, II, p. 9). In the case of *adhikārins* of *śāmbhava upāya*, the *śuddha vikalpa* gradually leads the *sādhakas* to the realization of their integral nature, *Pūrṇa Aham*, as it gradually unfolds the divinity and fullness of their *Svarūpa*. (Cf. *T.S.*, III, p. 10.)

all kinds of taints consequent on the complete destruction of all *malas* following the descent of divine grace in an extremely intense form. Consequently, following *dīkṣā*, when aspirants have the direct glimpse of their real *svarūpa (Aham)* within themselves, its light, it is said, at once illumines their *buddhi*. This process of illumination of *buddhi* is technically referred to in the Trika system as the awakening of *śuddha vikalpa*[83] *(śuddha vikalapodaya)*.

With their *buddhi* illumined by the self-effulgent *(bhāsvara)* light of Pure Self, everything in this field of experience undergoes tremendous change. They no longer experience discrepancy and duality in this world. The perennial conflict of the world is resolved once and for all. Instead, the world appears to them as a play of their divine Śakti in delight, a self-projection. All this transformation, consequent on the eradication of *aśuddha vikalpa* and the simultaneous rise of *śuddha vikalpa*, takes place so suddenly and instantaneously in the aspirants of *anupāya* and *śāmbhava upāya* that they are more often than not, aware of the transition, the transformation having taken place in them. And indeed it is for this reason that the Trika system does not even make any mention of the replacement of *aśuddha vikalpa* by *śuddha vikalpa* in connection with the discussion of *anupāya (mārga)* and the *śāmbhava upāya (mārga)*.[84]

But *aśuddha vikalpa* is subjective ignorance and it has its seat in the *buddhi*. It is not a tangible object which can be easily pulled out or gotten rid of like a poisonous plant. It is therefore said that the only way to destroy it lies in its transformation, or as the Trika system puts it, "purification" *(saṁskāra)*.[85] In other words, what is required of aspirants following the *śākta upāya* is incessant endeavor in transforming it into the *śuddha vikalpa*.

In this act of transformation or "purification of *vikalpa*" *bhāvanā* or mental act is said to be not only very useful to the *sādhakas*, but also indispensable. Because, as a matter of fact,

---

83. That is to say, the Self-realization as *Aham*.
84. *T.S.* II, p, 9; ibid. III, p. 10.
85. The process of purification of *vikalpa* actually signifies the performance of such acts as *śravaṇa*, *manana*, etc., by which the *śuddha vikalpa* can be made more manifest *(sphuṭa)* to *sādhakas* in gradual stages (cf. *T.A.* IV, 2, Comm. 2).

mental act or *bhāvanā*[86] is nothing but a kind of mental discipline in which the *sādhakas* are required to make sustained efforts to experience their pure *svarūpa* on the mental plane, i.e., in their *buddhi*. In this connection, it may be pointed out that the Trika system lays so much emphasis on the practice of *bhāvanā* (mental discipline) in the *śākta upāya* only for the obvious reason that the *aśuddha vikalpa* is of a kind of veil of ignorance *(ajñāna)* covering *buddhi;* hence it can be removed only by mental discipline. Thus, the *bhāvanā* is an essential part of spiritual discipline in the *śākta upāya,* without which it is impossible for the *sādhakas* of *śākta upāya* to dislodge and ultimately destroy the persisting vestiges of *ajñāna* from their *buddhi,* in order to liquidate their false sense of ego *(Aham)* in not-ego *(Idam).*[87]

It is no doubt true that the *sādhakas* of *śākta upāya* may not succeed in their first attempts to dislodge the *ajñāna,* but that should not dishearten them or make them give up their attempts. The *ajñāna* is deep-rooted, hence they have to make concerted efforts. It is only after continuous concerted efforts in practising *bhāvanā* for a long period that the *aśuddha vikalpa* begins gradually giving way and disappearing from their *buddhi.*

But to begin the practice of *bhāvanā,* (mental discipline) the *sādhakas* must first obtain an intuitive glimpse *(sākṣātakāra)* of their real *svarūpa* within themselves. On the basis of it, they must also develop in their *buddhi* a vague feeling that their present experience of self *(ahaṁ-abhimāna)* does not represent their real *svarūpa,* but that it is based on ignorance *(ajñāna).* They must also realize that the *svarūpa,* revealed to them in an intuitive flash, as it were, in their inner consciousness *(bodhagagane),* is their real *svarūpa,* which they would have to try to experience on their mental plane or the *buddhi* (sometimes called *cidākāśa*). In other words, with the awakening of real *svarūpa* within them following the descent of divine grace and *dīkṣā,* they must be convinced, at least mentally, of the falsity of their present sense of self (i.e., ego), which consists of the experience of Self in not-Self *(Idam).* Unless this is there, they would not feel the necessity of any *sādhanā,* much less of practicing any discipline. In fact, no discipline can begin with

86. *T.S.* IV, p. 21.
87. Ibid.

vacuity as the basis; it must have some positive experience to begin with and give it a direction. It is indeed for this reason that the Trika system lays so much emphasis on the awakening of real *svarūpa* from within, technically designated as the *śuddhavidyodaya* (lit., the awakening of *śuddha vidyā*) in the Trika system. The awakening of *śuddha vidyā*, pure spiritual knowledge, it is said, forms the basis of the *sādhaka's* integral Self-realization, and its rise in him marks the beginning of his spiritual journey.

In every *sādhaka*, the *śuddha vidyā*, as a rule, is said to arise from within immediately after the transmission of divine grace and *dīkṣā*; and normally if the *sādhaka's buddhi* is absolutely pure, he becomes at once conscious of its awakening within him. This automatically leads to the rise of *śuddha vikalpa*[88] in his *buddhi*, which is nothing but consciousness of the awakening of *śuddha vidyā*.

But all aspirants, such as the *adhikārins* of *śākta upāya*, do not normally possess perfectly pure *buddhi*, hence the rise of *śuddha vikalpa* in them is neither spontaneous nor direct. They have to depend on some external factors; they have to take recourse to certain expedients prescribed in the Trika system to purge their *buddhi* of traces of impurities and to arouse the *śuddha vikalpa*.

Of these, the "*āgama*" is the chief one that is prescribed for those aspirants of *śākta upaya* who have a thin film of *ajñāna* covering their *buddhi*. It must be pointed out here that by *āgama* the Trika system does not mean certain published texts on the subject, which are said to embody the Āgamic tradition, hence, popularly known as the Āgamas. *Āgama* here is the pure knowledge that exists eternally as Vāk—the self-expression of Supreme Reality in the form of Vāk *(svāmarśotpanna Vāk)*.[89] Such pure knowledge is impersonal and eternal. To this knowledge only persons endowed with pure intellect have an access through intuition.[90]

---

88. This is technically designated as the *sattarka* (lit., pure intuition). Cf. *T.A.*, IV, 34, p. 39; ibid 40, p. 44. The *sattarka* is supposed to be the best form of *jñāna* (Self-knowledge), because it arises independently of any other external medium (Cf. *T.A.*, IV, 34, p. 39) and the *sādhaka* who has it is considered to be the best *adhikārin*. (*T.A.*, IV, 43, p. 47.)
89. *I.P.V.V.*, I. 1, pp. 14–15.
90. Cf. *T.A.* IV, 45, Comm. p. 49.

Still there are aspirants whose *buddhi* is not sufficiently cleansed in order that they can have a direct access to the hidden *(rahasya)* knowledge[91] of the Āgamas. To such aspirants of *śākta upāya,* a *guru* in physical body is indispensable. His task is to "deliver" the hidden knowledge of the Āgamas to aspirants,[92] to initiate them into the mysteries of spiritual life. Ordinarily, the aspirants "exist" on the physical plane of existence as they have their sense of ego arising from the identification of this physical body with false *Aham (aśuddha aham).* Hence the *guru* belonging to his corresponding level is the most suitable person to reveal the pure knowledge of *āgama.* While defining the function of *guru* in this context, Abhinavagupta observes: "The chief function of *guru* is to reveal the secrets of the Āgamas".[93] While the *guru* reveals the hidden knowledge of the Āgamas from without, the disciple receives it from within himself, because the pure knowledge can never be imparted from without; it is always revealed from within, the innermost core of being. That is why the Trika system calls the self-revealed, self-acquired *(sopalabdha) Prātibha Jñāna* (highest knowledge) as the *sāmsiddhika* (inherent in oneself) knowledge,[94] as distinguished from the ordinary knowledge which is known as the *sāṅketika* knowledge.

Thus, roughly speaking, the *adhikārins* of *śākta upāya* fall under three categories, according to the state of their *buddhi* or development of their capacities. First, there are aspirants who have perfectly pure *buddhi,* hence the *śuddha vikalpa* arises directly in their *buddhi* from within, without any external aid.[95] Second, there are others, somewhat inferior to those of the first category, who have to have recourse to the study of *sadāgama* to create conditions conducive to the rise of *śuddha vikalpa.*[96] And third, there are still others, to whom the hidden Truth of *sadāgama* is not re-

91. Even the Upaniṣads speak of Truth (in the sense of knowledge) hidden to ordinary beings' view (cf. *Satyasya apīhitam mukham*).
92. *T.S.*, IV, p. 23.
93. Ibid.
94. *T.S.*, IV, p. 23. *Prātibha jñāna* and *sattarka* are more or less synonymous terms.
95. Ibid.
96. Ibid.

vealed so easily; hence they have to seek the help from the *sadguru* for its exposition and revelation.

There are still others possessing lesser capacity who are unable to obtain the pure knowledge of real self from either of the three sources mentioned above, viz., from within *(svataḥ)*, or from the study of the Āgamas *(śāstrataḥ)*, or from the teachings of the *sadguru (gurutaḥ)*. They are, therefore, unable to practice *bhāvanā* in the manner described above. For such *sādhakas*, the Trika system prescribes alternative means of *sādhanā*, such as the performance of *dhyāna* or *yoga*, *japa*, *vrata*, *yāga* and *homa*,[97] by practicing which, it is said, the *sādhakas* can purify their *aśuddha vikalpa*, and thus strengthen the *śuddha vikalpa* in themselves.

The manner in which the *sādhaka* is required to practice *dhyāna* and *japa*, or observe *vrata*, or perform *yāga* and *homa* is very much different from that of the *bhāvanā*; still there is some similarity between them insofar as the aim and the spirit are concerned. It is for this reason that the Trika system interprets them in a different way, and lays its emphasis on the inner side of the *sādhanā*[98] more than on the external *kriyā* aspect. And it is therefore enjoined on the *sādhakas* that they should perform these alternative means of *sādhanā* under the direct and personal supervision of the *guru* so that he can explain and reveal, at the time of performance, the true significance of these means of *sādhanā*.

In this connection, it may be observed that the Trika system considers the conventional ways of *sādhanā* such as the six *yogāṅgas*,[99] *yamas*, etc., as useless in *śākta upāya* as anywhere else, since they fail to awaken the *śuddha vikalpa* in the *buddhi* of the

---

97. *T.S.*, IV; p. 25. In *T.A.*, IV, 53, p. 60, Abhinavagupta mentions *śvapna* in place of *homa*.
98. For the details of the "inner" meaning of different means of *sādhanā* see *T.S.* IV, pp. 25–27.
99. The well-known six *yogāṅgas* are *prāṇāyāma* (breath control), *dhyāna* (concentration), *prātyāhāra* (abstinence), *tarka* (study), *dhāranā* (abstraction), and *samādhi* (perfect absorption of thought into the object of mediation.) The *yamas* are five in number, viz., *ahiṁsa* (non-injury), *satya* (truth), *asteya* (non-theft), *brāhmacarya* (abstinence), and *aparigraha* (not taking from others). (Cf. *T.A.* IV, p. 23.)

aspirants. Abhinavagupta analyzes the spirit behind the *yogāṅgas* and the *yamas,*[100] and concludes by saying the utmost limit that can be reached by the aspirants following these conventional ways is the achievement of identification of *dhyātā* (i.e., the aspirant) with the *dhyeya* (i.e., the Supreme Being), in which *dhyeya* is nothing but a figment of mental construction.[101] The *dhyeya,* in the sense of his Essence, (i.e., his *svarūpa*) can never be revealed to the aspirant unless he is an *adhikārin* of a very high order, such as the *adhikārins* of *anupāya* and *śāmbhava upāya.* The *adhikārins* of high order do not need any *sādhanā* at all, since the Supreme Realization is achieved by them immediately after the *śaktipāta* and *dīkṣā.* In the *adhikārins* of *śākta upāya,* who are *sādhakas* of relatively lower order, the question of spontaneous revelation of pure *svarūpa* in their *buddhi* does not arise at all. Truly speaking, there is nothing that exists apart from the Supreme Reality that limits or veils its *svarūpa.* The Supreme Reality is One and All. As it is the Supreme Reality who limits himself in exercise of his divine freedom and thus creates dichotomy as it were in himself and manifests himself as the multiplicity, it is he himself who brings about the restoration of his intrinsic *svarūpa,* as it were, in exercise of his corresponding aspect of divine freedom *(svātantrya).*[102] And in fact, this constitutes the Essence of his divine freedom.

Viewed from this angle, the futility of the conventional ways of *sādhanā* in restoring man to his real Essence, the *Śivatva,* is obvious.[103] Besides this, the scope of achievement by various conventional means of *sādhanā* is very limited, inasmuch as all of them aim at the purification of *adhāra* (the body-substratum) only. This, according to Trika view, is not sufficient; the purification of *ādhāra* is not all. It alone cannot deliver the *summum bonum.* What is really necessary to root out the ignorance from the *ādhāra,* the *dvaita vikalpa* from the *buddhi,* is to awaken the *śuddha vidyā* from within, to arouse the *advaita vikalpa* in *buddhi.* This cannot be achieved by mere purification of *ādhāra.* Hence, *śaktipāta* is essential, nay indispensable, for its accomplishment. The practice of various conventional ways of *sādhanā* cannot achieve it.

---

100. Ibid. pp. 24–25.
101. *T.A.* IV p. 25.
102. Ibid.
103. Ibid.

Though the final Goal is achieved only after the descent of divine grace and *dīkṣā*, the individual effort on the lines indicated above is necessary in the case of *adhikārins* of *śākta upāya* to make up the deficiency of the mildness of *śaktipata*, of which they are the recipients.

As soon as they fulfill their part and are thus absolutely rid of all kinds of impurities *(kārma* and *māyīya)*, their divine *svarūpa* awakens from within and illumines their *buddhi* with its light, and they have the integral realization of Self as *Śivatva*.

5. THE ĀṆAVA UPĀYA

Of all the aspirants belonging to the ordinary class, there are a large number who are incapable of adapting the way of spiritual discipline laid down under the *śākta upāya*, having received divine grace in a very mild form and therefore possessing an imperfect body-apparatus. Such aspirants are forced to adopt the most arduous path of spiritual discipline prescribed under the *ānavopāya* and perform rigorous yogic practices to attain the Supreme Goal.

Being recipients of divine grace of the mildest intensity, they are said to have the dominance of the *kārma-* and *māyīyamalas* in their body-apparatus which continue veiling their *buddhi*. Despite the destruction of the *āṇavamala* following the descent of divine grace, its residual impressions persist, which sustains, as it were, the *kārma-* and *māyīyamalas* in the form of a thick veil. Consequently they fail to obtain a glimpse of their real Self after the infusion of divine grace and the performance of *dīkṣā* by the *guru*. Normally, the light of spiritual knowledge *(śuddha vidyā)* illumines the *buddhi* of the aspirants from within immediately after the descent of divine grace which eradicates all the three kinds of *malas*, but this does not happen if the divine grace is very mild. As a matter of fact, the aspirants who receive divine grace in mild form are very often not even aware of its descent and the consequent rise of pure spiritual knowledge in their *buddhi* after initiation by the *guru*, unlike the aspirants who are fit to follow the *śākta upāya* and undertake immediately the task of transformation of their false ego-sense (technically called *aśuddha vikalpa*) into the experience of Self in the real Self (known as *śuddha vikalpa*) with the help of *jñāna śakti.*[104] The aspirants fit for adopting a rigorous mode of *sādhanā,* i.e., *āṇava upāya,* are forced to take recourse to other means for accomplishing this task of transformation of *vikalpa,* technically called *vikalpa samskāra* (lit., purification of self-experience). They have to take help from other supporting instruments, technically called *ālambana,*[105] in order to affect transformation of their *aśuddha vikalpa* (experience of Self in not-Self) into the *śuddha vikalpa* (experience of Self in the pure Self). They are required to take recourse to the *kriyā śakti.* It is indeed for this reason that the mode of their yogic discipline is said to be entirely different from those of the aspirants fit to follow the other *upāyas,* including the *śakta upāya.* Their mode of *sādhanā* is relatively more gross and rigorous than that of other aspirants who are considered to belong to a higher class due to a relatively perfect body-appratus, following the descent of grade in relatively intense form.

Again, all the aspirants fit to follow the *āṇava upāya* do not possess body-apparatuses of uniformly imperfect character; therefore their capacity for performing spiritual discipline also cannot be the same. This means that they cannot adopt one particular *ālambana* (supporting instrument) for their yogic discipline. Therefore, keeping in view their varying capacity, the Trika system has suggested *buddhi* (intellect), *prāṇa śakti* (vital breath), *deha* (body), and *grāhya vastu* (external objects)[106] as *ālambanas,* arranged in order of grossness and proximity to the Self. The *ālambanas* are commensurate with their capacity, and they represent a number of alternative means for adoption,[107] as it were. The aspirants fit to follow *āṇava upāya* are required to adopt one *ālambana*[108] out of the four mentioned above.

The highest class of *sādhakas* among those who are fit to follow the *āṇava upāya* are capable of adopting their *buddhi*[109] as the instrument of their yogic discipline. The *buddhi* existing in close

104. *T.A.* V, 3–4 comm. p. 313; *T.S. Āh* V, p. 38.
105. *T.S. Āh.* V. p. 35.
106. Cf *T.A.* V, 6 Comm. p. 313.
107. Ibid.
108. Ibid.
109. *T.S. Āh.* V, p.35.

proximity to the Self that is of the nature of *samvid* is the best medium to reflect and reveal its real nature and its divinity. This *buddhi* is of a crystal-clear nature, like a mirror. In the aspirants, the *buddhi* is seen as covered by a veil of ignorance, hence it is generally incapable of revealing the true nature of Self. Rather, it manifests the opposite, the false experience of Self *(aśuddha Aham)*, which is a product of false identification of not-Self *(Idam)* with the false Self, which is imagined *(kalpita)* and superimposed. Thus the ignorance-covered *buddhi* is the prime locus of all ignorance which lies at the root of bondage. Hence the aspirants who are required to employ their *buddhi* as a means of spiritual discipline are required to strive to purge *malas* from their *buddhi* and achieve complete purgation of ignorance from it, so that it may serve as the perfect reflecting medium, like the spotlessly clear mirror, for the revelation of their Self-luminious nature *(bhāsvara-svarupa)* and divine Essence.

As is well known, the *buddhi* possesses the unique power of concentration *(dhyāna)*.[110] Hence those who adopt their *buddhi* as the instrument *(ālambana)* of their yogic discipline have to make use of its unique power, the power of concentration, focusing all their attention on their real Essence, the pure *Aham*. They are required to practice concentration, or *dhyāna*,[111] for a long time since their *buddhi* is generally covered by a thick veil of ignorance. It is said that the practice of concentration in the manner given below succeeds in removing ignorance completely, thereby making room for the awakening of *śuddha vikalpa*, i.e., experience of self in the real Self. The texts describe in detail the manner in which the concentration is to be carried out, which is given below.

The aspirant should first direct all his attention *(dṛṣṭi)* or "gaze" inward to the center of his being, called the "heart" *(hṛdaya)*, then concentrate his *buddhi* on the all-pervading *(sarva-tattvamaya)*, omnipresent, self-luminous *(svaprakāśa)* Self *(cit svarūpa)* in order to experience the same as existing within himself.[112] Abhinavagupta gives an analogy to describe beauti-

110. Ibid.

111. Ibid.

112. *T.S. Āh.* V p. 36; *T.A.* V, 19–20. Comm, pp. 329–30.

fully the actual method of achieving perfect concentration on the core of the aspirant's real nature. He says that a person desiring to obtain the inner portion or kernel in a flower has to remove the outer covers, i.e., petals, etc., one by one, and throw them away. In the same way, the aspirant practicing concentration should "remove" himself from the outer shells of his being, give up in gradual steps his intimate connection with gross physical body, suble elements, etc. He should thus withdraw himself in gradual steps from the gross physical world, go inwards to get near the core of his being, the real Self.[113]

Since it is very difficult to achieve perfect concentration in one or two attempts in a short time, it has been laid down that it should be attempted in stages stretching over a longer period of time. It is said that the aspirant should first attempt to obliterate the three poles of his experience, technically called the *tripuṭī*, by merging them into one, the *Saṁvid*, the Self. The three poles of experience, represented by *pramātā* (experiencer), *prameya* (object of experience), and *pramāṇa* (the means of experience), are invariably revealed at the time of all experiences as these are said to constitue the essential aspects of the operation of *jñāna śakti*, the power of knowledge. It is therefore enjoined that the aspirant should concentrate on the union *(sanghaṭṭa)* of these three poles of experience *(pramātā, pramāṇa, prameya)* symbolically represented by the *agni*, the *sūrya* and the *Soma* respectively.[114] When the aspirant is able to achieve the unification of these three aspects of his nature as the conscious Self through concentration, this signifies an important step,[115] as the achievement of complete introversion depends on his accomplishing this.

It has been said that as soon as the aspirant is able to achieve complete unification of the three poles of experience through concentration, he experiences the blazing forth of the great *Bhairava* Fire *(Mahābhairava Agni)* within himself *(hṛdaya-*

113. Ibid. Also see *T.A.* V, 22. Comm, pp. 331–32.
114. *T.A.* V, 22, p. 332.
115. Ibid. V, 22–23 p. 332. This step is described as the aspirant's entering into the *madhyamadhama* (the middle 'castle') in the mystical language of the system.

kuṇḍa).[116] The great fire is nothing but the sudden revelation of his divine Essence in the form of great illumination. It is said that as his divine Essence is fully revealed, the "Flames of *Bhairava* Fire," which represents the divine Śakti in its innumerable aspects, appears to him as growing gradually *(sphītatām vrajet)* and forms a circle of fire *(cakra),* as it were.[117]

The "flames of the *Bhairava* Fire" do not appear to remain confined within the aspirant. In the next stage, they appear to him as coming out of his body-apparatus through the openings of his sense organs *(indriya dvāra)* as a manifestation of knowledge power *(jñāna śakti),* and manifests itself also as so many objects of experience *(prameya).*[118]

When this stage is reached, the aspirant experiences everything in the universe as held in and engulfed by the "Flames of Great Fire" or "Self Fire" *(ātma-vahni)* as it is described in the esoteric language of the system. The objects of experience *(prameya),* too, then appear to him as so many *viśrāntis* (lit., resting places) of the Self Fire in the form of knowledge power *(jñāna śakti).*[119]

The aspirant practicing *dhyāna yoga* then experiences that all the objects of experience in the world are nothing but so many forms of his self-manifestation *(svaprakāśa)* out of his free and indepent will *(icchā).* In this way, his vision undergoes great change, his outlook *vis à vis* the universe is completely transformed. He sees everything in the world in new light, the light of pure spirit, and experiences everything in a new garb, as it were. In everything he sees the prototype of his real Self[120] and experiences everything as nondifferent from his real nature. When this stage is reached, he achieves all that he aimed to achieve through the yogic discipline, viz. the *Śivatva.* If there still

---

116. Ibid.
117. The "Flames of Fire" are also likened to the Goddess Kālī who is said to manifest herself in twelve forms *(dvādaśa Kālī) T.A.* V, 22. p. 333, *T.S.,* p. 36.
118. *T.A.,* 27, p. 337, *T.S.* V, p. 36.
119. Ibid 28–29; Comm., p. 338; Ibid.
120. *T.S.* V, 36.

remain any residual impressions of his desire for enjoyment latent in his *buddhi,* they are automatically achieved on reaching this stage.[121] It has already been stated that not all the aspirants among those who are fit to follow the *ānava upāya* are capable of adopting their *buddhi* as the instrument of their yogic discipline on account of their possessing less perfect body-substratum (which, again, is linked with the descent of divine grace in milder form). The Trika system prescribes *prāṇa śakti* as an instrument for yogic discipline as it is relatively gross and can be handled with ease by those aspirants who cannot employ their *buddhi* for their spiritual discipline.

The *prāṇa śakti* is the vital force which resides in the bodies of all creatures and sustains their life.[122] It is said to have its seat in the "heart" wherefrom it moves to and fro, up and down through certain channels, called *nāḍīs,* sustaining life. It is said to pervade and permeate in every cell of the physical body,[123] in the form of consciousness. As vital power responsible for living, it is omnipresent in the body.[124] It is manifested in gross form as exhalation and inhalation of breath *(niḥśvāsa-praśvāsa).*

The *prāṇa śakti,* while functioning incessantly in the bodies of all living beings, especially in man, is said to manifest itself in two forms: gross and subtle. Generally it is manifested in gross form as breath. As breath, it is said to have five forms, technically called *vṛttis,*[125] which control all life-sustaining functions in the body. In some however, it is said to be manifested in its special subtle form, as *varṇas,*[126] through which the spontaneous, inarticulate sound *(anāhata)* is manifested. It goes on ceaselessly in the heart of every living creature, but it is normally not audible. Only the privileged few who possess the innate capacity for introversion are able to perceive *nāda.* Nada is associated with the two *bījnavarṇas,* technically called the *sṛṣṭibīja* and the *saṁhārabīja,* symbolized by the two *varṇas SA* and *HA* respectively.

---

121. Ibid.
122. *T.A.,* V, 18 Comm. p. 328.
123. Cf. *T.S.,* V., p. 38; *T.A.* V, 17–18., pp. 327 ff.
124. Ibid.
125. The *Vṛttis* are *prāṇa, apāna, udāna, samāna,* and *vyāna.*
126. *T.S.* V, p. 38.

Aspirants who employ the ever-vibrating *prāṇa śakti* as an instrument for their spiritual ascent have to make special efforts (on the lines laid down in the texts of the system) to elevate their normal consciousness or awareness from the plane on which matter and consciousness *(jaḍa-cetana)* lie in mixed state to a higher plane of spirit, i.e. consciousness. They have to follow certain yogic practices in order to free the spirit lying admixtured with matter, so that it can be liberated from the clutches of matter. The manner in which this is to be achieved is technically called the *uccāra*[127] *(lit.,* elevation). The Trika system gives the details of the process of the *uccāra* of the *prāṇa śakti,* which are given below.

In the beginning, the *sādhaka* should endeavor to arouse the *prāṇa śakti* within himself *(hṛdayākāse).*[128] In the normal state of being, the *prāṇa śakti* as the vitalizing *śakti* is said to exist in every being, and is said to be always functioning, but, men are generally not conscious of its existence or functioning within themselves. Hence, the first step should be that the aspirant should "wake up" and realize intuitively its existence and functioning within himself. The *sādhaka* should not only realize the *prāṇa śakti* in the gross form of life—sustaining breath, he should also be able to see its true form, the subtle form as Śakti, viz., as the controller of revelation *(unmeṣa)* of the external creation, which is supposed to be caused by its functioning as identified with the Pure Self *(Saṁvid).*[129]

In the next stage he should try to "feel" intuitively the *prāṇa śakti* functioning outside himself, pulsating and animating the external creation *(sṛṣṭi).*[130] The external world, being only a self-manifestation of the *Saṁvid,* therefore nondifferent from it in essence, is said to be permeated and pervaded by the cosmic *prāṇa* that reveals it—the cosmic *prāṇa* being nothing but an aspect of *Saṁvid* itself,[131] in the aspect of divine Śakti. The *prāṇa śakti,* which vitalizes the very being of all creatures, and the cos-

---

127. Ibid.
128. *T.A.*, V, 44, Comm., p. 349 ff.
129. *T.S.*, VI, p. 36.
130. *T.S.*, V, 45, Comm., pp. 349 ff.; *T.S.*, v p. 48.
131. *T.S.;* VI, p. 46.

mic *prāṇa,* which animates the external creation, are thus not different in essence, because both are the aspects of the same *Saṁvid.* Hence, in the next stage, what the *sādhaka* should endeavor is to discover this affinity, this intrinsic oneness of *prāṇa śakti* functioning within him on the individual plane and the cosmic *prāṇa śakti* functioning without him on the cosmic plane.

When he succeeds in discovering the link between the *prāṇa śakti* functioning within himself and the cosmic *prāṇa śakti* functioning outside himself, or to put it in the language of the Trika system, "in awakening the *prāṇa śakti* in the external world,"[132] he begins to realize his identity with the external world.[133] The world now appears to him as a part and parcel of himself. The next step, naturally, should be to withdraw this world, as it were, within himself; to withdraw his self-extended form as the world. This is technically called the *saṁhāra* or the *grāsa* (lit., devouring).[134] This is essential to effect complete introversion, without which he cannot get near the core of his true Being. When the *saṁhāra* (dissolution) of the external world is fully accomplished by the *sādhaka,* he feels himself completely self-centered *(svātmaviśrānta)* and self-satisfied *(nirākāṅkṣa),* because he experiences nothing outside himself. In this stage, the *prāṇa śakti* does not appear to him as *prāṇa śakti,* the vital force of creation outside himself, but as the *apāna śakti,* the *śakti* causing the withdrawal of external creation into himself.[135]

In the next stage, the *sādhaka* should endeavor to balance the two *śaktis* opposed to each other into an equilibrium: *prāṇa śakti,* which is responsible for the *unmeṣa* (manifestation) of the external world, and the *apāna śakti,* which is responsible for its 'closing up' *(nimeṣa).* Because the functioning of *prāṇa* and *apāna śakti* cause only a lateral movement which must be stopped to create conditions favorable for the vertical movement of *śakti.* When the *sādhaka* succeeds in equilizing these *śaktis* opposed to each other, the lateral movement of *śaktis* causing alternatively

---

132. *T.V.,* V, p. 38; *T.A.,* V, 44–47, Comm., p. 350.
133. Ibid.
134. Cf. *T.S.* V, p. 38.
135. Cf. *T.A.,* V, 44–47, Comm., p. 350. For literal meaning of the term *apāna,* see p. 351.

the *unmeṣa* (or 'opening out') and *nimeṣa* (withdrawal) of this world automatically ceases, and all movements automatically become neutralized. In this stage of neutralization the *prāṇa śakti* appears to him in a new form, in the form of neutral *śakti*, technically called the *samāna śakti*, [136] which is said to be of the nature of perfect equilibrium. The rise of *samāna śakti* creates conditions conducive to the opening of the "middle path" *(madhyama-mārga)* through which the *sādhaka* can ascend to the level of his real Self *(parama dhāma)*.

In the following stage, the *sādhaka* should endeavor to rouse the "vertically ascending" *śakti*, technically called the *udāna vāyu*. The *udāna vāyu* has been described as being of the nature of fire *(agni)*[137] for two reasons: first, like common fire, it has an upward-rising tendency, and second, as it arises it obliterates the sense of *pramātā* and *prameya* in the *sādhaka*, so much so that even his earlier experience (that the entire creation exists in him as identified with him) is also blotted out.[138] The *pramātā* and *prameya* relationship in him is said to "melt," as it were, to form one unique experience, the experience of pure Self as the *saṁvid*. It is for this reason that the *udāna vayū* has been described in the Trika system as being of the nature of "all-consuming fire."

After all traces of objectivity have been effaced by the functioning of *udāna śakti* from the *sādhaka*, the stage is set for further development, further ascent. In the next stage, when the conditions are favorable, the *vyāna vāyu* automatically arises in the *sādhaka's ādhāra*. The *udāna śakti* is said to be of the nature of pervasion *(vyāpti)*;[139] hence its rise takes the *sādhaka* to a stage in which he becomes conscious of the all-pervading nature of his Pure Self, the *Ahaṁtā*, He reaches the summit from where he can see the all-pervasive nature *(vyāpaka)* of his Self.[140] When he reaches this stage, all bonds *(bandhana)* become automatically snapped and he begins to realize himself as the *pati*, the Lord. His divine glory is also revealed to him.

---

136. *T.S*, V, p. 38; *T.A.*, V, 44–47, Comm., p. 351.
137. Ibid.
138. Ibid.
139. Ibid. *T.A.*, V, 49 Comm., p. 353.
140. Ibid.

In this way, passing through the six stages of ascent or steps of realization, technically called the *viśrāntis* (lit., resting steps), the *sādhaka* finally reaches the end, the Supreme Goal.

During his passage through these steps of ascent[141] he experiences within himself a unique kind of bliss *(ānanda)* in each stage, technically designated in the Trika system as *nijānanda, nirānanda, parānanda, brahmānanda, mahānanda,* and *cidānanda*[142] respectively. These feelings of bliss arise in him from his *sthiti* (positioning) in the different stages of ascent in which he is said to come gradually nearer and nearer to his Pure Self, the *Śuddha Ahaṁtā.*

In the first stage, when the *sādhaka* succeeds in "rousing" the *prāṇa śakti* within himself, he experiences a unique kind of bliss, technically called the *nijānanda.*[143] The bliss arises from his first contact with the *prāṇa śakti,* which he experiences as identified with his Pure Self. In the next stage, he discovers the *prāṇa śakti* also functioning on the cosmic plane in the external world. He then experiences the external world to be constituted of the same "stuff" as his Pure Self, the external creation to be of the nature of *caitanya.* He is filled with ecstatic delight. The delight is so great that he forgets himself completely. His "attention" shifts, as it were, from within to without. Hence, the self-forgetting, ecstatic delight of this stage has been technically designated as the *nirānanda.*[144] Again, in the next moment, he experiences the external creation not only as of the nature of *Caitanya,* but also as a self-manifested form of himself, a self-projection which he can withdraw into himself at his free will. He then has the feeling of the entire universe as "contained" within him, which he can project out part by part at his free will. The experience of joy arising out of it is technically described as the *parānanda.*[145]

---

141. These are said to lie between the "heart" and "*dvādaśānta*" (cf. *T.S.*, VI, p. 48). The entire creation consisting of the thirty-six *tattvas* is said to exist there.
142. *T.S.*, V. p. 38.
143. Ibid.; *MVV.* II, 35, p. 107; *T.A.*, V. 44–47, Comm., p. 349 ff.
144. *T.A.*, V. 44–47.
145. Ibid.; *MVV.* II, 36, p. 107.

In the next moment, both the external creation and his Self, which are of the nature of *caitanya,* appear to be equally prominent in his experience. He experiences the universe with all its details as equally balanced with his Self, although as a matter of fact, the one (viz., the former) is contained in the other (the latter). The joy experienced in this stage is technically known as the *brahmānanda.*[146] In the following stage, the *sādhaka* experiences the dissolution, as it were, of the sense of *draṣṭā* (the seer) and the *dṛśya* (seen) in him. The universe as the *dṛśya* (object of experience) disappears. Simultaneously the sense of *draṣṭā* (the seer) also goes away in the *sādhaka*—a fact which has been symbolically represented in the Trika system by the imagery of the burning down of everything by the Consciousness Fire *(cidagni).* The disappearance of both the *draṣṭā* and the *dṛṣya* simultaneously from the *sādhaka's* experience gives rise to a feeling of bliss in him, technically called the *mahānanda.*[147] In the last stage, when the *sādhaka,* transcending all the stages, succeeds in securing his union with the Pure Self and experiences himself as the Transcendent Being that transcends and pervades at the same time, in every phase of existence, he then experiences the supreme bliss of his divine union, technically called the *cidānanda.*[148]

Again, simultaneously with the ascent of *prāṇa śakti* as the *sādhaka* raises himself to higher levels of existence, he is said to have in each step of ascent *(viśrānti)* a variety of experiences in successive moments. These experiences are indicative of his firm establishment *(sthiti)* in that particular stage of ascent as well as of his release in gradual steps from the clutches of matter. These experiences have been analyzed in the Trika system and classified under five principal heads, viz., the *ānanda, udbhava, kampa, nidrā* and the *ghūrṇi.*[149]

In the first moment, as the *sādhaka* enters into a particular stage of ascent, he experiences ecstatic delight *(ānanda).*[150] This experience of delight is caused by two factors—one, with his en-

---

146. *T.S.,* V. p. 38; *T.A.* V. 44–47, Comm., pp. 349 ff.
147. *T.S.* V, p. 38; *MVV.* II, 37, p. 108.
148. Ibid; *MVV.* II, 38; p. 108.
149. *T.S.* V. p. 40. Also see *M.V.V.* Adh 18.
150. Ibid; *T.A.* V, 101, Comm., p. 411 ff.

trance into a *viśrānti* (lit., a step for resting) he comes under the unique touch of absolute perfection *(pūrṇatā)* of his Pure Self, which fills him with unique joy, and secondly in consequence of the first, his intimate association with the matter in the form of his false identity with the not-Self, i.e. body, etc., begins to dissolve.

This dissociation of the *sādhaka's* self from the matter grows in the successive stages, until finally he experiences himself completely dissociated and separated from his physical body-apparatus. He feels disembodied, as it were, as a result of which he experiences a peculiar feeling of buoyancy or rising up, as it were, in the pure space of *caitanya*. This experience of the *sādhaka* is technically designated the *udbhava*[151]—the upward motion.

With the slackening of intimate connection of the Self with matter, the self-consciousness *(ātmabhāvanā)* grows in the *sādhaka*, and his attention is directed more and more inwards toward his Self. As a result of this, the body, which received the most attention previously, is deprived of all support and begins shaking before it goes out of the *sādhaka's* field of consciousness. This experience of the *sādhaka* is technically designated as the *kampa* (lit., shaking).[152]

With the complete dissociation of Self from the body, etc., the *sādhaka* is overtaken by sleep-like quiescence and peace, in which all movements cease; the mind has no outward movement nor any internal movements. This experience of the *sādhaka* is technically called the *nidrā*.[153]

In the next moment, with the absolute dissolution of the sense of identity of Self with body, the *sādhaka* gets an intuitive vision of true Self. This vision of his real Self makes him realize that his Self alone is, and that there is nothing in the universe apart from his Self. This realization automatically awakens the divine power of Self that was lying latent in him until that moment. He realizes his omnipresent Being. This experience of the *sādhaka* is technically called the *ghūrṇi*.[154]

---

151. Ibid.; *T.A.* V, 102, Comm., p. 411 ff.
152. *T.S.* V. p. 40; *MVV*, II, 57, p. 109; *T.A.* V, 103, Comm., p. 412.
153. Ibid. p. 40.; II, 60 p. 110. Ibid. V, 104, Comm., p. 412.
154. *T.S.*, V, p. 40; *T.A.*, V, 104–05, p. 414.

On the attainment of this state of *ghūrṇi* the *sādhaka* reaches the stage in which his self-experience is unlimited and unrestricted, the state of *mahāvyāpti*.[155] With the achievement of this state, he establishes himself firmly on that particular *viśrānti*, and acquires fitness for further ascent.

So far we have described the mode of *sādhanā* of those *sādhakas* who seek to realize their Supreme Goal through the ascent of *sthūla prāṇa śakti* (vital breath in gross form). But all *sādhakas*, according to the Trika system, who adopt the *prāṇa śakti* as their *ālambana* of *sādhanā* do not necessarily have to strive for the ascent of *sthūla prāṇa śakti;* there are, on the other hand, many highly gifted *sādhakas* who are capable of realizing their Goal by merely repeating and meditating on the significance of certain potent *varṇas* revealed to them from within in course of their *sādhanā*.[156]

These *varṇas*, it is obvious, are not letters from ordinary speech, which are, by their very nature, impure and impotent,[157] and hence incapable of delivering the goods. On the other hand, these are potent *varṇas*, revealed to the *sādhakas* from within, embodying and revealing the Absolute Truth.[158] The potent *varṇas* are, according to the Trika system, of the nature of uncreated Sound *(anāhatadhvani)* that arises from within, revealing the unmanifest Absolute Reality *(avyakta)* in the form of Sound.[159] The Trika system holds that the Supreme Reality in the form of divine Śakti is ever-functioning and ever-vibrating, and its vibration is revealed spontaneously by the uncreated Sound which is technically known as the *Nāda*.[160] Though this *Nāda* is said to be arising eternally in the inner most part of all,[161] it is not revealed to all

155. *T.S.*, V. p. 40; *T.A.*, V, 105–07, Comm., p. 415 ff.
156. *T.S.* V p. 42.
157. The *varṇas* of ordinary speech are impotent *(nirvīrya)*, because they do not have the touch of *saṁvid's* vibration *(saṁvid-spanda-sparśa)*. The letters of conventional speech are therefore called the *sāṅketika varṇa*. Cf. *T.S.*, V, p. 42.
158. *T.S.*, V, p. 42.
159. *T.A.*, V, 131, Comm. p. 444.
160. *T.A.*, VI, 216.
161. *T.A.*, V, 131, Comm., p. 444.

sādhakas owing to their inherent incapability of receiving them. It is, on the other hand, revealed to the gifted *sādhakas* in the form of different *varṇas* in the course of the ascent of *prāṇa śakti* in gradual steps.

The *varṇa,* in the form of *Nāda,* is one and indivisible *(akhaṇḍa).*[162] It is for this reason that the *sādhaka,* being limited by nature, is not capable of receiving the *varṇa* in its one and integral form. The *varṇas* are, therefore, revealed to him in *khaṇḍa* form, one by one as a multiplicity of them. The *sādhaka* perceives them as interlinked and intimately interconnected as the garland of letters *(varṇamālā).*

The *varṇamālā* as a whole reveals the functioning of the totality of divine Śakti in its innumerable phases and aspects. There are, however, two principal *varṇas* in the *varṇamālā,* which are capable of revealing the integral nature of the *varṇa* to some extent, and are, therefore, technically called the seed *varṇas (bīja-varṇa).* The first is the *'A' varṇa,* symbolizing the *anuttara,* from which the entire creation-process *(sṛṣti)* has emanated; the other is the *'HA' varṇa,* which stands for the dissolution *(saṁhāra)* of the entire creation.[163] The entire creation, beginning from the *anuttara* down to the earth *(pṛthvi),* is said to be contained in potential form in the *varṇas* beginning with *'A'* and ending in *'HA',* because all the phases *(kalā)* of the divine *Śakti,* which are responsible for the manifestation of the universe as divine glory of the Supreme Lord, lie hidden in these *varṇas.*[164] It is therefore said that if the *sādhaka* succeeds through his efforts to realize the hidden Truth *(rahasya)* that lies behind the *varṇas* from *'A'* to *'HA',* he is able to know the secret of the three processes of creation, maintenance, and destruction of the universe.

It is therefore enjoined in the Trika system that the *sādhaka,* in order to accomplish the process of ascent of *prāṇa śakti* and thereafter realize his integral *svarūpa,* should repeatedly utter and meditate on the significance of *Ahaṁ,* which is to be constituted

162. *T.A.*, VI, 216.

163. Technically called the *sācka varṇa* and the *anacka varṇa.* Cf. *T.A.* V. 133, p. 446.

164. For a detailed discussion of the nature of *varṇas* see *Parā Trim.* pp. 166 ff.

by a combination of the seed *varṇa (bija-varṇa)* '*A*', penultimate vowel '*AM*', and the last vowel, '*HA*' (which is also a seed *varṇa*), in the order of '*A*'-'*HA*'-'*M*'.[165] This *Ahaṁ* is not only a symbolic representation of the Supreme Self, it also represents the Essence of Parāvāk. The repeated *japa* (utterance) of *Ahaṁ*, followed by meditation on its significance,[166] reveals to the *sādhaka* his integral *svarūpa*, and also opens the path to its perfect realization.

As has been observed above, all those *sādhakas* who are unable to adopt *buddhi* or *prāṇa* as their *ālambana* of *sādhanā* to achieve the supreme Goal, owing to its being a subtle internal organ, are forced to adopt a relatively gross *ālambana* such as the *karaṇa* for their *sādhanā*.

By *karaṇa*, the Trika system means all such instruments of *sādhanā* (they are many in number) that the *sādhaka* is required to employ in order that he might discover his true Self, and finally, realize his integral divine nature, i.e., the *Śivatva*. Such *karaṇas* are numberless in this world because everything in this world, being of the nature of *saṁvid*, has the potentiality of revealing his true nature to him, though of course, not of showing him the path leading to his Self-realization.

Taking a broad view of things, the Trika system has made a list of *karaṇas* most suitable for the purpose (viz., Self-realization), and has indicated also the way to utilize them in *sādhanā*. The *karaṇas* are said to be seven in number, viz., *grāhya*, *grāhaka*, *saṁvitti*, *sanniveśa*, *vyāpti*, *ākṣepa*, and *tyāga*.[167] The mode of their employment is as follows:

In the first step, the *sādhaka* should endeavor to realize the true nature of all objects of cognition *(grāhya)*.[168] Though all objects of experience outwardly appear as made up of matter, they are essentially of the nature of *saṁvid* as all of them are said to be only the self-manifested forms of the supreme Reality, the *parāsaṁvid*. Being covered by a veil of *ajñāna*, the *sādhaka* normally

---

165. *T.A.*, V, 133, p. 146.
166. The repeated *japa* of *Ahaṁ* accompanied by meditation on its significance is said to cause the remembrance of the integral *Svarūpa* in the *sādhaka* (cf. *T.A.*, V, 133, Comm., p. 445).
167. *T.A.*, V, 128–29, Comm., p. 439.
168. Ibid. p. 440.

is not able to perceive their real nature, which is of the nature of *saṁvid*. Hence, it is enjoined on every *sādhaka* following this mode of *sādhanā* to approach and seek the help of the *guru* in unmasking and understanding the real nature of all objects of experience.[169]

After realizing the essential nature of all objects, he should, in the next step, turn his gaze on himself. To realize his true Self, he should take the help of the *jñāna śakti;* that is to say, he should endeavor to understand the relationship between his real Self, the *grāhaka,* and the objects of experience, the *grāhya.*[170] If he makes an attempt in this direction through the help of the *guru,* he will realize that the objects of experience, being of the nature of *saṁvid,* are essentially one and identical with the subject *(grāhaka),* the real Self, which is also of the nature of *saṁvid.* If he meditates further and goes a step forward, he would experience them not only as one and identical with the Self, the subject, but also as the former being contained and sustained by the latter, i.e., the Self.

Thus, the firm realization of the identity of *grāhya,* the object of experience, and the *grāhaka,* the *sādhaka's* self, (which includes his entire psycho-physical being besides pure Self) goes a long way in revealing the true nature of the Self to him. Hence, this realization of identity, technically called the *saṁvitti,*[171] is also regarded as an instrument *(karaṇa)* of Self-realization.

In the next step, the *sādhaka* is enjoined to meditate on the identity of subject *(grāhaka)* and the object *(grāhya)* in such a way and until the time that they are merged into one and become united. As a result of this union effected through his intense and concerted efforts, the glory of his true and integral nature is revealed spontaneously to him. This step, technically called *sanniveśa,*[172] leads the him to his integral Self-realization; hence it is also considered as a *karaṇa.*

Most often, the realization of identity of *grāhya* with *grāhaka* that is experienced at the stage of *saṁvitti* does not lead *sādhakas*

169. *T.A.,* V, 130, p. 441.
170. Ibid., V, 128–29, Comm., p. 440.
171. Ibid.
172. Ibid.

to the achievement of perfect *sanniveśa*. Hence, the Trika system prescribes two more *karaṇas*, the *ākṣepa* and the *tyāga*,[173] to help and expedite the process of *sanniveśa*. The *ākeṣpa* means the process of conscious and deliberate experience of the identity of a particular object of experience with the subject, which implies some effort on the part of the *sādhaka*. And the *tyāga* implies a process of *sanniveśa*. It is a process of deliberate discrimination of what is not of the nature of *saṁvid* i.e., the elimination of the material part from the object of experience, which is to be experienced as identified with the subject. Though these *karaṇas* are actually employed by the *sādhaka* at every stage of *yogic discipline*,[174] they are especially helpful in the achievement of *sanniveśa*.

The revelation of the *sādhaka's Svarūpa* and his glory leads him to the realization of his all-pervasive *(vyāpaka) Svarūpa*. He then experiences nothing but himself, the all-inclusive, all-pervasive, Supreme Self. This step is technically called the *vyāpti*. The achievement of *vyāpti*[175] (lit. pervasion) is final the *karaṇa*, which is responsible for the *sādhaka's* firm establishment in his integral *Svarūpa*, the *Śivatva*.

Finally, there are aspirants who are unable to employ the various kinds of *karaṇas* as instruments of their spiritual discipline. Such aspirants must follow one of the six other paths, technically called *ṣaḍadhvas*, which are classified under external rites *(bāhyavidhi)* in the Trika texts.[176] These paths are to be followed under the guidance of the *guru* who alone can make them experience the significance of each step and guide them to reach the Ultimate Goal.

Abhinavagupta has described these six *adhvas* (lit., paths) which an aspirant has to follow depending on his capacity. The *adhvas* are broadly classified under two heads. Under the first category, *varna*, *mantra*, and *pada* are included, and are related to knowledge *(pramāṇa)*. The other three, viz. *kalā*, *tattva*, and *bhuvana* constitute the second category which have connection with

173. *T.A.*, V, 130, p. 441.
174. Ibid.
175. Ibid.
176. *T.S. Āhs.* VI, p. 45.

the object of knowledge *(prameya)*.[177] The aspirant has to adopt one of them to achieve his Goal under the advice of his teacher *(guru)*. All these paths are intimately connected with the functioning of cosmic *prāna śakti* which is the source of its nourishment. Hence when an aspirant adopts any one of the above paths, he indirectly is helped by the *prāṇa śakti* (life-force) that is pulsating and vitalizing the entire creation.[178] As a matter of fact, the ever-active cosmic *prāṇa śakti* is a form of *vimarśa śakti*, or the divine Sakti, which is always vibrating and making the universe appear and disappear in the "view" of the Supreme Lord. As such, the cosmic *prāṇa śakti* occupies the position between *vimarśa śakti* and material power *(jada śakti)* which is responsible for the manifestation of the gross world.

As we have already shown, *varṇa* represents the primordial Sound *(nāda)* that is arising eternally within the body of the aspirant as a result of the movement of *prāṇa* in conjunction with the ceaseless vibration of the divine Śakti.[179] The *varṇas* are extremely subtle and as such they can be experienced only by the aspirants who have achieved complete introversion. The *varṇas* are of three kinds: transcendent *varṇa (paratama varṇa)*, which is the same as the *nāda;* the subtle *varṇa (paratama)*, and the gross *varṇa (sthūla varṇa)*, which forms a part of our speech. The aspirant is required to move from the gross and externally manifest-*varṇa* to the subtlest *varṇa*, i.e. *nāda* (primordial sound), with the help of *prāṇa śakti* under the guidance of his teacher *(guru)*.[180] The total number of *varṇas* is said to be fifty.

The *mantras* constitute a relatively grosser path, which also leads the aspirants to realize themselves as the pure experiencer *(śuddha pramātā)*, ultimately culminating in their Self-realization. The *mantras* are essentially of the nature of *vimarśa*, whereby the Supreme Lord has the Self-experience as *Aham*. They are of the nature of pure consciousness and represent a state of Self-experience within the pure experiencer, and therefore are spoken of as identified with the pure Experiencer. It is therefore enjoined

177. Ibid. *Āh.* VI p. 47.
178. Ibid.
179. *T.S. Āh.* VI, p. 48.
180. Ibid.

that an aspirant should concentrate on the *mantra* while uttering the same, after receiving it from his teacher, to discover the underlying conscious force which it represents, and thus accomplish perfect concentration.[181] The *mantras* are said to be ten in number.

The *padas*, too, represent the grossest path, which is related to knowledge.[182] It is said that when the pure consciousness *(Caitanya)* as the experiencer *(pramātā)* projects itself out, the objects of experience *(prameya)* come into being. This represents a kind of "disturbance" *(kṣobha)*, a deviation from the experiencer's normal and natural Self-experience as *Aham*. As a result of this "disturbance" in the experience of the experiencer, two things emerge: experience, or knowledge *(pramāna)* and the object of Knowledge *(prameya)*. All the three, experiencer *(pramātā)*, experience *(pramāṇā)*, and object of experience *(prameya)*, are held to be of the nature of divine light *(prakāśa)*. The *pada* symbolizes that light of knowledge *(prakāśa)* which is responsible for the manifestation of objects as knowledge. It is enjoined that aspirants following this path of *pada* should attempt to grasp, with the help of the *guru*, that light, the light of pure consciousness or Self which underlies all the three—the experiencer, the experience, and the experienced—with the help of *pada*. The *padas* are ten in number.

The term *kalā* means that aspect of the Supreme Lord's divine power which underlies a particular group of *tattvas* constituting the universe. It is responsible for the self-manifestation as the universe, hence it is named *kalā* (from the root *Kal*, to manifest). The entire creation consists of five *kalās*, in descending order, viz., *nivṛtti kalā*, comprised of *prthvi tattva; pratiṣṭhā kalā*, which contains the levels of creation beginning with *jala tattva* up to *prakṛiti; vidyā kala*, made up by *puruṣa tattva* to *māyā tattva; śāntā kalā*, embracing the levels of creation from the *śuddha vidyā* to *śakti tattvas;* and *śāntyātita kalā*, which exists on the level of *śiva tattva*.[183] The aspirant must discover with the help of his teacher *(guru)* the underlying substratum of all levels of creation which is divine Śakti, and which is also their locus. Through Śakti he

181. *T.S.*, *Āh.* VI, p. 49.
182. Ibid.
183. *T.S.* *Āh.* X, p. 109.

must approach the *saṁvit* (pure consciousness) and establish himself in the highest Reality. When he realizes that the entire creation has proceeded from the Supreme Lord, he dissolves the *kalās* step by step to reach the Supreme Goal. For example, he dissolves the *nivṛtti kalā* in Brahmā, who is the lord of *brahmāṇda,* i.e., gross physical world, *pratiṣṭhā kalā* in Viṣṇu, and so on. Abhinavagupta has described a sequence in which the *kalās* and *tattvas* are to be dissolved to reach the *anāśrita,* i.e., level of the Void, and then the level of *Paraśiva,* i.e., Supreme Śiva, the supreme all-pervading level of existence, containing all in the reverse order of creation, i.e. dissolution.[184] The aspirant must follow this path under the direction and supervision of his *guru.*

We have already described thirty-six *tattvas* which emanate from the divine *Śakti* when it functions somewhat differently, associated with the Supreme Lord, and manifests his glory as the universe. The aspirant finds in the world that the various objects (such as house, courtyard, market, temple, garden, forest, and trees) are different from one another and they shine in his consciousness *(bodha)* not only as mutually distinct but also as different from him (as the experiencer). The aspirant following this *tattvādhva* path must discover the underlying unity that is divine Śakti which holds the diversity of objects.[185] He first has to see the play of Śakti that is going on perennially around him and then merge the innumerable manifestations of the Śakti in himself as the Seer, pure experiencer *(pramāta).* He can accomplish this with the help of his *guru.*

The *bhuvanas* also symbolize expansion of divine Śakti. They hold within them the multiplicity of subjects and objects of experience on the different levels of creation.[186] It is said that *nivṛtti kalā* contains sixteen *bhuvanas, pratiṣṭhā kalā* fifty-six *bhuvanas, vidyā kalā* twenty-eight *bhuvanas,* and *śantā kalā* eighteen *bhuvanas,* making a total of 118 *bhuvanas.* Abhinavagupta has described in detail the location of all these *bhuvanas* together with the names of their presiding deities. The aspirants are required to discover the underlying Reality, i.e., divine Śakti, which constitutes the

184. Ibid.
185. *T.S. Āh.* VIII, p. 41.
186. Ibid. Āh VII, p. 59.

locus of creation as *bhuvanas,* then merge them all in gradual steps in the Supreme Cause *(mūla kāraṇa)* from which they have emanated. He is then to realize his identity with this ever-vibrating divine Śakti and thus reach the Supreme Goal.

The Trika texts describe in detail various external rites which are to be performed by the aspirants daily after initiation. Such rites fall under three categories: first, the obligatory rites *(nityakarma),* which include ablutions, sitting in a particular direction before the deity; *nyāsa* (establishment of sacred *mantra* in the different parts of the body), followed by show of *mudrā; dhyāna* (concentration), followed by *japa* (repetition of sacred words), etc. All these have to be performed under the guidance of the *guru* four times daily. A worshiper should daily worship his deity, who symbolizes the Supreme Being, imagining it to be a clear "sky" with all the essential attributes of consciousness and all other deities present in it. This helps the aspirant to experience his identity with the deity and the highest *mantra.* Secondly there are occasional rites *(naimittika karma)* which are to be performed on certain occasions in the prescribed manner. Thirdly, there are *kāmya karma,* which are to be performed by the aspirant on the fulfilment of some desire.[187] Abhinavagupta does not attach much importance to such *karmas,* hence he has not gone into details. He considers daily worship to be very important in securing oneness with the deity, which culminates in the experience of his identity with the Supreme Lord.[188] He has therefore gone into details which we need not reproduce as these are required to be performed under the supervision of the *guru,* who alone can explain the significance of each step. Meditation and worship carried by the aspirant in the prescribed manner ultimately result in the introversion and thereafter realization of the Supreme Goal, i.e. *Śivatva.*

Here we do not wish to enter into the details of the *sthūla kriyā,* and describe how the *sādhaka* realizes gradually their significance, by meditation and through the grace of the *guru.* It would suffice here to state that, as we have already observed, the aim of the performance of the external *kriyā* is to direct the "gaze" of

187. *T.S. Āh* XXI, pp. 193 ff.
188. Ibid Āh XXII pp. 198 ff.

sādhakas inward. When the *sādhakas* are able to achieve complete introversion and realize the significance of all acts they perform under the supervision of their *guru,* they realize the Supreme Goal.

In this way, through one of the five alternative means, the *adhikārins* of *āṇava upāya* are finally able to achieve the Supreme Goal, i.e., *Śivatva.*

CHAPTER 6

The Perfect Integral Self-Realization, *Śivatva*

IN THE PRECEEDING chapter the mode of *sādhanā* under the different *upāyas* prescribed for the *sādhakas* of varying capacities has been discussed in detail. In that connection it has also been observed that, though the mode of *sādhanā* differs in each *upāya* from that of the other exactly in the same proportion in which the capacity of individual aspirants *(sādhakas)* differs, all the different *upāyas* are said to lead the aspirants to the same destiny, viz., the Self-realization as Śiva. In this chapter it is proposed to consider the nature and content of the supreme realization, the *śivatva*.

The aim of all kinds of *sādhanā,* according to the Trika system, is the perfect realization of the integral divine *svarūpa (akhaṇḍa svarūpa),* and the firm establishment in it. The self-experience at that time of perfect realization is said to be of the nature of *pūrṇa aham.*

Although all the different ways of *sādhanā* aim at the achievement of this perfect Self-realization by aspirants *(sādhakas),* and also are said to lead them to this goal, the realization that they have at the end of their *sādhanā* is not always exactly one and the same. There are, as a matter of fact, slight differences in the content of their self-experience they are said to have at the end under each *upāya.* Though these differences are minor in nature and superficial in character, there can be no doubt, however, about their existence. And it is indeed for this reason that the Trika system gives different names to different *samāveśas*[1] (divine union or the union with one's divine nature), which they are said to have following each *upāya*. For instance, the moment the *adhikārins* for *anupāya* receive the divine grace in a very intense form, through the medium of the *guru* in the form of his *upadeśa* (precept), they achieve the *Pārameśa Samāveśa* instantaneously[2] when they are said to have not only the perfect realization of their integral divine nature *(svarūpa)*, but they are also said to have firm and direct establishment in their pure Self *(nirvikalpa svarūpa)*. Then they are said to have the self-experience as *pūrṇa aham*. The external creation, i.e., the multiplicity of the world, then does not disappear from their view; they continue to have its experience, not as existing apart from themselves but as existing within themselves as reflected in the pure space of consciousness *(bodhagagane)* as the glory *(aiśvarya)* of their divine nature *(svarūpa)*.[3]

The *adhikārins* for the *śāmbhava upāya*, being less perfect in comparison to those of the *anupāya*, are unable to secure perfect and firm establishment directly in their integral *(nirvikalpa) svarūpa*.[4] They are, however, not required to exert or perform any *sādhanā* to hasten the process of ultimate Self-realization. They have to approach the supreme goal through the divine Śakti and experience the revelation of divine glory *(aiśvarya)* of divine Śakti. It is for this reason said that, simultaneously with a descent of divine grace, they have only the awakening of the *śuddha vidyā*, when they have the self-experience as the *śuddha ahaṁ* (real Self). The self-experience as *śuddha ahaṁ* does not lead them immediately to the Self-realization of the Pure Self *(nirvikalpa svarūpa*. On the other hand, the self-experience as *ahaṁ* grows distinct and develops into the Self-realization of pure Self *nirvikalpa svarūpa)*, when the glory hidden behind the pure divine

1. *T.S.*, II, p. 9; Ibid., III., p. 19, cf. Ibid., IV, p. 22 ff; Ibid., V, p. 35. The *āṇava jñāna* leads them to the achievement of the *āṇava samāveśa*, while the *śākta jnāna* leads them to the *śākta samāveśa*.
2. Ibid., II, p. 8.
3. Ibid., II, p. 9; see also *I.P.V.* IV, 1, 12.
4. Ibid., III, p. 10.

nature *(svarūpa)* is manifested and revealed to them in gradual steps. This *samāveśa* (divine union) is technically called the *śāmbhava samāveśa*.[5] At the end, when they are able to establish themselves in their pure Self *(nirvikalpa svarūpa)*, they have the self-experience as *pūrṇa ahaṁ*. In their case, too, as in the case of all others, the experience of the external creation, i.e., the world of multiplicity, is not negated;[6] they continue to experience the external creation with all its details as reflected in the pure "space of their consciousness" as the divine glory. With the destruction of their physical body, however, in course of time, they become one and identified with the Supreme Lord.

The *adhikārins* of the *śākta upāya*, on the other hand, being covered by a thick veil of ignorance *(buddha-ajñāna)*, are unable to experience their pure *svarūpa ahaṁ* immediately after the descent of divine grace and *dīkṣā*. Hence, the question of the direct realization of their integral *svarūpa* does not arise at all. After they have the pure knowledge of their *svarūpa* (i.e. *Śuddha Vidyā*) awakened from within automatically or through the study of *śastras*, or by listening to the *guru's upadeśa*, they have to exert themselves to remove the veil of *ajñāna* (ignorance) from their *buddhi*, and endeavor to rid their *ādhāra* (psycho-physical apparatus) of the impurities[7] which are at the root of the continuance of *aśuddha vikalpa*. Following the way of *sādhanā* laid down under the *śākta upāya* when they succeed in their attempts, they have, in the beginning, the Self-experience as *śuddha ahaṁ* (i.e., the *śuddha vikalpa*) which, with the achievement of purification of their body-apparatus, later develops into the perfect Self-realization of their integral *svarūpa* as *pūrṇa aham*. The *śamāveśa* which they are said to have is technically called the *śākta samāveśa*.[8] Later, when their physical body-apparatus becomes destroyed in the course of time, they become one with the Supreme Lord.

The *adhikārins* of *āṇava upāya*, the other hand, have their *buddhi* laden with such a thick veil of ignorance *(buddha ajñāna)* that when they have their pure *svarūpa* awakened from within with

---

5. *Śiv. Sū.* I, 5, Comm., p. 19.; *T.S.*, III, p. 19.
6. *T.S.* III, p. 19.
7. *T.S.*, IV, p, 21.
8. Cf. *Śiv. Sū.* I, 6, Comm., p. 22.

the performance of *dīkṣā* by the *guru* they have no knowledge of it. Hence, they have to follow the most arduous path of *sādhanā* as laid down under the *āṇava upāya* to remove the veil of *ajñāna* from their *buddhi,* to have the self-experience as *śuddha aham*. The *śamāveśa* which they are said to have at the end under this *upāya* is technically designated as the *āṇava samāveśa.*[9] When their *ādhāra* is completely purged of impurities due to their incessant efforts, they have the perfect Self-realization of their integral nature,[10] the *pūrṇa aham*. It is only then that they are able to establish themselves firmly in their divine nature, the *nirvikalpa svarūpa*. In their case too, the external creation is not negated from their experience.[11]

In this way we find that *sādhakas* following the different *upāyas* are ultimately able to realize their integral divine nature and establish themselves in their *nirvikalpa svarūpa*. It must be noted here that although the *adhikārins* of the different *upāyas* are said to have different kinds of *samāveśas* at the end of their *sādhanā*, the content of the self-experience in all the *samāveśas* is almost of the same name, i.e., the *śivarūpa*, there is essentially no difference. All the four kinds of experiences lead the *sādhakas* to the same supreme Self-realization, viz., the *śivatva*.

From what has been stated above, it is clear that the *sādhaka* cannot have perfect Self-realization directly from the self-experience as *pūrṇa aham*. They have in the beginning self-experience as *aham* after the destruction of the *āṇava mala,* which grows distinct and pervades the entire field of experience with the destruction of the *māyīya* and *kārma-malas* in gradual steps. It culminates at the end in the revelation of their divine nature as *pūrna aham*. The perfect Self-realization or the realization of their integral divine *svarūpa* implies not only a knowledge or experience on their part of their real nature, it also involves a conscious recognition by them that they are *the* divine being, the Supreme Self. In other words, in order to have integral Self-realization of their divine *svarūpa*, the *sādhakas* should not only experience their pure *svarūpa* as *aham,* they must also realize simultaneously that

9. Cf. *Śiv. Sū.*, III, 6, p. 83.
10. Cf. Ibid., IV, 4, Comm., p. 79.
11. *T.S.*, VIII, p. 37.

they are the divine being, the Śiva, the supreme Self *(pūrṇa aham)*, and that the universe is nothing but his divine glory, his self-expansion *svaśaktisphāra)* out of his free and independent will. This recognition *(pratyabhijñā)* of his divine *svarūpa* constitutes the core and kernel of their supreme self-realization, the Self-realization as Śiva, because it implies not only the full development of their latent divine powers but also indicates the achievement of their individual perfection. It is indeed for this reason that the Trika system lays so much emphasis on the recognition *(pratyabhijñā)* in addition to the self-awakened knowledge of Pure Self (i.e., the self-experience as pure *aham*), and assigns it an important place in every mode of *sādhanā*, i.e., the *upāyas*.

The Trika system describes four stages or steps[12] through which the self-awakened pure knowledge (i.e., the *śuddha vidyā*) develops into the integral Self-realization in the course of *sādhanā*. To start with, every *sādhaka*, who has received the divine grace from the highest source and has had the *dīkṣā*, has first the intuitive "vision" of his real Self awakened from within when he has the self-experience as *pūrṇa aham*. This knowledge, arising from his intuitive vision, is technically called the *śuddha vidyā*, and the step in which he has it is designated the *ātmavyāpti*.[13]

But merely getting a glimpse of real *svarūpa* or the awakening of self-knowledge is not enough. In the majority of cases, the awakened self-knowledge is so weak[14] that it is unable to penetrate and remove the thick veil of *ajñāna* lying on their *ādhāra*. Hence, it becomes imperative that they should endeavor through their *sādhanā* to remove the veil of *ajñāna* from their *ādhāra* so that the awakened self-knowledge might illumine their *būddhi* also,

---

12. The higher class of *sādhakas*, such as the *adhikārins* of *anupāya* and the *śāmbhava upāya*, do not experience the succession of these steps; they achieve their goal almost simultaneously. Cf. *T.S.*, *Āh.* XI, p. 120.
13. *Śiv Sū.*, III, 7, Comm., p. 87.
14. In a few rare cases, such as in the case of the *adhikārins* of *anupāya* and *śāmbhava upāya*, the awakened self-knowledge is so powerful and overwhelming that it not only dispels all *ajñāna* in a moment, it also enables them to have the firm realization of their integral nature. Cf. *T.S.* IX, 119 ff.

whereby their false ego-sense might be destroyed. Hence it is enjoined on the *sādhakas* that they should direct their "gaze" inwards and "wake up" *(jāgrata)*[15] to realize their true Self, the *pūrṇa aham*. They should strive to conquer the *moha* (delusion) that is due to their self-ignorance and intimate association with matter in the form of body, etc.[16] They should also realize their present fettered condition in the light of self-awakened pure knowledge and endeavor to get rid of it. This step is technically designated as the *pāśāvalokana*.[17]

Once the *sādhakas* are conscious of their real Self and their present fettered condition, and start exerting to remove their fetters through the prescribed ways of *sādhanā*, the success is almost assured. As they endeavor for the destruction of the *malas* covering them, their pure *svarūpa*, the *śuddha aham*, becomes gradually uncovered so that when ultimately all the *malas* are totally annihilated, they get a full "vision" as it were of their pure *svarūpa*, the *pūrṇa aham*. The step leading to this is technically called the *śivavyāpti*.[18]

When they have the full "vision" of their pure *svarūpa*, their divine powers such as omniscience, omnipotence, self-contentment, eternity, etc., that were so long latent in them, develop and become automatically manifest.[19] With this, their integral *svarūpa (akhaṇḍa svarūpa)* is revealed to them and their divinity restored. They then rest in their divine nature. The universe is not negated from their view; it remains and they continue to experience it, though in a different form altogether. The universal manifestation no longer appears to them as different from them or existing outside themselves; it appears in its true form of his divine glory and his self-expansion *(svaśakti-sphāra)*, resting in themselves. They then are able to experience as it were, "I am the One. I am All. All is my own Self-manifestation."[20] The contradiction and inconsistency between

15. *Śiv. Sū*. III, 8, Comm., p. 88.
16. Ibid., p. 86.
17. Ibid., p. 87; Cf. *T.S*. IV. p. 32.
18. Ibid.
19. Ibid. III, 7, Comm., p. 87; cf. *T.S*. IV, p. 32.
20. Cf. *I.P.V*. IV, 1, 12, p. 309 (*Bhāskarī* Ed).

one and many, stability and movement, truth and falsehood, light and darkness then disappear as it were, in the light of all-embracing Supreme Self-experience, the *pūrṇa aham*. They recognize their divine nature as the Supreme Lord, the Supreme Agent, the Supreme Spectator, and rest in their *nirvikalpa svarūpa*.

The reason for such a view is not far to seek. The true rule of integral Self-realization is progressive comprehension. The Supreme Reality expresses itself in so many ways and forms, which all are co-existent in being, coeval in time and life. But if in passing from one domain to another, from material to spiritual, the *sādhakas* have completely to forsake the one that has been given to them forming their embodied personality, in eagerness for the other, for a new attainment; if in reaching the life of spirit they have to reject and renounce the material which is the basis of their embodied existence, they would certainly fail to realize their integral nature, the Supreme Reality's Self-manifestation as one and many. They cannot achieve their integral nature by rejecting and renouncing; they cannot become perfect by negating. By negations they will be only shifting the field of their imperfection from one plane to the other, from one altitude to another. To attain the divinity of their nature, which is integral and all-embracing, they need not abandon or cast away anything; they need only to understand and realize the true nature of things, comprehend the divine Śakti that is functioning in all spheres behind all manifestations. They need only to transform and transfigure what ordinarily appears as baser, material, and limited, and integrate them with and assimilate them in their pure *svarūpa*. Otherwise, they would get only a partial view. The Supreme Reality is one and integral and unifies all phases of its manifestation at the same time; it stands to reason therefore that the *sādhakas*, being the manifestation of his divine nature, should become integral and all-embracing.

In this context, it would perhaps not be out of place to compare and contrast the Trika view of supreme self-realization with that of the Sāṁkhya-Yoga and Advaita Vedānta of Śaṅkara for the sake of better appreciation of the Trika viewpoint.

The Supreme Ideal in the Sāṁkhya-Yoga system is the achievement of *kaivalya* or the purification of the individual soul (i.e., the *puruṣa*) to its utmost extent, and its liberation from the action of *prakṛti* and its *guṇas*. The liberation of *puruṣa* from the clutches of *prakṛti* or the separation of the spirit from the matter does not involve any change taking place in the nature of *puruṣa*, the individual soul, or imply the aquisition of any new property that was not there in it. It simply means the release of soul from the influence of ever-evolving *prakṛti*, after which it rests in itself, stable and serene. It implies only the recognition of soul as a reality that is beyond the space, time, and causality, above body and mind, and therefore essentially free, eternal, and pure.

With the dawn of *viveka-jñāna* when the individual soul achieves liberation, the *prakṛti* ceases to affect him. The individual soul retires as it were from active life in the world, to rest in its pure Being *(sattā)* and Consciousness *(cit)*. The *prakṛti* ceases to act and evolve the world to the liberated soul, so that the liberated soul does not see the *prakṛti* in its ever-functioning and ever-evolving form. The process of its creative activity ceases as it were for him.

The Advaita Vedānta does not state that the individual soul can achieve liberation by mere separation of self *(ātmā)* from matter *(jaḍa)*, and its purification. On the other hand, it believes that the liberation of the individual soul can be achieved only by intellectual intuition of the identity of individual soul with the universal *brahman*, the impersonal absorption of the individual soul in the universal Self, the *brahman*. The absorption of the individual soul in the universal Self again implies and involves the intuitive experience or knowledge of the real nature of Self as pure being *(sat)*, consciousness *(cit)* and delight *(ānanda)*, which is also the nature of the Supreme Reality, the *brahman*. It also implies the recognition of Self as a reality that is beyond space, time, and causality.

When the individual soul, according to the Advaita Vedānta of Śaṅkara, achieves liberation, the *māyā* ceases to exist for him. He does not experience *māyā*, hence he does not experience the world; the external world which is a product of *māyā* is negated from his view. He lies immersed, as it were, in his pure Being.

In none of these ideals, the Trika would say, is the Perfection reached. The achievement of Perfection implies the *recognition* of Perfection which involves, in its turn, the full development of the hidden powers of pure Self, including the absolute will, absolute knowledge, and absolute action,[21] which constitute the divinity of the pure Self. The Self is divine by nature, and it must regain its natural condition through the development or evolution of divine Śakti, which lies dormant in it. The Sāṁkhya and the Vedānta ideals do not fulfill this condition; hence their conception of Supreme Realization is incomplete and imperfect in the eyes of the adherents of the Trika system.

Even the ideal of the Siddhānta school of Śaivism is not perfect when compared to that of the Trika system. The dualist Śaivites hold that the *mūkta Śiva*, although free from matter of all shades and restored to original divine status, retains a semblance of distinction from the Absolute, the Supreme Lord, while the Trika system holds that there is absolutely no difference between the liberated individuals, the *mukta Śivas*, and the Supreme Lord, the *Parama Śiva*.

21. *Sp. Kā.*, I, 10, p. 41.

CHAPTER 7

Jīvanmukti and Related Issues

IN THE FOREGOING chapter the nature and content of the Supreme Realization has been discussed, which all *sādhakas* are said to experience when they realize their Essence, the *Śivatva*, and secure their firm establishment in it.

But as has been pointed out, all *sādhakas* do not possess the capacity of achieving the realization of their integral *svarūpa*, owing to differences in the intensity of divine grace received by them. Such *sādhakas*, when they achieve complete liberation in their embodied state, are technically called *jīvanmuktas*.[1] In the following paragraphs it will be shown which *sādhakas* are eligible to attain the state of *jīvanmukti*, and the nature and content of their realization in that state will be examined.

From what has been observed in the foregoing chapter, it is clear that according to the Trika system, all *sādhakas* who have attained the knowledge of their Essence and have had the self-experience as *Aham*, do not necessarily become disembodied immediately with the achievement of such knowledge. On the other hand, the Trika system believes that there are *sādhakas* who, after the achievement of the supreme knowledge and their establishment in their pure *svarūpa*, may continue to exist in embodied form for some time to come, provided they have previously rip-

1. Cf. *I.P.V.*, IV, 1, 14, p. 306 ff. *(Bhāskari)*.

ened *karma* (i.e., *prārabdha karma*)[2] sustaining their present embodied condition, and possess keen desire for enjoyment *(bhogavāsanā)*. Such *sādhakas*, when enlightened, are said to become the *jīvanmuktas*. The *jīvanmuktas* do not live in a different world[3] or walk about and behave differently from ordinary mortals. They exist, on the other hand, with ordinary mortals; they perform *karma* and participate in all the activities of the world like ordinary mortals, yet their actions do not affect them. They remain as they are, emancipated beings. They perform *karma* only to keep themselves in embodied form and to satiate their desire for enjoyment *(bhoga)* in this world, but in this process they do not acquire any fresh *karma*. Unlike ordinary mortals, they do not have accumulation of the fruits of new *karma* to their credit. As soon as the fruits of their ripened *karma*, i.e., the *prārabdha karma* which were sustaining them in their embodied form, are enjoyed and exhausted, they lose their body-apparatuses once for all and become one with the Supreme Lord. They do not have further birth after the present one.

But all *sādhakas* cannot achieve this state, the state of *jīvanmukti*. Of the four distinct kinds of *sādhakas* into which the Trika system has broadly classified all the *sādhakas* from the point of view of their varying capacities and their being recipients of the divine grace in different degrees of intensity, the *adhikārins* of *anupāya*, for instance, are incapable of attaining this stage of *jīvanmukti*. They are the recipients of a very intense form of *śaktipāta*, for which reason they are said to have their integral Self-realization in an instant as it were, when their body-

2. It is said that there are three distinct types of *karma* in all. Firstly, there are those *karmas* which are ripe and have started bearing fruits, technically called *prārabdha karma*. Secondly, there are *karmas* which are unripe and therefore lie accumulated, technically called *sañcit karma*, and last, there are those *karma* which are being gathered during the present life of the aspirant, technically called *sañcīyamāna karma*. With the achievement of the knowledge of pure *svarūpa*, it is said that the second kind of *karma* is destroyed, and the third is prevented from accumulating, while the first is allowed to remain to enable the *sādhaka* to exist in embodied form.

3. Because the achievement of *mukti* does not imply the achievement of something 'unachieved'. (Cf. *Par. Sār.* v-60, p. 115 ff.).

apparatuses fall off and they are firmly established in the divine nature *(nirvikalpa svarūpa).* Hence, the possibility of their attaining the state of *jīvanmukti* is not there at all.[4]

In the case of the aspirants following *śāmbhava upāya,* the chances of their becoming a *jīvanmukta* appear bright, though nothing definite can be said about them. The reason for such a view is not far to seek. After the descent of divine grace in intense form, they stay in their physical body for a short time, but not as short as the aspirants following *anupāya,* viz., until the traces of *māyīya-* and *kārmamalas* are automatically destroyed and the revelation of the glory of their divine Self takes place. When the traces of the persisting veil of *malas* disappear, they are said to establish themselves in their pure *nirvikalpa svarūpa,* when their body-apparatuses automatically fall off. The destruction of the body-apparatus is said to be essential for the perfect realization of the Essence, the *Śivatva.* Hence, in their case, the possibility of attaining the state of *jīvanmukti* is there, though it might be for a short duration only.

In the case of the aspirants following the *śākta upāyas,* however, the prospects of their attaining the state of *jīvanmukti* are very bright, because in their case the process of the destruction of physical body is not immediate; it is a long-drawn affair. Being *sādhakas* of lesser capacity, and therefore possessing relatively less perfect body-apparatus when they receive the divine grace in relatively less intense form, they have the *kārma-* and *māyīyamalas* persisting in their body apparatuses even after the descent of divine grace. Hence, to realize their pure divine *svarūpa,* they have to exert and perform *sādhanā* as laid down under either of the two *upāyas* (as the case may be). And when they succeed in their efforts, they have the *śākta* and the *āṇava samāveśas* respectively, but they do not at once become disembodied. They continue to exist for some time in embodied form, and it is during this period that they have the chances of attaining the state of *jīvanmukti,* provided they fulfill necessary conditions for its attainment and possess requisite qualifications.

There are, according to the Trika system, three essential conditions which must be fulfilled by all *sādhakas* attaining the

---

4. *T.S. Āh.* XI, pp. 119 ff.

state of *jīvanmukti*. Firstly, the *sādhakas* should have perfect realization of their pure *svarūpa* in which they should also secure their perfect establishment. This, no doubt, implies the destruction of the false identification of self with not-Self, the complete eradication of the *aśuddha vikalpa*, with which the false ego-sense also disappears; in other words, the *sādhakas* should have the self-experience of *Aham* in their pure *svarūpa*, the *śuddha aham*.

Second, the *sādhakas* must also possess pure *bhogavāsanā* (desire for enjoyment). The *bhogavāsanā*, we have stated, is of two kinds—the *bhogavāsanā* of *śivadharmi bubhukṣu sādhakas*, who aspire for enjoyment from elevated positions such as of the *ādhikārika devatās* (the presiding deities),[5] and the *bhogavāsanā* of *lokadharmī bubhukṣu sādhakas*, who do not desire any elevation but prefer to remain in this world as *jñānins* (Enlightened Ones). It is the latter kind of *sādhakas* who are eligible for the attainment of *jīvanmukti*.

Lastly the *sādhakas* should have the appropriate form of *dīkṣā* performed by the *guru*. The *guru* should perform the appropriate form of *putraka dīkṣā* so that the accumulated fruits of their past and present *karmas*[6] become automatically destroyed. In doing so, the *guru* should not, it is enjoined, destroy the *karmabīja* altogether, he should allow the ripened fruits of past *karma*, i.e., the *prārabdha karma*, to remain in their body arraratuses so that they might continue in their embodied form performing the meritorious deeds and enjoying the fruits thereof.

When the *sādhakas* attain liberation from their embodied existence, they do not achieve anything new or other than the establishment in their pure divine *svarūpa*. Hence, outwardly no change is noticeable in them though inwardly of course, they undergo revolutionary changes which are mainly confined to their self-experience. For instance, with the advent of pure knowledge when the knot of *ajñāna* is resolved, the veil of self-ignorance (i.e., the *bhrānti*) removed from their *buddhi*, they attain liberation and have full and clear experience *(amalabodha)* of their real Self. They are then always conscious of their pure divine *svarūpa* when they are free and full, one and all, the Supreme Agent and the

5. Cf. *T.S.* XI, p. 118
6. That is, the *sañcita karma*.

Supreme Lord, etc.,[7] and experience themselves as Pure *Aham*. They then experience the universe as their self-manifestation out of their free will, divine sport.[8] As a result of this, they become "unembodied" *(aśarīri)*[9] as it were, though their body does not fall off immediately. They continue to be associated with a body in the form of a thin veil *(āvaraṇa)* only,[10] to fulfill their pure *bhogavāsanā* and exhaust the ripened *karma* (i.e., the *prārabdha karma*).

They perform *karma* like any ordinary unliberated individual, but they are said to be unaffected by the fruits. The reason for this is twofold: first, the are always conscious of their pure *svarūpa* which is not subject to *ajñāna*,[11] and perform actions from their existence in their pure *svarūpa*. And second, as such, they have no false ego-sense, which is said to be the repository of the fruits of actions performed by them from the state of ignorance.

After exhausting the seeds of ripened *karma* and satiating their *bhogavāsanā* through the performance of *karma* in this world, when in the end the *jīvanmuktas* are dissociated from their physical body-apparatus, they establish themselves firmly and perfectly in their integral divine *svarūpa*, and become the Supreme Lord himself. This is the culminating stage of their existence, technically called the *videha-mukti*.

The Trika system is purely a monistic system of philosophy, but it believes in both the theories of the unity and the plurality of souls (technically called the theories of *ekajīvavāda* and *bahujīvavāda*, respectively) from different points of view. Looking

---

7. *T.S.*, p. 123.
8. Cf. *Sp. Kā.*, II, 3, Comm. p. 85 ff.
9. In the sense that they cease to have *dehātmabodha* (feeling of oneness with physical body).
10. The Trika system holds that no *tattvavid* experiences his body-apparatus in two different ways in course of his establishment in his pure *svarūpa*. First, when he is covered by *ajñāna*, he experiences his body-apparatus as a material vestment made up of material elements *(bhūtātmakam)*. Second, when he realizes his pure *svarūpa* and is able to experience the true nature of universal manifestation, he experiences it to be of the nature of *bhāva* only (i.e., the Śakti). Cf. *Sp. Kā.*, III, 3, Comm., p. 90.
11. *Par. Sār.*, v-67, Comm., p. 127. Ibid., v-70, p. 134.

from the point of view of the manifested universe, it admits the plurality of *jīvās*, and looking from the point of view of the Supreme Reality, it believes in the unity of all souls. In admitting both the unity[12] and the plurality of souls at the same time, the Trika system does not think that there is any contradiction or incongruity involved in it, because in the Trika view, the multiplicity is only a self-projection and self-manifestation of the unity, which is the Supreme Lord, out of his free and independent will. The multiplicity of souls is, thus, in the Trika view, as real as the unity of the Supreme Lord; there is no inconsistency involved in the two.

This view holds good even in the field of ultimate Self-realization or liberation of individual souls, where the admission of both the theories of *ekajīvavāda* and *bahujīvavāda* raises the important question of the salvation of individual soul and that of all souls simultaneously.[13] The Trika system, for instance, does not believe that there is really any contradiction between the emancipation of one soul and that of all souls. The ultimate fate of each of the souls is bound up with that of the rest, so that, strictly speaking, there can be no absolute liberation of one soul to the exclusion of the others. Consequently, the liberation of one is simultaneous with, if not identical with that of the rest. Hence what is generally looked upon as liberation achieved by one individual soul is not, strictly speaking, a full and complete liberation, the attainment of absolute perfection, it is only a partial liberation, a state of relative perfection. The achievement of absolute perfection or liberation is possible only when all souls achieve liberation or perfection simultaneously and are merged in the unity of the Supreme Lord. Just as all the inner points of the radii of the circle are united in a common center, in the same way the plurality of souls, when they achieve absolute liberation, are said to meet on the same ground and be united in the fundamental unity of the Supreme Lord. This is the most supreme Goal, the Supreme Destiny, the Supreme End of all manifested beings.

12. Cf. *Sp. Kā.*, I, 3, Comm., p. 22.
13. This is only in principle, because for all practical purposes the individual being is said to achieve his Supreme Goal when he succeeds in establishing himself in his *nirvikalpa svarūpa*.

This view is not an exclusive view of the Trika system; it is one which is shared and supported by all monistic systems of philosophy. Even the Advaita Vedānta of Śaṅkara has a similar view. The Vedantin philosopher Appaya Dīkṣita (sixteenth century), for instance, says that the perfect realization, which is a realization not of one soul but of all souls simultaneously, has not yet taken place. The highest limit of advance that the individual souls could make by securing their personal salvation is confined to the state of *īśvara-sāyujya* (union with God). Unless all individuals simultaneously achieve their personal liberation or perfection, it will not be possible for them to achieve Absolute Perfection, which means perfection of one and all. Even in the Mahāyāna school of Buddhism, it is believed that the Buddha is still working for the liberation of entire humanity, and that he will not enter into *nirvāṇa* until and unless the entire world accompanies him to it. The emancipation of the entire creation is the Goal, the Supreme Destiny of mankind.

Glossary

A

Ābhāsa: Manifestation

Abheda: Nondual

Ācārya: Realized teacher, spiritual guide

Ādhāra: Body-apparatus

Adhikārin: Spiritual aspirant, practitioner

Adhva: Level of manifestation

Āgama Śāstra: Original scriptures of Kashmir Śaivism

Agni: Fire

Aham: Self-experience as pure "I"

Ahaṁkāra: "I"-ness, concept of individuality

Ahaṁtā: The pure Self

Ahetukī: Unconditional nature of something

Āhnika: Chapter

Aiśvarya: Divine glory

Aiñāna: Ignorance

Akalpita Guru: Fully realized teacher

Ālambana: Supporting instrument, medium

Āmarśana Śakti: Capacity of Self-revelation

Ānada: Bliss

Āṇava Mala: Impurity of Minuteness

Āṇava Upāya: Path of Self-limitation

Ankurāvasthā: "Sprouting stage" of creation

Anugraha: Divine grace

Anupāya: "Way Without a Way," the highest path toward realization

Anuttara: Absolute, highest

Anuttara Cit: Absolute Consciousness

Apratihata Icchā: Unlimited free will

Āsana: Posture

Āśrama: Stage, level

Aśuddha: Impure

Aśuddha Aham: Common ego

Aśuddha Vikalpa: Impure or false understanding

Ātman: The Self

Ātma-saṅkoca: Self-limitation

B

Bauddha Ajñāna: Intellectual ignorance

Bauddha Jñāna: Intellectual knowledge

Bhakti: Devotion

Bhāvāna: Mental discipline

Bhedābheda: Diversity-in-unity

Bhogadeha: Body of enjoyment

Bhogavāsana: Desire for enjoyment

Bīja: Seed; seminal

Bījavasthā: Germinal state of creation

Bindu: Dot, point

Brahma: Ultimate Reality, the Absolute

Bubhukṣu: Desiring enjoyment

Buddhi: Mind

C

Caitanya: Pure Consciousness

Caitanyātmaka: Spiritual Plane

Camatkāra: Shining forth of divine glory

Cārvāka: Philosophical school of Materialism

Cit: Consciousness

Citi: Pure light of Consciousness

D

Daiva: Celestial, divine

Dama: Control of the external sense organs

Deha: Body-apparatus

Devatā: A god, celestial being

Dhyāna: Meditation

Dīkṣā: Spiritual initiation

Dravya: Substance

Dvaitabhāva: Duality

E

Ekajīvavāda: Theory that there is only one self (*jīva*)

G

Guru: Spiritual teacher, medium for the transmission of divine grace

H

Homa: Fire Ritual

I

Icchā: Divine will, free will

Icchā Śakti: Śakti in the aspect of the divine will

Idam: This

Indriya: Sense organ

Īśvara: Lord

J

Jaḍa Śakti: Material power

Jaḍātmaka: Material plane

Japa: Repetition, recitation of the mantra

Jīvanmukta: One who is liberated while living

Jīvanmukti: State of being liberated while living

K

Kalā: Authorship, an aspect of *Śakti*

Kāla: Time

Kāla Śakti: Force of Time

Kalpita Ahaṁbodha: Imagined self

Kañcuka: Covering of the Self, constrictor

Karaṇa: Instrument

Kāraṇa Śarīra: Most subtle of the three subtle bodies

Karma: Action, deed, accumulated effects of actions

Kārma Mala: Impurity in the form of residual impressions of past actions

Karmabīja: Seed of past actions

Karmavāsana: Desire for works, actions

Kartā: Agent

Kleṣa: Defiling element

Krama: Order, stage

Kriyā: Function, action

Kriyā Śakti: *Śakti* in the aspect of action

L

Laya: Dissolution

Laya Avasthā: State of existing without a physical body

Līlā: Play of *Śakti*

Liṅga: (1) Mark, form; (2) Phallus

M

Madhya Śaktipāta: Moderately intense descent of grace

Mahāmāyā: Divine power operating as identified with the Supreme Lord

Mahāpralāya: Cosmic dissolution

Mahāyāna: "Great Vehicle," a school of Buddhism

Mala: Defilement covering the Self

Mala-paripāka: Maturation of an impurity

Manas: Mind

Manda Śaktipāta: Light descent of grace

Maṇḍala: A division or book of the *Ṛgveda*

Mantra: Sacred syllable or work imbued with power

Mānuṣa: Human

Mātrikā: An aspect of Śakti associated with the evolution of the Sanskrit alphabet

Māyā: Power of illusion

Māyīya Mala: Impurity associated with the web and illusion of *māyā*

Mīmāmsā: Philosophical school of Inquiry

Mūla Mala: Original impurity; alternate term for *Ānava Mala*

Mukti: Liberation

Mumukṣu: One who desires liberation

N

Nāda: Uncreated Sound

Nigraha: Self-limitation

Nimeṣa: Closing up

Niṣkāma Karma: Desireless action

Niyata Krama: Fixed order

Niyati: Restriction in regard to space, a cause of limited understanding

Niyama: Control from within

Nyāya: Philosophical school of Logic

O

Oṃ: The Eternal Word, consisting of *A, U,* and *M*

P

Parācit: Supreme Consciousness

Parama Śiva: Supreme Reality

Paramarśa: Self-experience

Parameśvara: Supreme Lord

Parapramātā: Supreme Experiencing Principle

Parāsaṁvit: Supreme Reality

Parāvāk: Supreme Speech, Supreme Sound

Pariṇatāvasthā: "Flowering Stage" of creation

Paśakṣaya: Destruction of the bond of *Āṇava Mala*

Paśupramātā: Fettered experience

Pati: Lord

Pauruṣa Ajñāna: Fundamental ignorance arising out of self-limitation

Pauruṣa Jñāna: Knowledge of the Self

Prakāśa: Pure Consciousness as Pure Light, Illumination

Prakṛti: Primal Nature

Pralaya: Cosmic dissolution

Pralayākala: A type of disembodied soul

Pramātā: Limited experiencer

Prārabda Karma: Actions that have borne fruits; "ripened" *karmas*

Prārabdha Karma Saṁskāra: Residual impression of past actions beginning their fruition

Pratibhā Jñāna: Highest knowledge

Pratyabhijñā: Recognition

Pūjā: Cermonial worship

Pūrṇa Aham: Perfect realization of one's true nature

Pūrṇatva: Fullness of Self-contentment

Puruṣa: Cosmic Man

Puruṣārthas: The four goals in a person's life

Pūrvāśrama: "Final Stage" of life

Puryaṣṭaka Śarīra: Second most subtle of the three subtle bodies

Putraka Dīkṣā: An advanced initiation; becoming the "son" of the *guru*

R

Rāga: Passion, attachment

Ṛṣi: Seer

S

Sadguru: Authentic teacher, realized spiritual guide

Sādhaka: spiritual aspirant

Sādhanā: Spiritual practice

Śaiva (English, Śaivite): Of or relating to Śiva and his worship; a devotee of Śiva

Sakala: Embodied being

Śākta: Of or relating to Śakti and her worship; a devotee of the Goddess

Śākta Upāya: "Path of Śakti"

Śakti: Divine Power; Female personification of Cosmic Energy; Dynamic aspect of the Supreme Lord

Śaktimān: Substratum of Power

Śaktipāta: Descent of divine grace

Śama: Control of internal sense organs

Samāveśa: Divine union, perfect merging of consciousness

Samāyika: According to convention

Śāmbhava Upāya: "Path of Śambhu or Śiva"

Saṁhāra: Dissolution

Sāṁkhya: Philosophical school of Enumeration

Saṁkoca: Self-limitation

Saṁsāra: The objective universe; this world

Saṁskāra: (1) Residual impression; (2) Purification ceremony, rite of passage

Saṁvid: Supreme Consciousness

Sañcit Karma: "Unripe" *karma*, actions whose effects have not yet come to fruition

Sañcīyamāna Karma: Karmas being incurred in this lifetime

Saṅkalpa: Divine Resolve

Sannyāsin: Ascetic, monk

Sarvajñātva: Omniscience

Sarvakartṛva: Omnipotence

Śāstra: Treatise

Siddha: Perfected being

Śiva: The Ultimate Reality; Lord; The "Auspicious One"

Śivatva: Essence of Śiva, "Śivahood," highest state of realization, ultimate goal of spiritual path in Kashmir Śaivism

Śivatvaprāpti: Divine union

Śivatvayojana: Divine illumination

Spanda: Flutter, throb

Sphāra: Self-projection

Sṛṣṭi: Creation

Sthiti: Preservation

Sthula Śarīra: Lowest of the three subtle bodies

Śuddha Adhva: Realm of pure spirit, pure order

Śuddha Ahaṁtā: True identity

Śuddha Prākaśa: Pure illumination

Śuddha Vidyā: Pure knowledge

Śuddhavidyodaya: True knowledge awakening within

Śuddha Vikalpa: Pure experience

Sūkta: Vedic hymn

Śūnya: Void, negation

Sūtra: Verse

Svabhāva: Integral nature

Svāmī (English, swami): Teacher, spiritual guide

Svānubhāva: Self-experience

Svarūpa: Essential nature

Svātantrya: Absolute freedom

Svecchā: Free will

T

Tarkasya Kartā: Logic

Tattva: A constituent of the universe

Tattvātīta: The Absolute

Tirodhāna: Concealment

Tiryag: Subhuman

Titikṣā: Tolerance

Tīvra Śaktipāta: Most intense descent of grace

Trika: "Triad," name of the "triune" philosophy of Kashmir

Trikoṇa: Primal triangle

Tṛṣṇa: Thirst

U

Uccāra: Ascent

Udāna Śakti: Vertically ascending *Śakti*

Ullāsa: Manifestation or play

Unmeṣa: Opening out

Upadeśa: Spiritual instruction

Upāya: Way, path, means of approach

Ūrmi: Wave of pain or passion

V

Vairāgya: Nonattachment

Vaiśeṣika: Philosophical school of Distinction or Particularity

Vaiṣṇava: Of or relating to Viṣṇu and his worship; a devotee of Viṣṇu

Vāk: Primodial Word or Logos

Varṇamālā: Garland of letters of the Sanskrit alphabet

Vāsanās: Desires

Vedānta: School of philosophy based on the Upaniṣads

Videhamukti: Disembodied state of liberation

Vidyā: Knowledge, wisdom, insight

Vijñāna: Intellect, consciousness

Vijñānakala: A type of unembodied being

Vikalpa: Concept or experience

Vikṣepa Avasthā: State of existing in a body

Vimarśa: Self-revelation, Pure Consciousness as Pure Energy

Visarga: Emanation

Viśrānti: Step, resting stage

Visvottīrṇa: Absolute, transcendent

Vivekajñāna: Discriminating knowledge

Vrata: Vow

Vyāpaktva: Omnipresence

Y

Yāga: Oblation, sacrifice, offering

Yama: Self-control, abstention

Yoga: Philosophical school of Divine Union

Yogin: Practitioner of Yoga

Yoni: (1) Womb; (2) Type

Select Bibliography

ORIGINAL SANSKRIT TEXTS

Āgama

Mālinī Vijayottara Tantra, edited by Madhusudana Kaul, Srinagar, 1922.

Mṛgendra Tantra, edited with *tīkā* of Rāmakaṇṭha, Srinagar.

Netra Tantra, edited with com. of Kṣemarāja Vol. I–II, Srinagar.

Parātrimśikā with *Vivaraṇa* com. of Abhinavagupta, edited by Mukundarama Shastri, Srinagar, 1918.

Svacchanda Tantra with com. by Kṣemarāja, edited by Madhusudana Kaul, Vol. I–VI, Srinagar 1921 *Seq.*

Svacchanda Tantra translated into Hindi by Vrajaballabh Dvivedi, Vols. I & II, Varanasi.

Vijñānabhairava Tantra with comm. partly by Kṣemarāja, Śivopādhyāya, and Ānandabhaṭṭa, edited by Mukundarama Shastri, Srinagar, 1918.

Vijñānabhairava Tantra translated into English by Jaidev Singh, Varanasi, 1986.

Other Texts

Ajaḍaparamtṛsiddhi, edited by Madhusudan Kaul, Srinagar, 1921.

Amaraugha Śāsana, Srinagar.

Anuttarāṣtikā of Abhinavagupta (*stotra*), pub. as an Appendix in *Abhinavagupta, A Study,* by K. C. Pandey, Varanasi, 1936.

Anuttara Prakāśa Pañcāśikā of Ādinātha, Srinagar, 1918.

Anubhava Nivedana of Abhinavagupta (*stotra*), pub. as Appendix in *Abhinavagupta, A study* by K. C. Pandey, Varanasi, 1936.

Bodha Pañcadaśikā of Abhinavagupta, Srinagar, 1918.

Bhāvopahāra of Cakrapāṇinātha, edited by Madhusudan Shastri, Srinagar 1918.

Bhāskarī (*Īśvara Pratyabhijñā Vimarśinī* of Abhinavagupta with com. by Bhāskara), ed. by K. C. Pandey and K. A. S. Iyer, Vols. I–III Allahabad.

Īśvara-pratyabhijña-Vimarśinī (*Kārikā* by Utpaladeva and *Vimarsinī* comm. by Abhinavagupta), edited by Mukundarama Shastri, Vols. I–II, Srinagar, 1918 seq.

Iśvarapratyabhijñā Vivṛti Vimarśinī (*Kārikā* by Utpaladeva and *Vivṛti Vimarśinī* by Abhinavagupta), ed. by Madhusudana Kaul, Vol. I–III, Srinagar, 1941 seq.

Īśvara Siddhi of Utpaladeva, ed. by Madhusudana Kaul, Srinagar, 1921.

Kramastotra of Abhinavagupta (*stotra*), pub. as an Appendix in *Abhinavagupta, A Study,* by K. C. Pandey, Varanasi, 1936.

Janmamaranavicāra of Vāmadeva, Srinagar, 1918.

Mahārthamañjarī of Maheśvarānanda with Parimala comm.

Mahānayaprakāśa of Rājanaka Śitikaṇṭha, Srinagar, 1918.

Mālinívijayavārttika of Abhinavagupta (*Vārttika* com. on the 1st verse of *Mālinīvijaya Tantra*), ed. by Madhusudana Kaul, Srinagar 1921.

Nareśvaraparīkṣā of Sadyajyoti with comm. by Rāmakaṇṭha, Varanasi, 1936.

Parmārtha Carcā of Abhinavagupta (*strotra*), pub. as Appendix in *Abhinavagupta, A Study,* by K. C. Pandey, Varanasi, 1936.

Paramārthasāra (*Kārikā* adapted by Abhinavagupta with comm. by Yogarāja), ed. by J. C. Chatterji, Srinagar, 1916.

Paramārthasāra, Trans. into English with notes by L. D. Barnett, *Journal of the Royal Asiatic Society,* London 1910, pp. 401–46.

Parāpraveśikā of Kṣemarāja, ed. by Mukundarama Shastri, Srinagar, 1918.

Parātṛmśikā Tātparya Dīpikā of Somananda, ed. by Jagaddhar Jadoo, Srinagar, 1947.

Parātrśikā translated into English by Jaideva Singh and revised by Svami Laksman Joo, Ed. Bettina Baïsner, Varanai 1988

Pratyabhijñā Hṛdayam of Kṣemarāja with com. by the author, edited by J. C. Chatterji, Srinagar, 1911.

Pratyabhijñāhṛdayam, translated into German by Emil. Baer, trans. into English Kurt F. Leidecker, Adyar, 1938.

Pratyabhijñā Hṛdayam trans. in English with notes by Jaidev Singh, Varanasi, 1963.

Pratyabhijñā Kārikā with *Vṛtti* of Utapaladeva, edited by Madhusudana Kaul, Srinagar, 1924.

Sattrimśattattva Sandoha with *Vivaraṇa tīkā* of Rājānaka Ānanda, edited Mukundaram Sastri, Srinagar, 1918.

Saṭtrimśattattva Sandoha, ed. with English trans., notes, etc. by D. B. Sensharma, Kurukshetra, 1977.

Siddhi Trayī of Utpaledeva, ed. by Madhusudana Kaul, Srinagar, 1924.

Śiva Dṛṣṭi of Somānada with com. by Utpaladeva, ed. by Madhusudana Kaul, Srinagar, 1924.

Śiva Dṛṣṭi of Somānada translated into Hindi by R. S. Chaturvedi, Varanasi, 1986.

Śiva Dṛṣṭi, translated by Raneno Gnoli with notes, chapter I only, in *East & West,* Vol. VIII (1957) pp. 16–22.

Śivasūtra with Vimarśini com. by Kṣemarāja, ed. J. C. Chatterji, Srinagar, 1911.

Śiva Sūtra Vimarśinī, translated into English by P. T. Srinavasa Iyengar, Allahabad, 1912.

Śivasūtra of Vasugupta with *Vṛtti* com., edited by J. C. Chatterji, Srinagar, 1926.

Śivasūtra of Vasugupta with *Vārttika* comm. by Rājānaka Bhāskara, ed. by J. C, Chatterji, Srinagar, 1916.

Śivasūtra of Vasugupta with *Vārttika* com. by Varadarāja, Srinagar.

Śiva Stotrāvalī of Utpaladeva with comm. by Kṣemarāja, Varanasi, Chowkhamba Sanskrit Series No. 15.

Spanda Kārikā with *Vṛtti* by Kallaṭa, edited by J. C. Chatterji, Srinagar, 1916.

Spanda Kārikā with *vṛtti* of Rāma Kaṇṭha, edited by J. C. Chatterji, 1913.

Spanda Kārikā trans. into English, Jaideva Singh, Varenasi, 1984

Spanda Nirṇaya of Kṣemarāja (*Kārikā* by Kallaṭa and *ṭikā* by Kṣemarāja), ed. with English trans. by Madhusudana Kaul, Srinagar, 1925.

Spanda Sandoha of Kṣemarāja, edited by Mukundarama Shastri, Srinagar, 1917.

Tantrāloka of Abhinavagupta with *ṭikā* by Jayaratha and Śivopādhyaya, edited by Mukundaram Shastri Vols. I–XII, Srinagar, 1918 seq.

Tantrāloka of Abhinavagupta ed. with introduction in English by R. C. Dwivedi and N. Rastogi, Vol I–VIII, Delhi, 1987.

Tantrasāra of Abhinavagupta, ed. by Mukundrama Shastri, Srinagar, 1918.

Tantrasāra translated into Hindi by H. N. Chakravarti, Vararasi, 1986

Tantravaṭadhānikā of Abhinavagupta, Srinagar, 1923.

GENERAL BOOKS

Agrawal, V. S., *Śiva Mahādeva, The Great God Śiva,* Varanasi, 1966.

Ayyar, C. V. N, *Origin and Early History of Śaivism in South India,* Madras, 1936.

Bagchi, P. C., *Studies in the Tantras,* Calcutta, 1939.

Bamzai, P. N. K., *A History of Kashmir,* Delhi, 1962.

Banerji, J. N., *Pañcopasana* (in Bengali), Firma K. L. Mukhopadhyaya Calcutta, 1960.

Bernard, Theos, *Philosophical Foundations in India,* London, 1945.

Bhandarkar, R. G., *Vaiṣṇavism, Śaivism, and Minor Religious Systems,* Poona, 1928.

Bhattacharya, B., *Śaivism and the Phallic World,* Vols. I & II, New Delhi.

Chatterji, J. C., *Kashmir Shaivism,* Srinagar, 1914; reprint, Albany, NY, 1986.

Chatterji, J. C., *Hindu Realism,* Allahabad, 1912.

Chattopadhyaya, S., *The Evolution of Theistic Sects in Ancient India,* Calcutta, 1962.

DasGupta, S. N., *A History of Indian Philosophy,* Vol. V. Cambridge, 1962.

Eliot, C., *Hinduism and Buddhism,* Vols. I–III, London, 1921.

Farquhar, J. N., *An Outline of the Religious Literature of India,* London, 1920.

Gierson G. & L. D. Barnett, *Lallā Vākyāni,* (Monograph) Asiatic Society.

Iyengar, P. T. S., *An Outline of Indian Philosophy,* Allahabad, 1918.

Jash, P., *History of Śaivism,* Calcutta, 1974.

Joshi, B. L., *Kashmir Śaiva darśana aur Kāmāyanī* (in Hindi), Chowkhamba, Varanasi 1968.

Kachur, D. P., *Utpala, The Saint-mystic* (Monograph), Poona 1945.

Katiram, S., *A Handbook of Śaiva Religion,* Madras, 1950.

Kaviraj, G. N., *Bhāratīya Sanskriti aur Sādhanā,* Vols. I & II (in Hindi) Patna, 1957.

———. *Tāntrik Vāngmaya meṅ Śākta Dṛṣṭi* (in Hindi) Patna, 1965.

———. *Bhāratīya Sādhanār Dhārā* (in Bengali), Calcutta, 1955.

———. *Tāntrika Sādhanā O Siddhānta* (in Bengali) Vol. I, Burdwan.

———. *Tantra O Āgamaśāstra Digdarśana* (in Bengali) Vol. I, Calcutta, 1963.

Kittel, F., *Origin of Phallic Worship in India,* London.

Marshall, J., *Mohenjodaro and Indus Civilization,* Vol. I–III, London, 1931.

Mehta, R. L., *Pre-Buddhist India,* Bombay, 1939.

Mehta, P. D., *Early Indian Religious Thought,* London, 1956.

Mishra, U., *Bhāratīya Darshan,* Lucknow.

Pandey, K. C., *Abhinavagupta, An Historical and Philosophical Study,* Chowkhamba, 1929.

Pandit, B. N., *Aspects of Kashmir Śaivism,* Srinagar, 1977.

Pathak, V. S., *Śaiva Cults in North India,* Varanasi, 1960.

Sankarachandra, *Is Śivalinga a Phallus,* Calcutta, 1957.

Sharma, L. N., *Kashmir Shaivism,* Varanasi, 1972.

Shivaraman, K., *Śaivism in Philosophical Perspective,* Delhi.

Siddhanta Shastri, R. K., *Śaivism through the Ages,* Delhi.

Sinha, J. N., *Schools of Śaivism,* Calcutta, 1970.

———. *History of Indian Philosophy,* Vol. II, Calcutta.

Subrahmanian, K. R., *Origin of Śaivism and its History in Tamil-land,* Madras, 1929.

Upadhyaya, B., *Bhāratīya Darshan*, Varanasi.

Venkatramanyya, N., *Rudra Śiva*, Madras, 1941.

Woodroffe, J., *Principles of Tantra*, Madras.

———. *Garland of Letters*, Madras.

———. *Śakti and Śākta*, Madras.

———. *Mahāmāya*, Madras.

Yaduvanshi, *Śaivamata* (in Hindi), Patna, 1955.

Index

V

Y